Advanced Perspectives in Applied Computing

2253

Springer

London
Berlin
Heidelberg
New York
Barcelona
Budapest
Hong Kong
Milan
Paris
Santa Clara
Singapore
Tokyo

The Springer-Verlag Series on Advanced Perspectives in Applied Computing is comprised of research monographs that span the full range of topics in applied computing technology.

Books in the series provide a review of theoretical concepts and research activity in computer science alongside a view on how research concepts can be applied in the development of effective computer systems.

The series should be essential reading for postgraduate students and researchers in computing and information systems.

Books in the series are contributed by international specialist researchers and educators in applied computing who draw together the full range of issues in their research area into one concise authoritative monograph.

Sarah A. Douglas and Anant Kartik Mithal

The Ergonomics of Computer Pointing Devices

Springer

Sarah A. Douglas, AB, MS, PhD
Anant Kartik Mithal, BTech, MS, PhD

Department of Computer and Information Science
College of Arts and Sciences
1202 University of Oregon, Eugene, OR 97403-1202, USA

Series Editors

Professor Peter J. Thomas, BA (Hons), PhD, AIMgt, FRSA, FVRS
Centre for Personal Information Management, University of the West of
England, Coldharbour Lane, Bristol, BS16 1QY, UK

Professor Ray J. Paul, BSc, MSc, PhD
Department of Computer Science and Information Systems at St. John's,
Brunel University, Kingston Lane, Uxbridge, Middlesex UB8 3PH, UK

ISBN 3-540-19986-1 Springer-Verlag Berlin Heidelberg New York

British Library Cataloguing in Publication Data
Douglas, Sarah Ann
    The ergonomics of computer pointing devices. - (Advanced perspectives in applied
    computing)
    1. Computer input-output equipment - Design and construction
    2. Human-computer interaction
    I.Title II.Mithal, Anant Kartik
    621.3'986
    ISBN 3540199861

Library of Congress Cataloging-in-Publication Data
Douglas, Sarah A., 1949-
    The ergonomics of computer pointing devices / Sarah A. Douglas and Anant Kartik Mithal.
        p.   cm. -- (Advanced perspectives in applied computing)
    Includes bibliographical references and index.
    ISBN 3-540-19986-1 (pbk. : alk. paper)
    1. Computer input-output equipment--Design. 2. Human engineering. 3. Mice
    (Computers)--Design. I. Mithal, Anant Kartik, 1960- . II. Title. III. Series.
    TK7887.5.D665 1997
    621.39'86--dc21   96-49162

© Springer-Verlag London Limited 1997
Printed in Great Britain

Typesetting: ReadyText, Bath
Printed and bound at the Athenæum Press Ltd., Gateshead, Tyne and Wear
34/3830-543210 Printed on acid-free paper

Contents

Preface

We first began looking at pointing devices and human performance in 1990 when the senior author, Sarah Douglas, was asked to evaluate the human performance of a rather novel device: a finger-controlled isometric joystick placed under a key on the keyboard. Since 1990 we have been involved in the development and evaluation of other isometric joysticks, a foot-controlled mouse, a trackball, and a wearable computer with head-mounted display. We unabashedly believe that design and evaluation of pointing devices should evolve from a broad spectrum of values which place the human being at the center. These values include performance issues such as pointing-time and errors, physical issues such as comfort and health, and contextual issues such as task usability and user acceptance.

This book chronicles this six-year history of our relationship as teacher (Douglas) and student (Mithal), as we moved from more traditional evaluation using Fitts' law as the paradigm, to understanding the basic research literature on psychomotor behavior. During that process we became profoundly aware that many designers of pointing devices fail to understand the constraints of human performance, and often do not even consider experimental evaluation critical to usability decisions before marketing a device. We also became aware of the fact that, contrary to popular belief in the human–computer interaction community, the problem of predicting pointing device performance has not been solved by Fitts' law. Similarly, our expectations were biased by the cognitive revolution of the past 15 years with the belief pointing device research was 'low-level' and uninteresting.

In due consideration of our evolving process, we set the following goals for this book. Our first goal is to provide the reader with a basic background on human performance research with pointing devices. We cover the psychomotor research on pointing, the ergonomics literature evaluating specific pointing devices, and the work on developing performance models, such as GOMS, which predict pointing time. Where it is necessary to provide an explanation of concepts or terms, we have attempted to do so, for work in this area is cross-disciplinary, and incorporates both computer science and psychology. Our second goal is to demonstrate the value of empirical and experimental methods with typical users in the evaluation and design of pointing devices. While we are aware of the difficulties of empirical study, requiring the investment of time, money, and expertise, we are committed to integrating usability studies into design. We believe that empirical study is the only way to *truly* understand a pointing device.

We provide, in this book, two examples of our own work as demonstrations of this approach. As our final goal, we wish to provide a perspective on the future, its exciting ideas and difficult challenges. We believe that the invention of innovative human–computer interfaces has just begun, and that input via the human psychomotor system will always be a critical component.

The target audience for this book is intended to be quite broad. We have aimed this book at the inventors and designers of pointing device hardware and software, human factors and ergonomics engineers, human–computer interaction specialists and psychologists researching human movement. We hope that individuals doing basic research in the psychomotor system will see the varied and difficult challenges presented by applied research – challenges which can create new hypotheses to test. At the same time, we hope that those working on a practical level will benefit from more insight into the theory and empirical findings that have accumulated – whether this influences the design of a new pointing device or the design of a software interface.

Acknowledgements

We would like to thank an active HCI community of pointing device researchers – Bill Buxton, Scott MacKenzie, Shumin Zhai, Christine MacKenzie, Ted Selker, Wanda Smith, David Meyer, Bonnie John, David Kieras, Richard Jagacinski and nameless reviewers – who have shown considerable patience and support as we developed ideas and presented the research in this book. The errors are of our own manufacture.

At the University of Oregon, Steven Keele and Michael Posner in the Psychology Department and Gary Meyer in the Computer Science Department graciously provided us with research background and guidance based on their considerable experience. Ph.D. students in the Interactive Systems Research Group (Ted Kirkpatrick, Eck Doerry, Chris Hundhausen, Donna McKeown and the Advanced User Interfaces Seminar) offered many helpful suggestions for improving the readability of the manuscript.

We thank the patient participants in our studies and experiments without whom experimental research would not be possible. Additionally, we thank the enthusiastic designers at Home Row, IBM, Interlink, and Fleetfoot whose creativity and belief in their products pushed us into this research area which we now find so fascinating.

The senior author, Sarah Douglas, wishes to acknowledge the intellectual contribution to the general approach of this book by Tom Moran and Stu Card at Xerox PARC and, posthumously, to Allen Newell, who, during her Ph.D. education, clearly demonstrated the importance of human performance in the design of interactive systems. That spirit is immanent in this book. Finally, she thanks her partner, Marie Vitulli, for the intellectual and emotional sustenance that only love can provide.

The junior author, Kartik Mithal, wants to thank Dr Shakuntala Mithal, M.B.B.S., Ph.D., who taught him the importance of the scientific method, and Wen–Li, who poked and prodded him into finishing the manuscript.

1. Introduction

Pointing with the hand is an activity so basic and pervasive to human experience that most of us fail to notice the complex neural and psychomotor functioning that makes it possible. But pointing is more than neuromuscular events: it is the expression of our focus of attention on a particular aspect of the world. Pointing is inherently the communication of our intentions to other people. It is a *demonstrative* activity. It is with this sense that the, somewhat peculiarly named, computer input devices – the mouse, the joystick and the trackball – have become known as pointing devices. In a highly interactive system with a graphical user interface (GUI), the act of pointing is an act of communication with the system. Computer-based pointing is an expression of human intention that selects objects and actions mutually 'known' to the human user and the program.

GUIs are now so common that this technologically mediated activity hardly seems problematic. Indeed, we experience pointing with the mouse as a unitary act of consciousness common to all skilled, physical tool use. Using a mouse to point to an icon is like using a hammer to drive a nail:

> When we use a hammer to drive in a nail, we attend to both nail and hammer, but in a different way. We watch the effect of our strokes on the nail and try to wield the hammer so as to hit the nail most effectively. When we bring down the hammer we do not feel that its handle has struck our palm but that its head has struck the nail. Yet in a sense we are certainly alert to the feelings in our palm and the fingers that hold the hammer.
>
> *Polanyi, 1958:55*

In just this way, we are not conscious of the mouse while we use it to point to icons on a computer screen. This apparent 'naturalness' in using the mouse is the result of good tool design. It creates the paradoxical condition that a good tool is one we are not aware of using. A good design is one we take for granted. However, since it is a good design, we would like to know how to generalize those design aspects to other pointing devices: both those which seem to function poorly as well as new and innovative devices.

The difficulty is that we do not know how to do this very well. We do not know how to characterize a good design and, thus, we do not know how to improve or create other devices. It seems that it should be simple: take a good pointing device such as the mouse, determine the features that contribute to its goodness, and replicate those features in other devices. Why is this hard?

There are three main answers to that question: the *definition, translation* and *stability* problems.

The definition problem. We are not sure what 'good' means. We do know that goodness in a pointing device depends upon the context of use. When we choose to optimize a design for goodness in a particular task and with particular users, we may not optimize it for other tasks and other users. There are design tradeoffs. A mouse may be an excellent device for pointing and a poor device for drawing. Novice computer users may find the mouse easy to use when pulling down menus and recognizing menu items in an unfamiliar interface, but expert users may abandon the mouse and type keyboard commands instead, since, on average, typing is approximately three to four times faster. The mouse may be a very fast pointing device, but long-term usage may lead to repetitive strain injury due the posture of the hand in using it. Thus, goodness depends on a particular set of human values that we select to optimize for a design: speed, ease of learning, comfort, etc. These values should become design goals but they are often unspecified and thus not satisfied.

The translation problem. Once we settle on the values that we wish to optimize in the functionality of the pointing device, we need to translate those into specific measurable features of the device. Certain of these are easy to achieve. For example, does the device fit the shape of the human hand? We can devise a shape and try it out. But does it fit all sizes of human hands? Again, we need to make a design choice. This choice is often made unconsciously by designers. Today's mouse fits an adult hand fairly well, but not a child's. There are mice specifically designed for children, as well as a trackball that has a very large ball. We really need to know, *empirically*, the average size of the hand for the intended user population. Furthermore, we must often make a tradeoff again. If it fits a child's hand, it may not fit an adult hand and vice versa. Sometimes, in these design decisions we get lucky and find that our device satisfies multiple design goals without tradeoffs. For example, the single-button mouse works equally well for either right- or left-handed use. But did we think of that when we chose our design goals? Achieving a well-fitting shape, while it seemed easy at first, becomes difficult. More difficult still is translating design goals for psychological measures such as speed or ease of learning. Psychology does not yet have the ability to predict many specific aspects of human behavior. Instead, we have only the rough outlines to guide the design process.

The stability problem. Finally, replicating good design is hard because just when we get a handle on it, the technology rapidly changes. We have chosen to characterize this as technology *change*, not *evolution*, because frequently the change does not follow 'survival of the fittest', where the best design wins. Instead, it follows the dynamics of the marketplace. Some laptop and notebook computers have embedded finger-controlled isometric joysticks because the context in which these computers are used does not always provide the necessary surface for mouse movement – not because the pointing speed of the isometric joystick improves on the mouse. The design of pointing devices is frequently a victim of chance, subject to planned obsolescence, product differentiation, and niche saturation. This makes it difficult to perform long-term studies that could provide the necessary knowledge to guide design.

1.1 Approach

This book seeks to address the problems of definition, translation and stability of good pointing device design in the following ways. First, we will define design goals from the ergonomic or human factors perspective. Secondly, we will argue for a major role of psychology in translating from those design goals into device design and evaluation. Psychology provides not only valuable insights into the nature of human performance, but also a rigorous methodology. We unabashedly advocate the integration of experimental methods into the design process. Finally, we believe that the first step to achieving stability is to promote the importance of pointing device design from an ergonomics or human factors perspective. Until inventors, developers and manufacturers are persuaded that good design supported by solid empirical study increases profit, or decreases lawsuits, they will not pay attention to, nor support, ergonomics research.

1.1.1 Definition Problem: Defining the Design Goal

The notion of a tool or artifact's goodness from the point of view of how well it fits human physical, psychological or social capacities and constraints is usually termed its ergonomic or human factors aspects. The word *ergonomics* is defined in the Oxford English Dictionary as 'The scientific study of the efficiency of man in his working environment' with first mention in 1949 (second edition, 1989, p. 369). An alternative word more common in American usage is *human factors engineering*. In some usage the word ergonomics denotes only physical anthropometry, health and safety factors, reserving the word human factors as broader in scope. In this book, the words ergonomics and human factors will be used interchangeably and are intended to connote all aspects of design related to use. The general term *human computer interaction* (HCI) will be used to denote all ergonomically-oriented work with interactive computer systems.

The new International Standards Organization document 9241, *Ergonomic requirements for office work with visual display terminals*, which includes a section on hand-operated pointing devices, expands the usage of the term ergonomics to the broader concept of *usability*. ISO 9241 defines usability as the effectiveness, efficiency and satisfaction with which specified users achieve specified goals in particular environments. In turn, effectiveness is the accuracy and completeness with which specified users can achieve specified goals in particular environments; efficiency is the resources expended in relation to the accuracy and completeness of goals achieved; and satisfaction is the comfort and acceptability of the work system to its users and other people affected by its use.

These definitions are still not precise enough to measure whether design goals have been achieved. They lack an expression of effectiveness, efficiency and satisfaction in language which allows us to observe and measure human behavior. In studying pointing devices, the most commonly used measures are time to learn to use a device, error rates during learning, practiced task time, practiced error rates, physical comfort, muscle fatigue and stress, and user acceptability. Some of these measures such as practiced task time are human performance measures; others are indirect measures such as muscle stress, and still others are subjective and qualitative such as user acceptability. All of these must be measured within a particular task. For computer pointing devices, the most common measure is practiced task time for simple pointing tasks, even though pointing devices are also used for moving (dragging) and drawing. The focus on practiced task time is due both to the fact that it is a well-understood measure in psychological studies, as well as to the values placed in the work environment for maintaining or improving human productivity. As longer-term use of pointing devices in the workplace causes increased legal liability due to repetitive strain injury, measures of muscle fatigue and stress will become more important. It is our experience that human performance measures correlate with overall usability and attitudinal measures, such as preference and acceptability of a device.

1.1.2 Translation Problem: Translating the Design Goal into Practice

The translation of design usability goals into design practice requires the integration of bodies of knowledge and a particular method. There are two bodies of knowledge that we will incorporate into this book: the basic psychological research that theorizes on a description of human movement with pointing devices, and the existing ergonomics literature on pointing devices. Our psychological approach is from a psychomotor perspective based on the analysis of aimed movement. We will not focus in any depth on the control systems (linear feedback) theory that has dominated earlier human factors and psychological modeling of tracking tasks. Our reason for doing this is that recent experimental research (e.g. Meyer *et al.* 1982, 1988, 1990), leads us to believe that the human motor-control system is a complex, non-linear programmed system.

The ergonomics literature on computer pointing devices now covers almost 20 years of research. We will limit our discussion in this book to *continuous* pointing devices that move the display cursor by a continuous pointing motion. In contrast, *discrete* pointing devices allow step movements of the cursor, such as cursor control keys and step keys. Discrete devices function as keying devices and their ergonomics is best described in terms of keystrokes, not of pointing movements. We will cover the mouse, the joystick, the trackball, the touch screen and touch tablet, foot-operated controls, head and eye tracker, and the dataglove.

To create background knowledge for design, we will survey the ergonomic literature of those devices, relating their device features to human performance. The ergonomics literature is not comprehensive regarding usability and focuses almost entirely on evaluating and predicting practiced performance time for pointing. There is a lack of information on other tasks undertaken with pointing devices – such as dragging and drawing. In any case, the ergonomics literature does not present evidence that it is possible to generalize from device features to human performance. Thus, most design questions about innovative devices must be answered with specifically designed empirical studies.

As we stated earlier, translating design usability goals into practice requires a method and this is, perhaps, the most important contribution of the past 20 years of ergonomics research. As we shall see, ergonomics research has discovered that there is a very complex interaction of factors which determine human performance *directly* and attitude *indirectly*. The type of user interacts with the type of task, the type of device (its characteristics) and the limb used to control it. This complexity makes it difficult to determine what affects device performance. Experimental methods are, appropriately, the only way to determine differences in performance measures. Experiments control factors as well as manipulate them. They provide a common context for evaluation. This does not imply that other empirical methods are not appropriate for gathering information during design. Qualitative studies including videotaping of task performance may be crucial during very early design. Questionnaires, interviews, and focus groups may all gather important information for marketing. All these methods, provided they sample enough of the user population, are useful. But the only way, at present, to truly evaluate the human performance of a pointing device is to perform a well-designed experiment. This can be done during development of a design with prototypes. It can rigorously compare performance between a baseline or benchmark device and the newly designed one.

There are still limitations with the experimental method. Despite 20 years of research to find an absolute rule for relating the design features of devices to human performance, it has not been found. Initially, Fitts' law, which predicts the time of human movement for rapid aimed tasks, appeared to provide such a tool. Early work by Card, English and Burr (1978) demonstrated that Fitts' law applied to pointing movement with a computer-mediated device: the mouse. After 15 years, as we shall see, the promise of Fitts' law as an absolute metric has failed to materialize (MacKenzie, 1992). What is clear from the research literature is that while it is possible to compare performance between devices within an experiment, it is risky to compare across experiments.

Critical readers will no doubt raise the issue of why they should invest in conducting time-consuming and expensive experiments. We offer three examples where these methods work. They are all experiments conducted within the framework of Fitts' law and psychomotor modeling in general. They provide a critical lens through which we can study pointing device performance. The first example is the study of the *power mouse* by Jellinek and Card (1990). A power mouse is a mouse with an accelerated driver – the faster the mouse moves, the greater the distance moved on the screen. Their experiment uses Fitts' law to determine whether participants' pointing-times were significantly different with the power mouse compared to a regular mouse driver. Their results show that the accelerated driver had no effect on performance.

The second example was conducted by the authors (Douglas and Mithal, 1994) and will form a case study in this book. That experiment tests the hypothesis that an isometric, finger-controlled joystick embedded in the keyboard saves overall task-time because the user does not have to move her or his hand to the mouse. Again, the measure is Fitts' law and we will show that the savings in having the joystick installed on the keyboard do not overcome its significantly slower pointing-time.

The third study (Mithal, 1995; Mithal and Douglas, 1996) is also incorporated into a chapter of this book. In that experiment, detailed empirical data is gathered during movement – both with a mouse and a finger-controlled isometric joystick – in an attempt to understand why pointing with the joystick is so much slower than the mouse. The real-time, sampled data is compared to an existing psychomotor model called the *stochastic optimized submovement* (SOS) model. A very surprising result is found which may, indirectly, explain why some joysticks are difficult to learn and control.

Likewise, before dismissing the practicality of an experimental method during design, we should compare it to the current method. We do not feel that it is too harsh to characterize the design methods for pointing devices as *ad hoc*. They seem to lack principle and are not guided by ergonomics research. Developers go through cycles of building a device, informally observing how a few users perform (usually part of the development group or their friends), tweaking various parameters and then re-testing. The cycle is repeated until a vague level of satisfactory performance has been achieved. The design of isometric joysticks is an example of this approach (Bentley, Custer, and Meyer, 1975; Rutledge and Selker, 1990).

The problem with this technique is that it only focuses on the overall pointing task, i.e. how it feels to use it. While this is critical for a first cut at a usable design, it is not a reliable or broad empirical assessment. As a result, when the designers make a change in the pointing device, they do not know how the change affects the human performance, and therefore cannot predict, or even evaluate, whether or not the change will improve their device.

An experiment consisting of a range of benchmark tasks, random selection and adequate sample sizes of the target users, and relevant performance measures should all be specified to provide a focused method of design change. Furthermore, a new technique can be used – one we will demonstrate in a case study – that gives an insight into how the device works. This technique analyses the details of the movement process using real-time sampled data. All this empirical information can help designers converge on an improved design. We will expand on these methods and present more detail on these types of usability studies combined with traditional experimental methods.

1.1.3 Stability Problem: Understanding Why a Design Is Good

Currently, a wide range of pointing devices exist – which might make us believe that new pointing devices are not required. However, novel pointing devices are constantly being developed; new uses are found for computers and new situations arise which necessitate new types of pointing device. For example, as mentioned earlier, the laptop computer has become possible because of increased circuit miniaturization. The lack of a desktop for the mouse has spawned a range of keyboard-integrated, finger-controlled pointing devices: trackball, touchpad, and isometric joystick. As another example, the development of virtual reality presents new challenges to understand human performance with the combined pointing devices of eye tracker, Polhemus spatial tracker, and dataglove. Little is known about human effectiveness, efficiency and satisfaction with this 'immersion' interface.

Despite the continuing demand for new pointing devices, the current state of pointing device design is such that these new devices are not built on the good design of earlier devices. This is partly due to the fact that there has not been much in the literature to guide developers about which successful human performance aspects of an older device they should incorporate into a new device or the importance of doing so. Proprietary issues often prevent public disclosure of the details of a design and its human performance aspects. Even more of an obstacle is the fact that few developers are able to understand both the technological complexities and the psychological complexities. For example, in preparing this book, we have searched the literature in several major areas: human–computer interaction, human factors engineering, human motor behavior, and electrical engineering. Although it may be difficult to require expertise in all areas, it is critical to begin the development of a unified literature and team approach with a focus on relating design to human performance. This may help pointing-device design achieve stability in an ever changing marketplace which, at times, looks like a cottage industry of bad ideas that have been tried before.

1.2 The Organization of This Book

Broadly speaking, research on pointing, and pointing devices, can be divided into two areas based on whether the research concerns manual pointing or pointing mediated by a computer input device. However, many recent studies of manual pointing use the computer as a means for presenting the experimental task and thus blur the distinction between the two areas. Figure 1.1 illustrates these two areas as overlapping circles with research on manual pointing represented by the left circle and pointing devices represented by the circle on the right.

Most research on manual pointing has been done by psychologists doing both applied and basic research; most research on computer pointing has been done by people working in *human computer interaction* (HCI). The two areas intersect with an interest in Fitts' law (Fitts, 1954).

Fitts' law describes a property of the gross parameters of rapid aimed movement. It relates the time it takes to move to a target to the target distance and the target width. Research on models explaining Fitts' law has, in part, been prompted by the fact that the law holds across a wide range of conditions, which strongly suggests that there is some powerful unifying mechanism that controls pointing movement.

The accuracy of the predictions of Fitts' law are so unique and valuable for research in ergonomics, that it has been upheld as a vital principle in the field (Card, Moran, and Newell, 1983) based on the fact that in the late 1970s it was established that Fitts' law holds for pointing with a mouse and the isometric joystick (Card, English and Burr, 1978). Thus, pointing with the hand and pointing with a computer-mediated pointing device are, in some manner, the same.

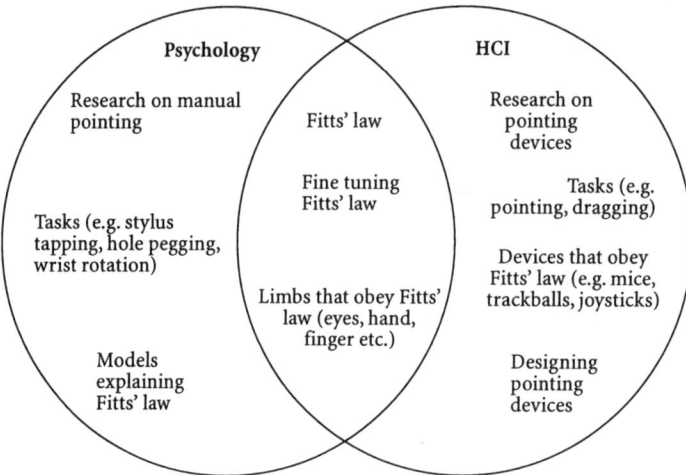

Figure 1.1: Framework of research on pointing and pointing devices.

Figure 1.1 shows reassuring parallels and surprising differences between the research done in the two areas. If we call the range of conditions under which Fitts' law holds a 'space', then both psychology and HCI have tried to map the space in which Fitts' law is applicable. These spaces are somewhat different – yet strikingly similar. One common dimension of the space is the task, where the attempt has been to determine what kinds of task conform to Fitts' law. A second common dimension is the limb used in the task. The pointing device used makes for a third dimension in the space for HCI research, although the pointing device and the limb used to control it are related. Thus, psychology has studied the mix of limbs and tasks that follow Fitts' law, while HCI has examined the limbs, tasks and devices that follow Fitts' law.

In the next three chapters we will present overviews of the psychomotor and ergonomic research literature. Chapter 2, *Human Motor Performance*, will present the requisite background from the psychological literature. These include Fitts' law, psychomotor models of movement, generalized motor control, perceptual feedback, and skill learning. Chapter 3, *Factors in Applying Psychomotor Studies to Pointing Devices*, introduces the reader to three factors that are fundamental to the application of psychomotor studies to the ergonomics of pointing devices: operation and features of the device, limb control, and task types. Chapter 4, *A Survey of Ergonomic Studies*, summarizes the ergonomic studies that have been done with different pointing devices and discusses the research on predicting human performance and comparing between devices.

In Chapter 5, *Evaluating New Devices: A Case Study*, we present our first case study which is an experimental comparison of an isometric joystick located on a keyboard and a mouse. The joystick was in the later stages of development when this study was conducted. The basic hypothesis tested is whether having the joystick on the keyboard saves device-switching time and, thus, overall task time. The design of the experiment is a mixed design with a between-subjects factor of device (joystick or mouse), a within-subjects factor of tasks (pointing, dragging, device switching), and a within-subjects factor of time (blocks of trials). The following performance measures are included for each task: learning performance time, learning error rate, practiced performance time, practiced error rate, and practiced device/mode-switching time. The three tasks were all designed to test Fitts' law relationships and presented participants with a wide range of combinations of target size, distance, and angle of approach. The results show that the savings in having the joystick installed on the keyboard do not overcome its significantly slower pointing time.

In Chapter 6, *Using the Microstructure of Movement to Understand Device Performance*, we present our second case study: another comparison of a finger-controlled isometric joystick and a mouse. Our goal in this study is to better understand why the joystick is such a slow pointing device when compared to the mouse. While experiments such as the one described in Chapter 5 are useful in predicting movement time under a range of conditions, these studies are not designed to be detailed enough to understand real-time performance at the millisecond level. Such an analysis requires detailed time and displacement data as the cursor moves towards the target – data that, typically, are not gathered in a Fitts' law experiment. Once collected, the data are used to verify a particular psychomotor model. Very little is known about whether human pointing mediated by a computer device is described by psychomotor models for manual pointing.

The *stochastic optimized submovement* (SOS) model has been shown to be applicable to manual pointing movement (Meyer, Abrams, Kornblum, Wright, and Smith 1988; Meyer, Smith, and Wright, 1982; Meyer, Smith, Kornblum, Abrams, and Wright, 1990) and to computer-based pointing with the mouse (Walker, Meyer and Smelcer, 1993). The SOS model, which is explained in detail in Chapter 2, describes a single pointing action as a sequence of submovements and predicts the relative size and accuracy of those submovements. Chapter 6 applies a psychomotor study to the isometric joystick and the mouse. A phenomenon is found which may explain why some joysticks are difficult to learn and control.

Chapter 7, *Performance Models*, is a review of the literature that integrates pointing performance into overall task-time prediction for a GUI interface. We have included performance modeling because it is a major focus of HCI research and attempts to directly link empirical research findings with the practice of user interface software design. In this chapter we first review the historical background for task analysis and work measurement in preparation for a description of the basic Card, Moran, and Newell (1983) GOMS and *keystroke level model*. We then discuss extensions to these models with Kieras' NGOMSL (1988); John's CPM-GOMS (1988); Kieras, Wood and Meyer's EPIC (1995), and Foley, Gibbs, Kim, and Kovacevic's UIDE (1989). We discuss the reliability of performance models and their usefulness in predicting pointing device performance.

Finally, Chapter 8, *Challenges of the Present and Future*, presents further integration of ergonomics into the design of pointing device hardware and software from the viewpoint of usability studies. It also includes an extensive discussion of the new ISO 9241 standard for pointing devices. The second part of this chapter anticipates innovations in pointing device technology, both in specific devices and in interfaces. Finally, the chapter concludes with a list of future research directions in pointing device ergonomics.

1.3 Importance and Future of Pointing Device Ergonomics

As computer science turns toward an emphasis on interactive systems, it will become ever more critical to apply knowledge and methods from the psychological and social sciences to problem definitions, engineering development and the evaluation of products. As one example, virtual reality presents computational demands that cannot be met if the goal is to produce realistic 3D images in real-time. Applying knowledge of how the human visual system uses perceptual cues to determine depth can be used to concentrate computation on creating just those features of the image, and ignoring less salient ones. Virtual reality presents exactly the same challenges for input from 3D devices controlled by limbs or head movement. Very little is understood about pointing, grasping, and gesturing in virtual 3D environments.

Although virtual reality environments present the most obvious and, to some, the most exotic challenges in future research on pointing devices, there are nevertheless other active and interesting horizons for pointing device research:

- development of mobile computer pointing devices;
- usage of 2D pointing devices such as the mouse in 3D environments;
- development of 3D input devices;
- development of telesensory and telepresent devices;
- development of multi-modal interfaces integrating speech and pointing;
- integrating force-feedback or other tactile sensory input into pointing devices;
- development of gesturing interfaces;
- development of interaction techniques and devices for two-handed or multi-limb interaction; and,
- development of interaction techniques for pointing in distributed work environments with shared workspaces.

The future presents exciting possibilities for ever-more interactive computing. Again, advocacy is needed for ergonomics and usability as values in the design, development and marketing process. We hope that this book is a small contribution in that direction.

2. *Human Motor Performance*

Many physical skills require a person to rapidly change the position of a limb from one location to another. These skills are used in tasks such as reaching for a pen or an elevator button, hitting the reset button on a computer, using a mouse to select a screen icon, and fitting a bolt into its hole. These actions are examples that can be collected under the category of *rapid aimed movement*.

Pointing is a type of rapid aimed movement and can be defined as the act of moving a limb from a starting position to some target location with some tolerance in the final resting position of the limb.

Pointing actions are fundamental to the understanding of mechanical skills in humans (Keele, 1986; Meyer *et al.*, 1990). The analysis of pointing actions has therefore been a major concern in the field of motor performance, with notable research being published as early as 1899 by Woodworth.

In preparation for the ergonomic studies that will be discussed later in the book, the purpose of this chapter is to present a basic introduction to the human psychomotor aspects of pointing movement. The previous chapter described a framework for categorizing research on pointing, and differentiated between research on manual pointing and research on pointing with pointing devices. Fitts' law predicts movement time in both these areas. With that in mind, this chapter starts by describing the original Fitts experiment, followed by a description of research studies of manual pointing and psychomotor models of pointing movement. The chapter ends with a brief discussion of some generalized aspects of motor behavior: perceptual feedback, neuromuscular control, timing of movement, sidedness, attention and cognition, and learning.

2.1 Fitts' Law

Research into pointing movement came to the fore in psychology at a time when worker efficiency was of major concern. The early experiments performed with pointing movements reflected the tasks that might be performed by workers on a production line. In a Fitts' law description of pointing, the parameters of interest are the width of the target, the distance from the starting location to the center of the target, and the time it takes from the start to the end of the movement (Fitts, 1954). This is illustrated in Figure 2.1.

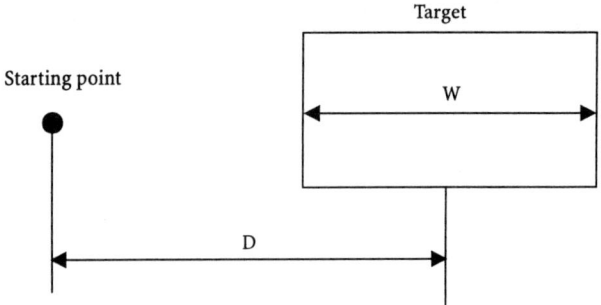

Figure 2.1: The parameters of interest in a pointing action.

Fitts' law provides industrial engineers with predictive tools for minimizing task time on a production line. Subsequent research was able to establish that Fitts' law holds in a wide range of conditions, and that its predictions are unusually robust and accurate.

2.1.1 Fitts' Law and a Description of Fitts' Paradigm

Fitts' original work (Fitts, 1954) established a mathematical relationship between:

1. the time it takes to move to a target;
2. the movement distance;
3. target width.

Fitts' original work has importance for two reasons. First, and strictly speaking, the parameters and variables in the Fitts' law equation must be interpreted according to Fitts' original experiment. Second, this research has been used as a research paradigm for a number of studies (Fitts and Peterson, 1964; MacKenzie, Sellen, and Buxton, 1991). It is therefore important to describe this experiment in some detail. Fitts' experiment was an attempt to extend information theory to human motor systems. He started with Shannon's Theorem 17 (Fitts, 1954):

$$C = B log_2(S/N + 1) \qquad (2.1)$$

where:

C is the effective information capacity of a communication channel

B is the bandwidth of the channel

S is signal power

N is noise power

Fitts then suggested that the distance of movement (A for amplitude) was analogous to the signal power, and the width of the target (W) was analogous to allowable noise (Figure 2.1). He noted that it takes longer to hit a target further away, and that it is easier to hit a larger target. With this starting point, he derived the following equation, which is now known as Fitts' law:

$$MT = a + b\,log_2(2A/W) \qquad (2.2)$$

where:

MT is the movement time

a, b are empirically determined constants. *a* is sometimes considered to include a constant time such as depressing a mouse button

A is the target amplitude (distance of center of target from starting location)

W is the width of target

The term $log_2(2A/W)$ is described as the *index of difficulty* (*ID*), acknowledging that it forms a measure of the difficulty of the pointing task. The *ID* is measured in terms of 'bits', a term that owes its name to its information processing heritage. Fitts also describes an *index of performance* (*IP*), which is analogous to the channel capacity (*C*) from Shannon's theorem. We can say:

$$IP = ID/MT \qquad (2.3)$$

IP has units of bits per second (bits/second). In an idealized Fitts' law task, the constant *a* is zero, so *IP* is taken as $1/b$.

2.1.2 The Original Fitts Experiment

To test his hypothesis, that movement time is a function of target distance and width, Fitts conducted an experiment using the apparatus shown in Figure 2.2.

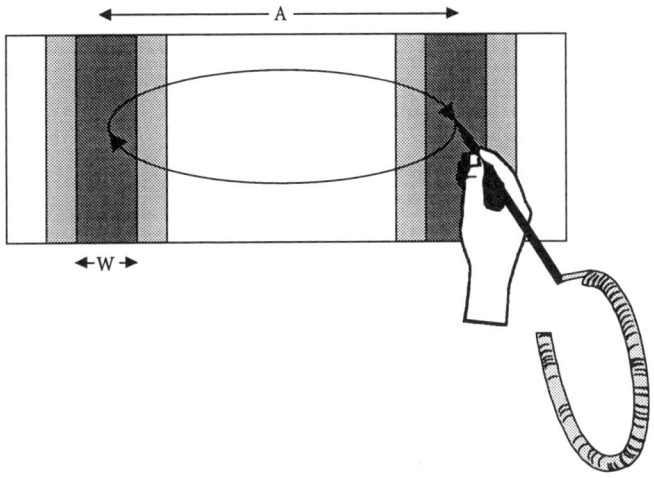

Figure 2.2: The original Fitts' law experiment.

Participants were asked to alternately tap a metal stylus in the central shaded areas. The instruments collected electrical impulses indicating a hit inside the target area (dark-gray shading) or outside (light-gray shading). The separation of the target centers was called the amplitude (A). The other dimension of interest was the width (W). The target height was 6 inches. The distance between the plates was varied between 2, 4, 8 and 16 inches, and the widths were varied between 0.25, 0.50, 1.00 and 2.00 inches. These amplitudes and widths were chosen to provide many different combinations of A/W. Note that the amplitudes and target widths are of the form $n2^0$, $n2^1$, $n2^2$, $n2^3$, $\cdots n2^m$ where n and m are positive integers. They were selected in this fashion because of the logarithmic term in ID. This pattern of increasing width and distance by powers of 2 has been followed by most subsequent studies. Two styli were used: a 1oz. and a 1lb. stylus.

Fitts found that the data matched Fitts' law (Equation 2.2) closely, with a correlation coefficient of 0.97. While such a high coefficient is unusual in other studies of human factors, studies of pointing and pointing devices commonly have correlation coefficients higher than 0.95. The task had an index of performance of ≈ 10.5 bits/second. The weight of the stylus did not have an effect on IP.

This study was performed during a period of history in which there was an emphasis on time-and-motion studies aimed at workers on production lines. The kinds of pointing tasks tested here are similar to the kinds of repetitive tasks that factory workers might perform. (As we shall see in Chapter 7, section 7.1.2, a major preoccupation of industrial engineers was work measurement, specifically the time to perform a taxonomy of common movements.)

Fitts' experiment and the Fitts' law equation highlight the factors that are important in a pointing task – namely pointing speed (or the time it takes to point), target distance and target size, and accuracy. Fitts' law gives us a means for comparing tasks, limbs and devices both in manual as well as in computer pointing. For example, if two pointing devices have to be compared, an experiment based on a Fitts' law paradigm, i.e. a task similar to Fitts' task, can be used to determine their *indices of performance* (IPs). The device with the higher *IP* is the faster device – *on average*.

At the same time, note that Fitts' law alone does not give us any means of predicting the performance of a limb or device, and is, therefore, no basis for predicting the human performance of a particular device's design. It is a *post hoc* test, but does not tell us what the performance will be without conducting an empirical study. Note also that the Fitts' law equation does not consider what happens during movement; it only describes the aggregate movement time, ignoring what happens during movement.

2.1.3 Fitts' Law and Manual Pointing

Fitts' law is an important result because pointing is fundamental to human movement, and because it is a very accurate predictor of movement times. Psychologists have tried to determine the extent to which Fitts' law holds for different limbs and different tasks.

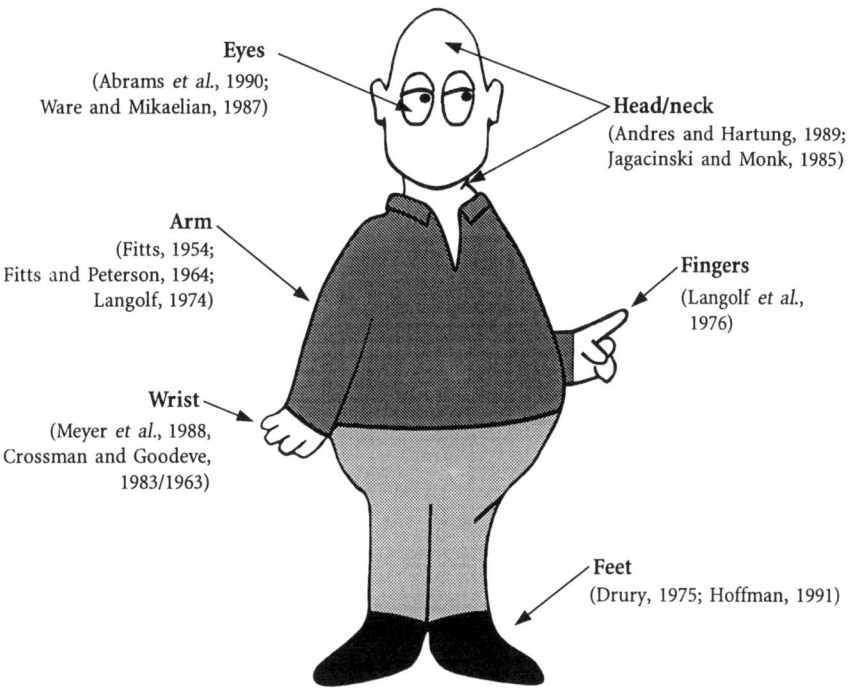

Figure 2.3: Limbs that have been shown to follow Fitts' law.

2.1.4 The Applicability of Fitts' Law to Different Limbs

Over a number of years, research has shown that Fitts' law holds for a number of limbs, as shown in Figure 2.3. Fitts' experiments (Fitts, 1954; Fitts and Peterson, 1964) indicated that movements of the arm followed Fitts' law. Fitts speculated whether the equation would be applicable to other limbs, and whether different limb segments might show different indices of performance. This idea was tested by Langolf who studied Fitts' law under various amplitude ranges (Langolf, Chaffin, and Foulke, 1976). Langolf's experimental setup included operations under a microscope, and extended to operations requiring movement of the whole arm. He found that:

> If the reciprocal of the slope, $1/b$, in the relationship $MT = a + bID$ infers the information processing capacity of the motor system, then the fingers showed an information processing rate of about 38 bits/sec; when the hand flexed and extended about the wrist the rate was 23bits/sec; and the rate for the arm was 10bits/sec.

> *Langolf et al., 1976:118*

Langolf's studies thus extended the scope of Fitts' law to fingers, wrist, and elbow, and suggested that the *IP* of the smaller limbs (fingers) is higher than the *IP* of larger limbs (the arms). Langolf's work has not been replicated to our knowledge, and he used only three participants. Thus, caution should be taken with his results.

The mobility of the head is an issue for physically disabled persons. A number of researchers studied head movements and showed them to follow Fitts' law (Andres and Hartung, 1989; Jagacinski and Monk, 1985; Lin, Radwin, and Vanderheiden, 1992).

In many situations, workers make extensive use of their hands and do not use their feet. This led to speculation that feet could also be used as controllers. Studies by Drury and Hoffmann showed that Fitts' law holds for feet (Drury, 1975; Hoffmann, 1991).

A number of researchers such as Meyer, Crossman and Goodeve, and Schmidt became interested in wrist rotation because they noted that:

1. such movement had a single degree of freedom, making it easier to model;
2. because the ratio of torque to inertia is high, the wrist submovements would not be smoothed out by mass inertia and would be visible in the data;
3. the movement had to be stopped primarily by antagonistic muscle action, thus reducing the effect of impact from an object such as a stylus.

Therefore, it is useful to study wrist movement to validate models of movement, and in the course of conducting such studies, wrist rotations have been shown to follow Fitts' law (Crossman and Goodeve, 1983; Meyer *et al.*, 1988).

The actions studied in these experiments are referred to as *rapid aimed movements*, because the movements are rapid and aimed at a target. Research has shown that in rapid aimed movement involving the hands, the eyes start moving towards the target before the hand starts moving, and arrive at the target before the hand gets there (Abrams, Meyer, and Kornblum, 1990). In addition, the eye is, in some sense, the 'natural pointing device' because it indicates the user's focus of attention. Researchers in HCI became interested in the eye as a pointing device, and Ware and Mikaelian showed the eye to follow Fitts' law (Ware and Mikaelian, 1987).

2.1.5 Tasks in the Fitts' Law Space

As explained above, researchers have extended the applicability of Fitts' law to various limbs. The other dimension along which Fitts' law has been explored is the *task*. This has led to the use of the term *Fitts' law tasks*.

Broadly speaking there are three types of movement: Type A, Type B, and Type C (Keele, 1968). Type A movements are movements that are stopped by impact with an object – such as hitting a nail with a hammer. These are the fastest movements. Type B and Type C movements are stopped by antagonistic muscle action, and therefore take longer. In Type B movements, the exact location where the movements stop is not important, making them faster than Type C movements. The upstroke of a hammer is an example of a Type B movement. Type C movements, which require precision, are the slowest of the three. All manual pointing movements are of Type C. Thus, Fitts' law applies to movements of Type C.

There is an inherent tradeoff between speed and accuracy in Type C movements, i.e. pointing tasks. The more accurate a person's movements need to be (the smaller the target), the slower they tend to become. The exact form that this tradeoff takes could be logarithmic, polynomial or linear, depending on the task. The Fitts' law equation represents the outcome of a logarithmic speed–accuracy tradeoff. A linear speed–accuracy tradeoff is described later in this chapter and in Chapter 3, section 3.3.3.2.

Fitts' original experiment explored the applicability of Fitts' law to different tasks (Fitts, 1954). In addition to the pointing (stylus tapping) task, Fitts also conducted two additional experiments. One, which was similar to the 'Towers of Brahma' problem (sometimes referred to as the 'Towers of Hanoi' problem), had two posts with disks on them. Participants moved the disks from one post to the other as rapidly as possible. The second experiment had two rows of holes with pins, and participants had to move the pins from one set of holes to the other. Both tasks closely conformed to the law. Langolf, in replicating part of Fitts' work, also used a peg-transfer task that conformed to Fitts' law (Langolf *et al.*, 1976).

Fitts differentiated between discrete and continuous tasks. The task studied in his first experiment was a continuous task. He later conducted a second experiment where the plate to be struck was indicated by a light stimulus. The participant waited with the stylus on a mark midway between the plates until perceiving the stimulus, and then struck the plate indicated by the light (Fitts and Peterson, 1964). Consequently, there were distinct pauses between each movement. This is a discrete task and it also followed Fitts' law and had an *IP* greater than that from the earlier experiment. Fitts and other researchers have speculated that the continuous experiment includes a 'dwell' time on each plate (Kantowitz and Knight, 1976).

Jagacinski studied tasks with two kinds of endpoint conditions, one where the endpoint of a trial was reached when the participant stopped on the target, and the other where the endpoint was reached when the participant held the pointer steady over the target for a specified amount of time (Jagacinski, Repperger, Moran, Ward, and Glass, 1980a). Both movements conformed to Fitts' law.

Fitts' studies were one-dimensional to the extent that the movement was along a line. Jagacinski extended Fitts' law to two dimensions by placing targets in a circle (Jagacinski and Monk, 1985). Fitts' original experiment is considered to be in one-dimension because the targets were placed in a straight line. On the other hand, the stylus moves through a three-dimensional arc while carrying out the movement, an important distinction that will be discussed later in this chapter.

These studies blend together to show that there is a wide range of combinations of tasks and limbs in which Fitts' law holds.

2.1.6 Manual Tasks That Do Not Follow Fitts' Law

A number of interesting studies have produced cases where Fitts' law does not
hold, or where a variation of Fitts' law holds – such as the study by Kerr. Keele
describes a study by Kerr which looked at movement under water in a tapping task
(Keele, 1986). Kerr analyzed the effects of target width and distance separately
(Kerr, 1978), obtaining the functions:

$$MT_{land} = 34\,\text{ms} + 111 log_2 D + 109 log_2\left(\frac{1}{W}\right) \tag{2.4}$$

$$MT_{water} = 145\text{ms} + 155 log_2 D + 115 log_2\left(\frac{1}{W}\right) \tag{2.5}$$

Keele notes:

> Thus, while distance and width have equivalent effects for land-based move-
> ment, underwater distance has a larger effect than width, presumably because
> viscosity of water slows down the fast distance-covering portion of move-
> ment.
>
> *Keele*, 1986:24

This suggests that there are two parts to a pointing action: one fast distance-
covering portion, and one slower error-correction portion, and that the fast dis-
tance-covering portion is slowed by the water. Note that distance and width play
the same roles in increasing and decreasing movement time respectively as they do
in the Fitts' law equation.

Jagacinski, Repperger, Ward, and Moran studied Fitts' law for moving targets
(1980b). In particular, they studied the effect of movement in the target on target-
acquisition time. They found that Fitts' law was not a good predictor of movement
time with moving targets, and empirically derived the equation:

$$CT = c + dA + e(V+1)\left(\frac{1}{W} - 1\right) \tag{2.6}$$

where:

CT is the capture time in seconds

A, V, W are amplitude, velocity and target width, respectively

c, d, e are the regression coefficients

The Fitts' law equation describes a logarithmic speed–accuracy tradeoff. Under
some conditions, this gives way to a linear speed–accuracy tradeoff. Schmidt *et al.*
performed an experiment in which the participants had to make single, aimed
tapping movements whose distances and durations were both supposed to match
specified values (Schmidt, Zelaznik, Hawkins, Frank and Quinn, 1979; Schmidt,
Zelaznik, and Frank, 1978). They found that the speed–accuracy tradeoff could be
characterized in terms of the equation:

$$S = A + B\frac{D}{T} \tag{2.7}$$

where:

S is the standard deviation (variable error)

D is the mean movement distance

T is the mean movement duration

This equation not only holds for stylus tapping, but also for wrist rotations (Meyer *et al.*, 1988). Meyer notes that this equation might have the same functional status as Fitts' law when the movements have to match a temporal goal (Meyer *et al.*, 1990).

2.1.7 Variations to the Fitts' Law Equation

It was pointed out in Chapter 1 that one area where efforts in HCI and psychology work together is in the attempt to fine tune Fitts' law. In Fitts' original experiment, he used $log_2(2A/W)$ as the *ID*, primarily to ensure that the *log* term did not become negative for any of the movement amplitude and target width conditions he had. Since then, researchers have proposed other forms of *ID* to provide a better fit to the experimental data. Three forms of Fitts' *ID* have been used by various researchers. Fitts' original study produced the first form (Fitts, 1954):

$$MT = a + b\,log_2(2A/W)$$
$$ID = log_2(2A/W)$$

$$(2.8)$$

This form was subsequently justified by Fitts saying that in attempting to hit a target of width *W*, a participant can make an error of at most $W/2$, giving a *log* term of $A/(W/2) = 2A/W$ as in the equation above (Fitts and Peterson, 1964).

In 1960 Welford proposed the following variation (Welford, 1968):

$$MT = a + b\,log_2(A/W + 0.5)$$
$$ID = log_2(A/W + 0.5)$$

$$(2.9)$$

This variation was used by Card *et al.* (1978) in their study of pointing devices. While Fitts picked his variation for *ID* primarily to ensure that the value of *ID* was always positive for his target conditions, Welford proposed the second variation based, in part, on the observation that this definition reduces the numerical value of the first constant, *a*, giving theoretical predictions of *MT* near zero for an *ID* of zero (Fitts and Peterson, 1964). In 1992 MacKenzie proposed the Shannon variation (MacKenzie, 1992):

$$MT = a + b\,log_2(A/W + 1)$$
$$ID = log_2(A/W + 1)$$

$$(2.10)$$

Note that the equations differ only in the *log* term, i.e. they differ only in *ID*. In all forms, increasing the movement amplitude increases movement time, and increasing target width decreases movement time.

The variation MacKenzie proposed was intended to match more closely Shannon's theorem (Equation 2.1). He suggested that this formulation is more faithful to the information theoretic origins of Fitts' original derivation. He showed that this formulation also had a better fit to the data from a number of experiments, including Fitts' original study (Fitts, 1954) and the study by Card et al. (1978). In addition, this formulation has the advantage that the ID can never be negative, a condition that was possible in both the original Fitts formulation as well as in the Welford variation. The effect of Welford and MacKenzie's variations is to better fit the data at the bottom of the curve – where ID is low. The graph in Figure 2.4 represents how the data appears with the original formulation of ID.

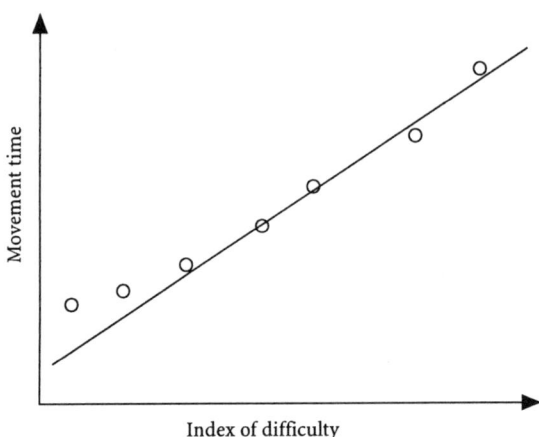

Figure 2.4: Curvature of data when compared to the Fitts' law regression line.

Index of difficulty

Unfortunately, MacKenzie adopts the information theoretic nature of Fitts' law too literally (MacKenzie, 1992). While Shannon's work on information theory was a good analogy to apply to the problems of human movement, there is no evidence at all that the theory applies to pointing tasks. In fact, other researchers have proposed different forms of the speed–accuracy tradeoff. For instance (as described earlier), Jagacinski and others investigating moving targets found a better fit using the empirically derived equation:[1]

$$MT = c + dA + e(V + 1)\left(\frac{1}{W} - 1\right) \qquad (2.11)$$

where:

c, d and e are constants

V is the velocity of movement of the target (Jagacinski et al., 1980b)

If $V = 0$, the equation becomes:

$$MT = c + dA + e\left(\frac{1}{W} - 1\right) \qquad (2.12)$$

Using this equation, Jagacinski got a better fit to the data for stationary targets in their task than the fit using the Fitts' law equation (Jagacinski et al., 1980b).

Kvalseth (1981) suggested a relationship of the form:

$$MT = aA^b W^c \qquad (2.13)$$

which, when $b = -c$, becomes:

$$MT = a(A/W)^b \qquad (2.14)$$

Meyer *et al.* note that values of b ranging between 0.25 and 0.5 often have a better fit to target acquisition data than Fitts' equation (Meyer *et al.*, 1990). These three contrasting models were studied by Epps, and he found Kvalseth's model to have the best r^2, though the Fitts and Jagacinski models had better mean squared error and predictive sum of squares (Epps, 1986).

Attempts to fine tune the Fitts' law *IP* are, perhaps, premature because we are still unsure of the factors that affect the speed–accuracy tradeoff. As Meyer *et al.* note, it is likely that differing tasks will have a better fit to one or other form of the Fitts' law equation, so finding a form that has a better fit to some subset of data is likely to yield results that cannot be generalized to other data (Meyer *et al.*, 1990).

2.2 Psychomotor Models

Psychologists have long understood the importance of a model describing the kinematics[2] of movement. This problem received the attention of modern psychology as far back as the nineteenth century. Once investigators started examining the basis for Fitts' law, the information theoretic reasoning that Fitts used was rejected as a model of movement, and various other theories were developed.

There are a large number of mathematical models that predict Fitts' law. Without anchoring the variables to a model of psychomotor behavior, there is no way of determining the validity of any one. Psychologists have therefore developed models that describe the manner in which people plan and execute movements. This section discusses various theories of movement which have been suggested, starting with work from the previous century by Woodworth, and concluding with current work by Meyer and others.

2.2.1 Initial Adjustment and Current Control

Some of the earliest work on models of movement was done by Woodworth in 1899 (cited in Meyer *et al.*, 1990). Woodworth thought that rapid movement had two phases, which he called *initial adjustment* and *current control*. The initial adjustment phase (also called ballistic movement) transports a selected part of the body quickly towards a target location. The current control phase (also called feedback control) subsequently corrects any errors made along the way, using sensory feedback to reach the target accurately (Meyer *et al.*, 1990). Based on experiments that compared movement accuracy of participants with closed eyes against participants with open eyes, Woodworth estimated that the initial adjustment takes place in the first 300ms of a movement, and the bulk of time required for movement is taken up by the current control phase.

Fitts' work with Shannon's theorem from information theory was the next major model of rapid aimed movements to emerge. Although his empirical results were easy to replicate, information theory has not been well received as a theoretical framework of movement control. Critics felt that the information theory hypothesis was strained at best, and totally wrong at worst, and this triggered a search for other ways of explaining the logarithmic speed–accuracy tradeoff (Meyer *et al.*, 1990).

2.2.2 Deterministic Iterative Corrections Model

In work originally presented in 1963, and subsequently re-published in 1983, Crossman and Goodeve raised doubts about Fitts' idea that there was noise in the initial adjustment phase of rapid movements (Crossman and Goodeve, 1983; Meyer *et al.*, 1990). They note that:

> There is an empirical difficulty of establishing the existence of the postulated 'noise' or initial uncertainty. … Thus the supposed 'noise' is apparently not present in the effector system.
>
> *Crossman and Goodeve*, 1983:253

They proposed an alternative model, which Meyer *et al.* call the *deterministic iterative corrections model* (Meyer *et al.*, 1990). Movements under this model are depicted in Figure 2.5. The horizontal axis represents movement distance and the vertical axis represents movement velocity. The curves correspond to successive hypothetical submovements between an initial home position (distance = 0) and a target region bounded by vertical lines whose center is A units from the home position and whose width is W units (Meyer *et al.*, 1988:343).

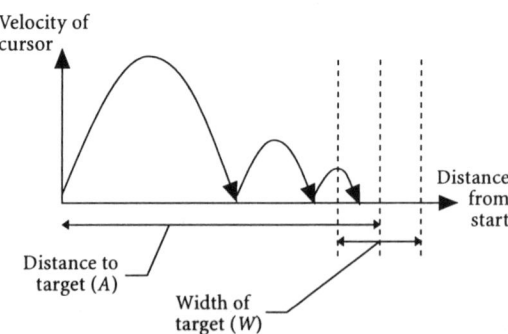

Figure 2.5: Movement characteristics of the *deterministic iterative corrections* model.

The model assumes that a movement to a target is made up of a number of sub-movements, of which each covers a constant portion (p) of the distance between the starting location and the target. For instance, the first submovement would travel a distance pA, the second would travel a distance $pA(1-p)$, the third would travel a distance $pA(1-p)^2$, and so on. The model's second assumption is that each of these submovements takes the same amount of time. The third assumption is that the submovements are guided by sensory feedback, either visual or kines-thetic. Movement ends when the distance to the target is less than $W/2$, where W is the width of the target. This gives a function representing movement time in terms of p, A and W, which has the same form as Fitts' law. Keele suggested a similar model (Keele, 1968). This model was rejected later in studies such as those of Jagacinski below.

2.2.3 Second-Order Under-damped Function

In 1976 Langolf, Chaffin and Foulke suggested using control system theory as an alternative to information theory as a means of explaining Fitts' law. They noted that a second-order, under-damped system with a constant damping ratio ξ will settle according to the equation:

$$MT = \frac{1}{\xi\varpi_n}\ln\left(\frac{2A}{W}\frac{1}{\sqrt{1-\xi^2}}\right) \tag{2.15}$$

They pointed out that such a system shows an oscillatory behavior, frequently characteristic of human movements. This function has a time versus displacement function as shown in Figure 2.6.

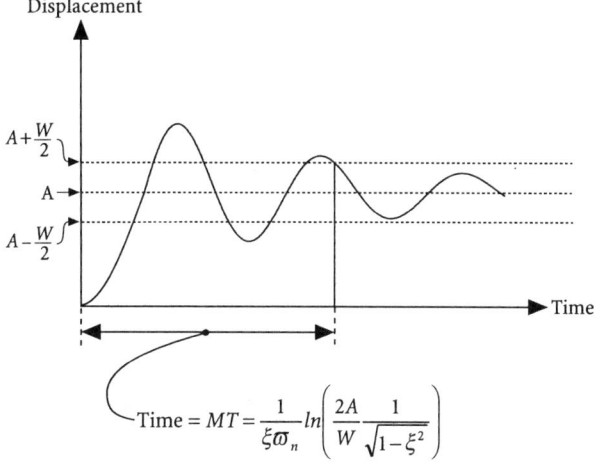

Figure 2.6: Movement characteristics predicted by an under-damped, second-order system (after Langolf et al., 1976:115).

Figure 2.6 shows how a system with damping ratio ξ will settle towards a signal of amplitude A. MT is the time after which the oscillations in the signal are within $W/2$ displacement units of the target distance A. This theory has not gained much popularity because it does not appear to describe the movement trajectories gathered in various studies, such as the one by Jagacinski described below. Langolf's model suggests that all movement will be characterized by a large initial movement, followed by a movement back to the start, followed by a movement towards the target, oscillating in this fashion until the oscillations are completely contained in the target. These characteristics were not found when movement data was gathered.

2.2.4 Dichotomous Movement Models

Jagacinski *et al.* (1980a) studied the microstructure of movement for joysticks employing position control and velocity control. Position and velocity control are discussed in detail in Chapter 3. Briefly, a position-control joystick controls the position of the cursor, while a velocity-control joystick controls the velocity of the cursor. Their experiment was aimed at determining which of two classes of model describing movement was valid. One class of movement models suggest a 'unitary convergence pattern' i.e., that all the submovements that form a movement towards a target are similar in form (Crossman and Goodeve, 1983; Keele, 1968; Langolf *et al.*, 1976). These are the models described earlier as *deterministic iterative corrections* models and the second-order, under-damped function. For example, in Crossman and Goodeve's model, the movements are of constant duration and accuracy. The other class of movement models suggest that there is an initial ballistic movement, initiated by a motor program, and subsequent movements are made under feedback control (also called current control). These are the type of models suggested by Woodworth (1899).

To determine which of the two classes of model was accurate, Jagacinski varied the ending criterion. One required participants to maintain the cursor over the target for a specified time (350ms), and the other required participants to hold position *as well as* keep the velocity of the cursor below a specified level (0.5 degrees/sec). Jagacinski hypothesized that if the unitary movement models were correct, there would be a significant change in the structure of the entire movement, while if the dichotomous model was correct, there would be a change only in the end of the movement.

Plots of cursor velocity against cursor position were made to examine the structure of the movements. The results showed that the trajectories did not resemble straight line, parabolic or spiral shapes, as would be expected from linear first- or second-order continuous systems. The movements usually consisted of a series of irregular episodes of acceleration and deceleration, which Jagacinski (Jagacinski *et al.*, 1980a) referred to as submovements.

In order to be able to measure and quantify these submovements, Jagacinski used a computer program to parse the input data to determine the beginnings and endings of submovement durations. A submovement was considered terminated when (a) the velocity changed sign, or (b) the acceleration changed sign. The submovements thus parsed were tabulated in terms of duration and accuracy.

He defined submovement accuracy as:

$$accuracy = \frac{|dist_{final}|}{|dist_{start}|} \qquad (2.16)$$

where:

$dist_{final}$ is the distance to the target at the end of the movement

$dist_{start}$ is the distance to the target at the beginning of the movement

The results clearly indicate that there is a marked difference between the first submovement and the rest of the submovements. The first submovements were both slower and more accurate than the rest of the submovements. This dichotomy is more marked for the velocity-control system than for the position-control system. The results also showed that the main effect of the position plus steadiness criterion was to increase the number of submovements that the participants made at the end of the movement, which is illustrated by Table 2.1 below.

Table 2.1: Number of submovements required for different control mechanisms and termination conditions.

	Number of submovements	
	Position criterion	Position plus steadiness criterion
Position control	2.1	3.1
Velocity control	2.5	3.0

The result that the first submovement was quite different from the subsequent movements rejects the deterministic iterative corrections models (Crossman and Goodeve, 1983; Keele, 1968). The finding also rejects Langolf's second-order, under-damped system (Langolf et al., 1976).

2.2.5 Stochastic Optimized Submovement Model

The stochastic optimized submovement model is the most developed model of movement currently available. By making a few simple assumptions, it attempts to predict a number of observed behaviors. The model has been proposed by Meyer et al. (1982, 1988, 1990), who argued that the deterministic iterative corrections model could not account for the experimental results from the Langolf and Jagacinski studies. The deterministic iterative corrections model postulates multiple submovements until the participant reaches the target, but a number of studies (Jagacinski et al., 1980a; Langolf et al., 1976; Meyer et al., 1988) found many occasions on which there are only one or two submovements, even when the ID is very large. Submovements measured in those experiments have not been found to have constant duration. In addition, submovements do not travel a constant portion of the distance to the target, and the initial submovement tended to be much longer and much more accurate than the subsequent movements (Jagacinski *et al.*, 1980a).

The deterministic iterative corrections model does not account for errors, but errors do occur (Fitts, 1954). A number of researchers have found that the error rate increases with increasing *ID* (Fitts and Peterson, 1964; Meyer *et al.*, 1988; Douglas and Mithal, 1993). Finally, Meyer notes that there are a number of cases where the speed–accuracy tradeoff is not logarithmic such as in the study by Jagacinski with moving targets (Jagacinski *et al.*, 1980b).

To explain these differences, Meyer *et al.* (1988, 1990) suggested the *stochastic optimized submovement* model (SOS model), which is illustrated in Figure 2.7. The model brings back the notion of noise in the motor system, which was originally introduced by Fitts (1954), then rejected in subsequent studies (Crossman and Goodeve, 1983). The model is influenced by the impulse–variability model (Schmidt, 1979; Schmidt *et al.*, 1978) which was originally described for time-matching movements such as making movements in time with some signal such as a metronome (Meyer *et al.*, 1990).

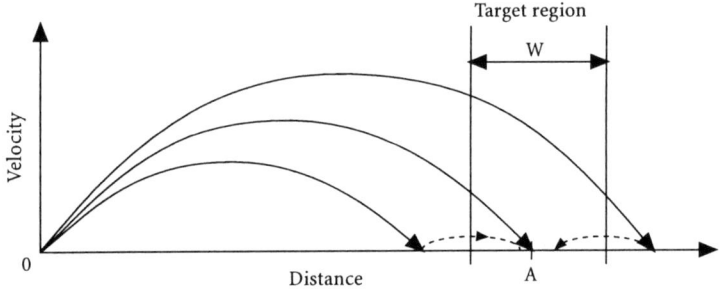

Figure 2.7: Movement characteristics predicted by the *stochastic optimized submovement* model.

The model makes a number of assumptions. These are listed below, with the caveat that this description assumes there are at most two submovements. The more general model is an extension of this model, and does not place a limit on the number of submovements.

Primary submovement. A movement begins with a primary submovement which is programmed to hit the center of the target region (illustrated by the middle trajectory of Figure 2.7). If the submovement is successful, the action terminates.

Motor noise and secondary submovements. Noise in the motor system may cause the primary submovement to miss the target shown by the upper and lower trajectories in Figure 2.7. This might cause a secondary corrective submovement to be made, based on sensory feedback. The secondary movement will, in most cases, hit the target but, on occasion, it will miss. In this limited case of the model, movement will cease – although as many as five submovements have been noted (Crossman and Goodeve, 1983). In most cases, there are only two submovements as shown by Figure 2.7.

Effects of noise on submovement endpoints. The model assumes that errors due to motor noise will increase with increasing velocity. In particular, primary submovements are assumed to have endpoints whose standard deviation (S_1) in space is proportional to the average primary submovement velocity (V_1):

$$S_1 = KV_1 = K\frac{D_1}{T_1} \tag{2.17}$$

where:

D_1 is the average distance traveled by the primary submovement

T_1 is the average time of the primary submovement

This assumption is based on studies that have shown that the variable error is a function of average movement velocity in a time-matching movement task (Schmidt *et al.*, 1979). Similarly, for the secondary submovement, we have:

$$S_2 = KV_2 = K\frac{D_2}{T_2} \tag{2.18}$$

Minimization of movement durations. The last key assumption is that the average velocities of the primary and secondary submovements are programmed to minimize the average total movement duration (T). Meyer *et al.* note that this assumption stems from the demands of the typical time-minimization movement task, where participants are presumed to try to reach the target region as quickly, and with as few errors, as possible.

The model makes a number of predictions. It predicts that the average total movement duration (T) is a quasi square-root function of the target distance/width ratio (Meyer, 1988):

$$T = 2K\frac{2\theta\sqrt{D/W} - \sqrt{W/D}}{\theta\sqrt{\theta - W/D}} \tag{2.19}$$

where:

K is a multiplicative constant from Equations 2.17 and 2.18

θ is a parameter whose value converges to $\sqrt{2\pi/Z}$ as D/W grows large

They are both experimentally derived constants. This function is very closely approximated by the function (Meyer *et al.*, 1990):

$$T = A + B\sqrt{\frac{D}{W}} \tag{2.20}$$

Meyer *et al.* note that they expect Equation 2.20 to come closer to the actual movement durations than a logarithmic equation. Kvalseth noted a better fit of the data to this equation (Kvalseth, 1981). Epps noted that the equation provides a better fit than Fitts' for some cases, but not for others (Epps, 1986).

The model predicts that the primary submovement duration will also follow an equation like Equation 2.19, and can be approximated by an equation similar to Equation 2.20. It predicts that the proportion of trials in which there are secondary submovements will increase with D/W.

The model also makes a prediction that error rates should increase monotonically with D/W:

> When target distance increases or width decreases, the primary submovements should slow down somewhat, but the decrease in their velocity would not be sufficient to maintain a constant rate of target hits. Instead, given the nature of the optimization, the primary submovements should miss the target more often, thereby requiring more corrections through secondary submovements.
>
> *Meyer et al.,* 1990:207

Meyer *et al.* have studied the SOS model for wrist rotations, and found its predictions to be fairly accurate. Thus, the model is possibly the best theory for explaining Fitts' speed–accuracy tradeoff that is available today. It is important to note, however, that the SOS model was developed for isotonic movement[3], and even among its authors, there are differences in opinion as to whether it will work for isometric movement.[4]

2.3 Other Aspects of Motor Behavior

In this section we discuss some general characteristics of overall motor processing: feedback, neuromuscular control, the role of attention and cognition during motor activity, and the learning of motor skills.

2.3.1 Feedback

We briefly introduced the notion of feedback in our discussion in section 2.2.2 where submovements are guided by sensory feedback. Feedback is the use of information to change the course of action and is a fundamental concept in the theory of control systems. Much of the early modeling of human movement depended upon models derived from this theory, which developed during the 1940s to understand and design self-guided weapon systems. In the psychological literature the focus has been on the following questions:

- Is there feedback during movement?
- What is the time course of action with integrated feedback?
- What is the sensory nature of the feedback?

Is there feedback during pointing movement? In a *closed-loop* system, such as the deterministic iterative corrections model and the second-order, under-damped function, feedback is crucial to the explanation of movement. In those models, corrective movements are made based on feedback from sensing relative positions of target and limb and comparing those to the goal. As we saw, the empirical data does not support an explanation of pointing movement based on a closed-loop control system. Instead, the data model supports a model that has two phases: an initial ballistic movement and subsequent corrective movements. This is a more complex non-linear model based on examining the microstructure of movement. In contrast to a closed-loop system, the ballistic motion is called an *open-loop* system. Open-loop system behaviors are explained by motor programs. A motor program is a set of muscle commands which are executed sequentially without interruption. Given values for a set of parameters (features), the same program can generate many different movements. The rapidity of movement is often cited as evidence for the existence of motor programs. There simply is not enough time to monitor feedback after each movement (Rosenbaum, 1991).

It is not known if, during movement, the human psychomotor system is closed-loop. Current research favors a mixed model with an initial ballistic phase unmonitored by feedback followed by a feedback-driven corrective phase. In a broader sense, it is clear that sensory feedback provides important information in subtle ways to guide the initiation and termination of movement, and the formulation of goals.

In the next two sections we will briefly review some of the research on visual and haptic perception as feedback and circumscribe answers to the third area of psychological questions: What is the sensory nature of the feedback and what is the time course of action with integrated feedback?

2.3.1.1 Visual Perception

People use visual feedback in movement. (See the discussion in section 2.3.3 on the role of attention and eye movement.) In an experiment conducted by Pew (1966), participants were asked to keep a moving target centered on an oscilloscope screen. To prevent feedback processing, the screen was blanked out for brief times of varying duration. Given the ability of participants to perform this task correctly, the time of visual feedback processing was estimated to lie between 200ms and 250ms.

The results from Pew were supported by other research conducted a few years later. In a classic study by Keele and Posner (1968) aimed at measuring the time of visual feedback, participants moved a pointer to a target. Participants were told to generate intended movement times of 0.15s, 0.25s, 0.35s and 0.45s. The experiment measured movement accuracy. Half of the time the lights were off so that the movement had no visual feedback. The lights were turned off randomly so that people had no intentional control over whether to use visual feedback or not.

The time required for visual processing was estimated as the shortest intended movement time for which accuracy was better with the lights on. A significant difference in error rate occurred initially at 0.25s. Therefore, the time to process visual feedback is assumed to be less than 0.25s. Participants took slightly more time than instructed, namely 0.19s, in the 0.15s condition. This leads to the conclusion that visual information feedback processing is between 190ms and 250ms.

In another study by Elliott (1985) on the role of visual feedback during rapid aimed movements, participants moved a stylus to a target 20cm away with movement times of approximately 225ms. Visual conditions were manipulated by the availability of light and prisms and the participants were informed in advance of the availability of visual feedback. The results indicate that participants are able to use vision rapidly to modify aiming movements but may do so only when the visual information is predictably available and/or yields an error large enough to detect, and early enough to correct.

Another important issue in visual feedback during movement is the perception of the trajectory of the moving limb. A study by Hay and Beaubaton (1986) tested three visual feedback conditions: no feedback, dynamic on-going feedback on the complete hand trajectory, and static error feedback on the movement endpoint. Accuracy was highest under the complete feedback condition. In a later study by Blouin, Teasdale, Bard and Fleury (1993), evidence was found for the significant contribution of vision during the initial phase of rapid pointing movements. Movements having directional requirements were more accurate when vision of the initial portion of the trajectory was available. Time-to-peak acceleration and velocity were shorter and their respective amplitudes were generally higher when vision was available for the first third of the trajectory than when it was not.

These studies argue for the value of visual feedback during rapid aimed movement, but they estimate it at a minimum of approximately 200ms. Since the ballistic phase of rapid aimed movements can occur much more rapidly, visual information processing of feedback is not assumed to play a role in the first phase of rapid aimed movement motor control – thus the popularity of the motor program theory. Nevertheless, some researchers believe that this estimate for visual feedback time is too high and has not been accurately measured. Evidence gathered by Hay and Beaubaton and Blouin *et al.* cited above supports this view. Most researchers believe that the time for the visual feedback loop is most certainly greater than 100ms (Rosenbaum, 1991). Other researchers believe that the sensory feedback from muscles could play a major role in motor control during the ballistic phase, since measuring neural signals from muscle just prior to observable movement gives processing time as low as 50ms for humans.

2.3.1.2 Haptic Perception

Haptic perception involves perception of information about texture, space, and form through contact with the physical world. Haptic perception is defined as a combination of tactile and kinaesthetic perception to provide information about distal objects and events (Loomis and Lederman, 1986). Tactile perception is perception triggered by cutaneous stimulation while the posture remains unchanged. Tactile perception is provided through receptors located in the skin for pressure, temperature and pain. Differences in pressure are sometimes translated into the perception of texture. Areas of the body vary in sensitivity. The fingers have the greatest sensitivity; the forearm about ten times less. Kinaesthetic perception is an awareness of the position of the body and limbs due to proprioceptive information from the joints. These receptors provide information about movement in a particular direction as well as position in space. Included within kinaesthetic perception is information about muscular effort. Information about balance is provided by the inner ears.

Very little research has directly addressed the role of haptic perception in pointing. However, it is quite clear that it is of critical importance to movement with a pointing device. Perception of shape, texture and temperature are critical in grasping. Proprioceptive information from joints determines whether the hand is correctly holding the device. Muscle and joint feedback from the hand during movement provide spatial position information as well as information for muscle contraction used for the device's mass inertia control.

The relationship between haptic perception and visual perception as feedback during movement are even less well understood. Gibson (1979) argued for the interrelatedness of perceptual systems. Perceptual information from a variety of senses, including kinaesthetic feedback related to self-directed body movement coupled to visual image changes, are crucial to our understanding of space and how the body moves through it.

2.3.2 Neuromuscular Control

In this section, we will introduce basic motor functioning from the point of view of the neurological system. This contrasts with this book's predominant perspective in terms of psychomotor functioning and performance. Our purpose here is to provide background for later discussions in the book on the effect of tremor and sidedness. It also serves to remind us that movement occurs within a biological system with its own complexity of constraints and abilities. The view we present parallels that of Rosenbaum (1991) and MacKenzie and Iberall (1994) in basing overall motor control in a motor program model.

2.3.2.1 Brain Anatomy and Functioning

The brain regulates muscular movement through a number of specialized areas: the cerebellum, the basal ganglia, the various parts of the motor cortex and the parietal lobe in the cortex. Figure 2.8 illustrates these principal areas in the brain. More than half of the neurons in the brain are located in the cerebellum. Its primary functions are the regulation of muscle tone, coordination, timing and motor learning. Damage to the cerebellum can permanently produce 'reaching too far' (hypermetria) and oscillation in conjunction with purposeful movements (intention tremor). Alcohol ingestion in otherwise normal individuals can produce similar effects. Overshooting targets during aiming movements can be viewed as a timing problem in the cerebellum (Eccles, 1977).

The basal ganglia in the forebrain appear to control ballistic movement, retrieve and activate motor plans, scale the amplitude of movements such as resting tremor, and integrate perception with motor activity.

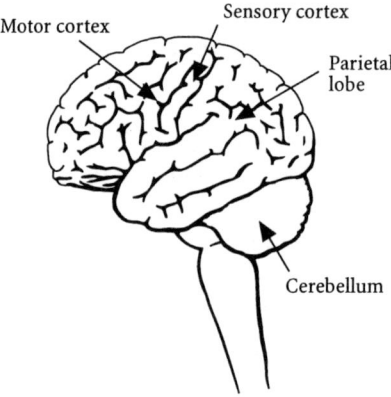

Figure 2.8: Areas in the human brain related to motor processing.

The motor cortex neurons fire just prior to motor movements (50ms). These neurons are functionally mapped to different muscle groups and limbs. The number of neurons is proportional to the precision of movement and they are responsible for the force and direction of movement. Motor-cortex neurons respond to muscle stretch with a reflex independent of volitional state. The premotor cortex prepares postural muscles for programmed movements and selects movement trajectories. The supplementary motor cortex is involved in planning extended movement sequences. The left hemisphere primarily stores learned movement sequences: the right hand receives motor commands directly from the left hemisphere, but the left hand receives them from the right hemisphere after the right hemisphere has received signals from the left hemisphere via the *corpus callosum*.

The parietal cortex appears to function in the memory representation for motor acts, that is, a person with damage to this area cannot pantomime the use of an object when asked to do so, but can manipulate the object successfully when it is physically present. This part of the brain gives evidence that motor activities have conceptual representations which can control the implementation and sequencing of motor acts.

2.3.2.2 Coordination and Sidedness

Because the limbs of the human body are bilaterally symmetrical, the psychomotor system must deal with allocation of tasks to different limbs and different sides of the body, and to coordination. One solution is to allocate a particular side of the body to a particular activity. The definition of the preferred or dominant hand, foot, eye or ear is that it is regularly used in tasks that require only one limb, eye or ear. Although reaching motion is done by either hand, pointing movement is usually performed with the preferred hand.

It is estimated that approximately 10% of the population is left-handed, although the causes are as yet unknown. The determination of the preferred sidedness of hand, foot, eye, or ear may vary by task. For example, a person may prefer to write with the left hand holding the pen, but play tennis with the right hand holding the racquet. Similarly, a person may prefer to use the right hand for writing, but the left foot for kicking a ball. The proportion of the population who are right-footed is 80%; right-eyed 70%; and right-eared 60%. Various tests are available for handedness and others for sidedness (Oldfield, 1971; Porac and Coren, 1981).

2.3.3 Attention and Cognition

Although the motor system is embedded in a complex neurological system that functions without any awareness on our part, many movements, including pointing, are voluntary acts. Both attention and cognition are involved. Most information about attention and cognition and its role in human movement has been obtained from studies of the human eye, particularly with saccadic and smooth pursuit movement (cf. Rosenbaum, 1991). Research has shown that when attention is directed to an object spatially located, the eyes move saccadically to bring the image of the object into the foveal region of the retina. The saccades are under voluntary control although not conscious awareness. They are triggered by the difference between the position of the object and the position of the eye, i.e. retinal position error. Although initiation of a saccade requires a shift of spatial attention, shifting of attention does not require a saccade (Posner, 1978).

Visual perception is not suppressed during a saccade. Multiple saccades appear to be programmed in advance, but subject to modification on the basis of visual feedback during execution. It is also the case that while people cannot report verbally on visual perception during a saccade, the psychomotor system is capable of using the visual information to guide aimed movements.

If an object is moving, mental attention is focused on the object and, if the target is away from the current eye fixation point, a saccade is made. Once the object is fixated, the velocity of the eye tries to match the velocity of the object in what is called a smooth pursuit movement. Although it appears that an object in the visual field must trigger the smooth pursuit movement, it is now known that eye motion reflects cognitive states. For example, people's expectations about the direction of movement of a target will cause the eyes to move in that direction before the object starts to move.

2.3.4 Learning

Many human movements, such as reaching and walking are so well-practiced that we usually cannot remember the process of learning them. However, new-skill acquisition can be characterized by a three-stage process model first proposed by Fitts (1964). The first stage is *cognitive* during which basic procedures for performing the task are established. This stage demands focused attention and is often accompanied by verbal cues. An *associative* stage follows during which the learner tries out different task components and associates their execution with success or failure. Actions not contributing to success are dropped. Feedback is thus very important at this stage. The final stage is the *automatic* performance of a task with less attention and often intermittent feedback.

Another characteristic of human learning is that the repetition of a motor task over a period of time results in a reduction in movement time. This is called the practice effect. The decrease in performance time as a result of practice can be quantified as the *Power Law of Practice* (Card *et al.*, 1983). The time T_n to perform a task on the *n*th trial follows a power law. That is, with practice, performance time decreases according to a formula of the form:

$$T_n = T_1 n^{-a} \tag{2.21}$$

Alternatively, the logarithm ('*log*') of the time to do a task on the *n*th trial is equal to the *log* of the time to do it on the first trial minus a constant, *a*, times the *logarithm* of the trial number:

$$\log T_n = \log T_1 - a \log n \tag{2.22}$$

This equation can be plotted as the *log* of the mean trial time for participants (*y*-axis) vs. the *log* of the trial block number (*x*-axis) and will yield a straight line if the data are well-behaved. In addition to a decrease in performance time with repetition, practiced human-motor movements become more graceful and efficient. This can be attributed to the fact that more degrees of freedom in limb movement are allowed to vary. Well-learned perceptual motor skills are very resistant to being forgotten and may be retained for years without intervening practice.

2.4 Summary

This chapter has provided a basic introduction to the results of the psychological research on human pointing. It will provide a basic introduction to issues related to human psychomotor functioning which will be addressed by ergonomics research covered in the remainder of the book. These issues will range from Fitts' law, to the SOS model of movement, to feedback and to handedness. However, the complexity of the human psychomotor system should not be underestimated: this brief chapter can only provide the barest review.

There is one issue that is not often addressed in the psychomotor research. That issue is the role of the computer in presenting the experimental task, and gathering and analyzing the data. We have drawn a strong distinction in Chapter 1 between studies of manual pointing and computer-based pointing. This chapter has presented the studies of manual (non-computer) pointing for the most part. However, there has been a slight amount of blurring. Early experimenters, such as Fitts, did not use the computer in any part of their experimental design. However, later research studies such as Walker *et al.*'s validation of the SOS model (1994) are entirely computer-based. Does the computer introduce experimental error which may not be accounted for by the design? Are we getting a true representation of movement? We will wrestle with this problem of scientific validation of psychomotor experiments again in Chapter 6.

A second aspect of this problem is illustrated by the experimental extension of Fitts' law phenomena to computer-mediated pointing. The computer is merely a representation of experiments such as Fitts' – an experiment which is a simplification of real movement. Any results are only as good as the strength and accuracy of the representation. Computer-based experiments, even those that closely mimic Fitts' study, differ from studies of real movement on two significant points:

1. Fitts' experiment took place in three-dimensional space even though the placement of the target varied only in one dimension. Computer-based experiments take place in a two-dimensional space: the computer's screen. Movements with a device such as a mouse on a mousepad take place on a two-dimensional plane, while the stylus used by Fitts' participants described arcs in three-dimensional space.

2. Fitts' experiment was, for want of a better word, direct, i.e. participants were moving the stylus in order to make the tip of the stylus connect with a target plate. In computer-based experiments, the object that participants are moving, e.g. the mouse, is not the focus of their attention. The focus of attention is the cursor on the screen.

There is also no direct mapping between the action performed on the pointing device and the movement of the cursor on the screen. This might be as simple as a linear mapping from displacement to displacement, as is normal for most mice, but it need not be so. In fact, devices such as power mice use non-linear mappings between mouse displacement and cursor displacement in an attempt to increase performance (Jellinek and Card, 1990), while devices such as isometric joysticks map force into velocity. A more complete discussion of this issue is deferred until Chapter 3, section 3.1. The importance of this is that while computers have played a valuable role in understanding human psychomotor movement, the differences between computer-based movement (virtual movement) and real-world movement (real movement) should always be kept in mind. In the next chapter we move from manual pointing behavior to computer-based pointing and discuss the application of Fitts' law and findings from other psychomotor research. Three factors become critical in the discussion: operation, types and features of devices; control by different limbs; and types of computer-based tasks.

2.5 Endnotes

1   Personal communication in e-mail from Richard Jagacinski, 28 October 1994.
2   Kinematics is the branch of mechanics that studies the motions of bodies, e.g. position, velocity and acceleration, without regard to the masses or forces involved.

3   Pointing devices are classified as *isotonic* or *isometric*. Isotonic devices use displacement of the device as an input variable. An example is the mouse. Isometric devices use force applied to the device as the input variable. Many joysticks are isometric.

4   Personal communications from David Meyer, 10 November 1993 and Charles E. Wright, 16 November 1993.

3. *Factors in Applying Psychomotor Studies to Pointing Devices*

In the previous chapter we briefly surveyed the extensive psychological literature that provides a background for understanding basic elements in human manual pointing, primarily as rapid aimed movement. In this chapter we turn to computer-mediated pointing and its ergonomics.

As we discussed in Chapter 1, the question that is always foremost in studies of the ergonomics of pointing devices is 'Which device is best?' That question is impossible to answer without considering complex relationships between multiple factors. Chapter 2 discussed, in depth, several psychomotor factors:

- the type of movement and task;
- the limb and preferred side for performing an activity;
- the skill level of the person.

These factors continue to have importance in computer-mediated pointing and must always be taken into account in empirical studies. This chapter focuses on three additional factors:

1. the device and its operation;
2. the controlling limb;
3. the computer-based task.

All these factors have been shown to exert a significant effect on dependent variables such as pointing speed, errors, time to learn, and whether the movement follows Fitts' law. We will spend this entire chapter providing technical background and discussing these three factors in terms of their isolated impact on motor behavior. We will postpone the analysis of the ergonomic research literature on each device and studies which compare performance between devices until Chapter 4.

In section 3.1, *Devices: Operation, Features and Types*, we will present background information on device operation, both hardware and software. We will pay particular attention to different types of transducer inputs and cursor control, the concept of transfer functions and the related concept of gain. We then describe features of devices that have special implications for pointing behavior such as control resistance, selection of screen objects and mode switching. Section 3.2, *Limb Control*, elaborates on the different limbs used for controlling pointing devices, multiple-limb input, preferred limb input, and the issue of sensory feedback. Section 3.3, *Tasks*, examines the basic types of tasks which can be done with pointing devices: pointing, dragging, tracking, and drawing. Finally, a comparison is made between experimental tasks and real work environments – the so-called ecological validity problem.

3.1 Devices: Operation, Features and Types

In this section we will briefly introduce the operation and features of pointing devices that have a significant impact on the ergonomics of their use. Readers who desire a more detailed technical engineering review are referred to Sherr (1988) for a discussion of computer input devices and to Frost (1972) for general device-control dynamics.

3.1.1 From Transducers to Drivers to User Interfaces

A key concept in the understanding of how pointing devices work, is the complex transformation of information sensed by a physical device into movement of the cursor on the screen. Figure 3.1 represents a system block diagram of a generic pointing device.

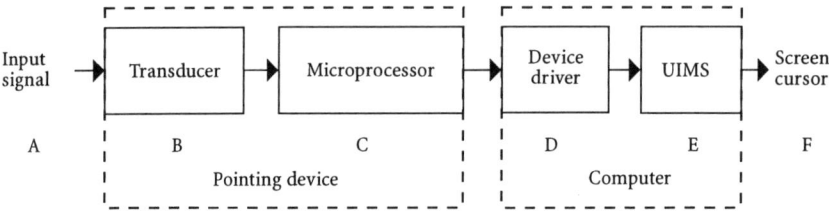

Figure 3.1: Generic block diagram of a pointing device.

The user manipulates a physical property of the device (A), such as position, which is sensed by the *transducer* (B) and input as changes in an electrical quantity, such as voltage, into a device microprocessor (C). For most modern pointing devices, the microprocessor translates the signal from analog to digital form using an A–D converter. The transducer and the microprocessor are usually packaged as part of the device. The microprocessor may also compute a sophisticated *transfer function* which takes the digitized signal and transforms it into displacement or velocity data. The pointing device is usually connected to the main computer through a standardized connection called a *port*. The microprocessor generates interrupts to signal that new data is available from the pointing device. This data is read by specialized software in the main computer known as the *device driver* (D) which generates pointing device events to that part of the operating system responsible for graphics and windows management. This is called the *user interface management system* or UIMS (E). The UIMS is responsible for the graphics which, finally, create cursor position and motion (F).

Although the software driver plays a critical role in determining the relationship between input parameters and output parameters, the UIMS and low-level graphics routines determine other ergonomic features. For example, the speed of the software routines may be critical for timely perceptual feedback during both pointing and dragging.

As the cursor moves across the screen, its position must be updated often enough to provide a natural sense of smoothness of motion. How the UIMS handles the sampling of events for cursor position is equally important; for example, is the sampling rapid enough to accurately represent changes in (x, y) position? Finally, the UIMS determines aspects such as whether auditory feedback is possible in addition to visual feedback and whether two-handed (parallel) input is supported.

3.1.1.1 Transducer Input

Different types of pointing devices sense different physical properties and can map to different properties of cursor control. For example, in the case of a touch-sensitive tablet, when the user moves a stylus, thereby changing its position, the position of the cursor is directly mapped to the screen. In other devices, the mapping between the input parameter and the cursor position is not so direct. For example, in a mechanical mouse the user changes the physical location of the mouse, which is sensed by rollers moved by the mouse ball. The displacement of the rollers, not the actual position of the mouse, is input to the microprocessor.

Thus, devices can be categorized by whether they operate in *absolute* or *relative mode*. This terminology is intended to characterize absolute mode devices, such as the touch pad, which directly maps the coordinate system between the input device to the screen. Relative mode devices use the initial position of the input device to establish a cursor reference position. The mouse is an example of a relative mode device. Subsequent movement of the input device is always represented on the display as relative to this initial reference position no matter where it occurs on the input device. Because there is no direct mapping of user input (movement) into the intermediate parameter for the software driver, users can pick up the mouse and put it down in another position without moving the cursor, i.e. users can move the mouse without affecting its sensor. Only relative devices allow this repositioning. There are 3D mice, such as an experimental one by Apple Computer Inc., which sense the position of the mouse in 3D space and are absolute mode devices.

The mapping between transducer input and cursor movement becomes even more indirect in the case of isometric joysticks which use force as the physical property sensed by the pointing device. An *isometric* device is one that does not change shape when force is applied to it – there is no discernible movement of the device itself. (In contrast, most pointing devices such as the mouse are *isotonic* and use displacement of the control itself as an input variable.) In isometric systems, force applied to the device is typically the input variable to the system. In an isometric joystick, users vary the amount of force they apply to the device, thereby changing the resistance of varistors attached to the joystick. A similar device can be built using strain gauges in place of the varistors. The change in resistance is used to control the *velocity* of the cursor. Frost (1972) cites some of the advantages of isometric devices:

1. they transduce force, as opposed to displacement, therefore no space is necessary for control movement;
2. the output returns to zero when the applied force is removed;
3. they have less problem of input under environmental forces, e.g. extreme gravitational forces ('G-force') flying a fighter plane;
4. as velocity-controlled devices, they have fewer errors (2:1) in tasks that involve tracking high-frequency target inputs.

On the other hand, isotonic devices, when compared to isometric, have at least two advantages:

1. visual feedback of control position is available;
2. they are less fatiguing because the amount of force applied is not an input variable which must be constantly monitored and maintained.

3.1.1.2 Cursor Control

Once the device sends its signals into the computer, other factors come into play. One such factor is the cursor display output control. Based on the type of output control, we can call devices *position control, velocity control* and *acceleration control* (or any arbitrary time derivative of input position that we choose to take). The type of output control is also called the *control order* of the device, from earlier control systems theory (Frost, 1972). For example, a mouse maps a displacement (of the mouse on the mousepad) to a displacement (of the cursor on the screen). This position control is basic to a *zero-order control device*. An isometric joystick that maps joystick force to cursor velocity control is referred to as a *first-order control device*. A small force results in less speed, while a larger force increases the velocity. If it mapped the force to an acceleration, it would be called a *second-order control device*. Similarly, third-, fourth- and higher-order control devices are possible. Computer system pointing devices are either zero- or first-order devices. The accelerator in an automobile and the rudder in an airplane are second-order control devices. Submarines have at least third-order control.

It is important to note that the input parameter sensed can be mapped onto any of these output parameters simply by changing the software driver. The mouse can be used to control displacement, velocity or acceleration. We could re-write the mouse's device driver so that its displacement from a central location controls the cursor's velocity. For example, we could write an algorithm that mapped one *mickey* (smallest unit of mouse movement) away from the central location, to a movement of one pixel per second away from the center. If (0,0) defined the center of the screen, and the mouse was at (2,–3) mickeys, it would have a velocity of (2,–3) pixels per second away from (0,0). This would result in a velocity-control mouse. Similarly, an isometric joystick is most often configured so that force controls the velocity of the cursor, but it could be configured so that force controls the absolute position of the cursor away from the center. Position control joysticks have been studied by Jagacinski and Monk (1985) and are common in some game-control situations.

The order of the device has often been suggested as a means of predicting human behavior. That is, the higher the order of the device, the more difficult the system is to control. Ultimately, this categorization appears somewhat unclear and the order of the device interacts as a factor with the input property and the task. For example, it is not clear that human behavior with an isometric (force) joystick that controls velocity – a first-order device – is the same as an isotonic (displacement) joystick that controls velocity – another first-order device. Instead, it is more precise to take note of the relationship between the input parameter and the output parameter for any pointing device and recognize that general experience has suggested that higher order devices may be more difficult to control for rapid aimed movement task situations.

3.1.1.3 Transfer Functions and Display/Control Gain

The transfer function is the mathematical model for representing the transformation that is made from the input signal to the cursor control. Many device drivers allow users to choose different transfer functions. For example, the Macintosh Control Panel (operating system version 7.5) for the mouse has seven speeds from very slow to fast.

Transfer functions are characterized as linear or non-linear, and can be simplified to a concept called *gain*. Gain is a term used in the early human factors literature and is derived from control systems modeling. Gain is expressed in terms of the ratio between display and control movements, for example, the inches of pointer movement per revolution of a knob. Sometimes, the term *display/control (D/C) gain* is used to make the relationship between the two variables clear. In a computer-based system, the gain is the ratio between the magnitude of displacement or velocity of the cursor on the screen and the magnitude of displacement of the control device. For example, a D/C gain of 2.0 means that the cursor will move two centimeters for every one centimeter of input device displacement. In contemporary ergonomics usage the reciprocal of gain, called the *control/display (C/D) ratio*, is sometimes used. Readers should be attentive to the differences between the two terms.

It should also be noted that it does not make sense to describe non-linear transfer functions (see below) in terms of a simple ratio such as D/C gain. The ratio itself is not constant; it increases the faster the device moves. In other words, when gain depends on velocity, fast movements will result in larger cursor displacements per unit of displacement of the input device. Secondly, it is impossible to quantify force as a measure of control movement, the 'C' term. In both these cases the correct specification of the transfer function is the function or even algorithm itself.

Any measure of D/C gain always should be sampled empirically, since lag caused by slow software routines or operating system demands can change the expected values. Likewise, monitors differ in their resolution, causing pixels to vary in size. This can cause a D/C gain of 2.0 to change to 1.75 since gain is measured in actual physical distance.

D/C gain was once thought to be a critical design factor in terms of human performance, often determining both the speed and accuracy of the device. (For a general discussion, see Chapanis and Kinkade, 1972.) However, research has found that there is a range within which the device is usable and, within that range, the display/control gain does not appear to have much effect (Jellinek and Card, 1990; Kantowitz and Elvers, 1988; Lin et al., 1992; MacKenzie, 1991). For the mouse, a gain of 2 is the normal setting, with increases to gains of 4, 8, 16, 32 having no effect on average overall movement time. A gain of 1 is *not* desirable: on a large screen, the mouse has to be constantly repositioned on the (smaller) mousepad.

In discussing why changes in gain have little effect on performance, Graham (1996) suggests that the hand motion in the initial ballistic phase is preprogrammed by the brain's motor control system for the actual distance to be covered by the hand, not the distance covered by the cursor on the display. Gain is bounded on the upper limit by the inability of the operator to make precise changes in position or force; on the lower limit by the maximum displacement or force the operator can achieve (Frost, 1972). Thus, very high gains create faster initial movements, but make fine positioning more difficult.

The transfer function described by Bentley, Custer and Meyer (1975) is an example of a linear transfer function for an isometric joystick. Bentley et al. designed the joystick used by Card, English and Burr (1978) in the latter's ground-breaking studies of mouse and joystick performance. Bentley et al. used the following transfer function which computed a constant coefficient difference equation to determine the position of the cursor on the screen based on the voltage (force) being applied to the joystick:

$$Cx_k = a_1Cx_{k-1} + a_2Cx_{k-2} + a_3Cx_{k-3} + b_0(Vx_k + b_1Vx_{k-1} + b_2Vx_{k-2} + b_3Vx_{k-3}) \qquad (3.1)$$

where:

Cx, Cy are the cursor coordinates

Vx, Vy are transducer voltages

$k-3, k-2, k-1$ are discrete sequential sampling times

a_i, b_i are constants

Since the isometric joystick in this case was controlled directly by the software application program, the program was able to update the cursor position directly. In modern computer systems, this is not possible because they are designed for many interchangeable pointing devices mediated by device drivers, and have a UIMS which manages the actual positioning of the cursor independently from application software. Thus, the device's transfer function has no information about actual cursor position. Although some devices have linear transfer functions, many have non-linear ones. Because pointing motions are generally initiated with a ballistic motion and then a series of fine positioning motions, some have proposed that the ideal transfer function is non-linear (Bentley, Custer and Meyer, 1975; Greenstein and Arnaut, 1988) and even non-linear and discontinuous (Rutledge and Selker, 1990). The transfer function developed by Bentley *et al.*, (Equation 3.1) can become non-linear by squaring or cubing the incoming digital value before the difference equation is computed. A second example of a non-linear transfer function is that of Rutledge and Selker (1990) for a finger-controlled, isometric velocity joystick called the Pointing Stick. (This device was marketed by IBM as the Trackpoint™ II). Rutledge and Selker describe experimentally determining the force-to-motion transfer function to optimize pointing speed. They report that the following characteristics are desirable:

1. a solid feel in which the cursor does not move even if the finger is not perfectly steady;

2. small target pointing with accurate control of low-speed motion, e.g. one pixel at a time;

3. long-distance pointing with high speed required;

4. users like to feel they can dash across the screen if necessary.

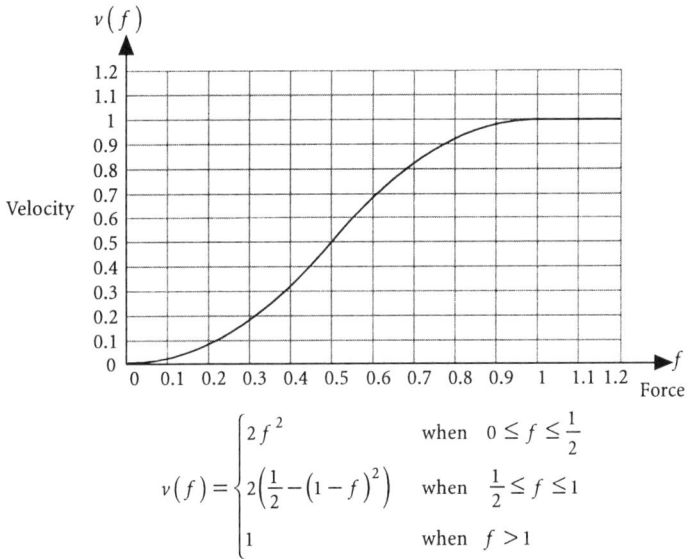

$$v(f) = \begin{cases} 2f^2 & \text{when } 0 \le f \le \frac{1}{2} \\ 2\left(\frac{1}{2} - (1-f)^2\right) & \text{when } \frac{1}{2} \le f \le 1 \\ 1 & \text{when } f > 1 \end{cases}$$

Figure 3.2: Sigmoid parabolic function (after Rutledge and Selker, 1990, Figure 1).

These characteristics define a non-linear function in which there is no motion at all for very small force, followed by a region of predictably slow motion somewhat independent of force, then followed by a rapid but smooth acceleration until reaching an upper plateau which lies just below the eye–hand tracking limit. Such a function, derived from a piecewise sigmoid parabolic, is illustrated in Figure 3.2.

To compute actual values of force to velocity for the device they developed, force, f, must be scaled by 225g mm^{-2}, and velocity, v, by 1.5 pixels/ms. This function, called '2Plateau' by Rutledge and Selker, was chosen as the best transfer function based on user testing for optimal user pointing performance when compared with several linear and parabolic functions.

The general problem of choosing a non-linear transfer function is very complex. First, there is a very large number of possible mathematical functions, and designers have to pick one. Second, having picked a transfer function, designers do not have any analytical means of picking the values for the constants in the transfer function, such as $k-3$, $k-2$, $k-1$ and a_i, b_i in the function used by Bentley *et al.* cited earlier. As a result, the design process is marked by a cycle of picking a transfer function, setting the control parameters, testing the device with users, changing the parameters and re-testing, and going through this cycle until acceptable performance is achieved. Such an approach has the problem that most solutions are not optimal. In addition, manufacturers' claims of 'improved drivers' (or transfer functions) are difficult to substantiate because few developers, if any, perform rigorous experiments with human participants to show that their drivers or transfer functions actually improve task-level pointing speed. Therefore it is not clear that any changes they made to the drivers are in fact 'better'. An acceptable experiment would be one such as the example described in Chapter 5. Such an experiment would compare the performance of the new transfer function to a benchmark device such as the mouse; have at least 10 participants randomly selected from the population of potential users; and extend over a period sufficient for users to reach a skilled level.

As previously explained, the literature frequently contains the speculation that non-linear functions would be better, given the nature of human rapid aimed movement. Unfortunately, the Bentley *et al.* and Rutledge and Selker studies of isometric-joystick transfer functions were not conducted in rigorous experimental environments that would allow a clear evaluation of the effects of the transfer functions. There are, however, two studies which specifically test the effect of non-linearity, that of Jellinek and Card (1990), and that of Graham (1996).

In a study of accelerated (non-linear) transfer functions in mice, Jellinek and Card (1990) found no significant difference in human movement time between mice with accelerated and non-accelerated transfer functions in a one-dimensional Fitts' task. For the non-accelerated (linear) condition, D/C gains of 1, 2 (normal setting), 4, 8, 16 and 32 were tested. For all gains of 2 or greater no differences were found between movement times. For the gain of 1 (1cm mouse movement = 1cm cursor movement), movement time was slower because participants had to keep picking up the mouse and repositioning it to move to the larger target distances. (The largest was 22.3cm.) For the non-linear transfer functions, the gain was varied as a continuous function of the mouse's velocity – as the hand moves faster, the gain itself increases. Again, no improvement in average overall movement time was attributable to the non-linear transfer functions; in fact, they appeared to increase pointing time.

A recent detailed study by Graham (1996) of pointing movement kinematics for the hand confirmed this result. The Graham study used an infrared tracking system to record motion of the hand while the user viewed a computer display with conventional targets and cursor. The cursor motion was modified in three transfer function conditions:

- constant gain (linear);
- discrete gain increase (discrete non-linear);
- continuous gain (continuous non-linear).

Discrete gain-change showed no advantage in overall movement time over constant gain, which was the finding of Jellinek and Card (1990). Moreover, continuous gain significantly degraded (increased) movement time. This degradation in the non-linear condition was also seen as an increase in the average number of corrective submovements and increases in effective target width compared with the constant gain condition. Graham attributes the non-linear condition performance degradation to difficulty, i.e. increased time, in decelerating to the target during the initial ballistic motion.

The results of the Jellinek and Card, and the Graham studies suggest that despite the apparent appeal of non-linear transfer functions, they do not improve performance time. *Why then are they so popular?*

Both the Macintosh and Microsoft Windows operating systems drivers for the mouse support accelerated (non-linear) transfer functions. Jellinek and Card suggest that the popularity of such transfer functions is that rather than reducing the speed of pointing, they are preferred because they reduce the size of the mouse 'footprint' (area needed to move the mouse) with large screens.

Most pointing devices today are designed with static transfer functions – that is, the transfer functions themselves are always the same no matter what the task or user. This is probably attributable to the early development of pointing device technology in the 1950s and 1960s. It is interesting to conceive of dynamic transfer functions which adapt over time to the performance of a particular user or task. This is entirely possible now that there is a microprocessor controlling the pointing device hardware.

The resulting complex combination of transducers, software drivers, graphic routines and UIMS creates the transformation of sensed physical property of the pointing device to control of the cursor. To summarize, there is no direct mapping between the action performed on the pointing device and the movement of the cursor on the screen (indicated in Figure 3.1). This might be as simple as a linear mapping from displacement to displacement, but it need not be so. Absolute devices such as touch tablets, and displacement devices such as mice and trackballs usually have a very simple overall linear transfer function. On the other hand, isometric joysticks have very complex and, most often, non-linear transfer functions. The final behavior of the cursor is also influenced by the speed of the graphics routines and UIMS and the monitor characteristics, including pixel density and shape.

3.1.2 Other Device Features

There are a few other design aspects of pointing devices that must be considered from an ergonomic point of view. These include the control resistance of the device, selection of screen objects and mode switching.

3.1.2.1 Control Resistance

Force must always be applied to move a control. There are four types of resistance:

1. elastic (spring loading);
2. static and sliding friction;
3. viscous damping;
4. inertia.

All physically manipulated controls have mass. Exceptions would be those controlled by eye tracking, brain waves or body states. Since most controls move across a surface or pivot within a mechanism, they also have static and sliding friction. Users interpret these forces as the 'feel' of the device and frequently use the sensory information as feedback. Chapanis and Kinkade (1972) provide an extensive discussion of the human factors issues of control resistance in general.

Designers of computer pointing devices typically must make decisions about whether a device will have elastic resistance (spring loading or not), inertial resistance (its weight and size), and viscous damping resistance. A non-isometric joystick can be spring loaded or not. If it is spring loaded, it will always return to a central rest position when released. When it is not spring loaded, it will remain in the last position it was moved to. Such factors can in turn affect other factors. For example, the spring-loaded device will more likely be used as a velocity control device, while the other will more likely be used as a position control device.

Such pragmatic considerations can sometimes be carried across to other devices. For example, if we designed a mouse which controlled velocity of the cursor, a spring-loaded mouse is conceivable. This would always return to a central location when released. Note that this return to the central location can either be performed explicitly by springs, or tacitly by software, which could return the cursor to the center of the screen after a few seconds of inactivity.

3.1.2.2 Selection of Screen Objects

A second aspect that must be considered is *selection*. The pragmatics of computer use require that the user signals the system explicitly for screen object selection after pointing. Selection guarantees that the system will fully correspond to the user's intentions to end a pointing activity and select a specific target. Continuous pointing devices must provide an additional device for selection, usually, though not always, in the form of a button. The selection device can be integrated into the pointing device or physically separated, such as a key on a keyboard. Alternative methods of selection include selection by tapping or other distinguishable semantic action, or by direct contact with the surface of the tablet.

3.1.2.3 Mode Switching

If a device can be used in two different contexts or modes, then we describe it as a *mode-switching* device. For example, a key used as both a typing device and a pointing device, such as in the Home Row 'J' Mouse®, can mode-switch. In the Home Row keyboard, when the key is held down for longer than some threshold of time, the device switches into pointing mode.

3.2 Limb Control

As we have seen, pointing devices differ greatly in their operation and features. This is the first major factor of which we must be aware. Even so, while devices might be grouped into general categories such as mice or joysticks and have major similarities as result of their basic operation, they still may differ markedly in human performance because of the limb used to control them. In Chapter 2, we saw that psychomotor research on Fitts' law has noted differences in human performance based on the limb used for pointing. In this section, we discuss some basic issues peculiar to limb control of pointing devices. This is the second factor that must be considered when adapting psychomotor studies to computer-meditated pointing.

3.2.1 Types of Limb

The most common body parts used for pointing device control are the hand and wrist. The mouse, the hand-operated joystick, the digitizer stylus, the trackball and the light-pen are all hand-operated (Card, English and Burr, 1978; Epps, 1986; Goodwin, 1975; MacKenzie, Sellen, and Buxton, 1991). The finger (Rutledge and Selker, 1990; Douglas and Mithal, 1994; Zhai, Milgram and Buxton, 1996), eyes (Ware and Mikaelian, 1987), head (Andres and Hartung, 1989; Jagacinski and Monk, 1985), knees (English, Englebart, and Berman, 1967) and foot (Drury, 1975; Pearson and Weiser, 1986; Pearson and Weiser, 1988) have also been used to control pointing devices.

Although limbs have been studied as an inherent part of device operation and limbs have been studied in manual pointing (see section 2.1.4), few studies have focused specifically on the factor of the limb in performance with pointing devices. One exception is a recent study by Zhai, Milgram and Buxton (1996). In this study of 6 degree of freedom (DOF) pointing devices, a hand-operated input device that included the fingers was compared to a device without finger control. (*Note*: these are essentially three-dimensional input devices. The normal mouse is a 2 DOF pointing device.) The experimental task was a 6 DOF stereoscopic docking task which required the participant to move a 3D cursor as quickly as possible to align it with a 3D target. The cursor and the target were two tetrahedra of equal size: 4.2cm. Since earlier studies such as those of Langolf *et al.* (1976) had found that the fingers have a higher *index of performance* than the hand, the Zhai *et al.* experiment predicted and confirmed that the input device which included finger control would out-perform the other device. After approximately an hour of practice, movement-completion times for the docking task were significantly faster for the finger-controlled device. (Means estimated at 7.5s for the finger-controlled device; 10.5s for the non-finger device.)

The issue of the index of performance of fingers versus hands will be raised again in Chapter 5 when the ergonomics evaluation of a finger-operated isometric joystick is discussed in comparison with hand-operated joysticks.

There is little research on parallel input from multiple limbs since most modern computer UIMS systems do not support this. One study suggests there is some evidence that two-handed input might speed performance (Buxton and Myers, 1986). This is supported by research on chording from earlier studies of the ergonomics of keying (Van Cott and Kinkade, 1978) and from a study of two-handed input by Kabbash, Buxton, and Sellen (1994). The Kabbash *et al.* study measured mean trial completion times, mental preparation times (planning, deciding, reflecting before the next action), errors, and preference. However, the conclusions of the latter study warn that while some methods of two-handed input improve performance, others can degrade it.

One study compared Fitts' pointing and dragging tasks using the preferred and non-preferred hands (Kabbash *et al.*, 1993). All participants were self-declared right-handers. A mouse, a trackball and a tablet with stylus were tested. The 24 participants selected for the experiment were divided into two groups of 12. One group used their preferred hand for all tasks and devices; the second, their non-preferred. Results confirmed that for small targets and short distances, the preferred hand was superior in movement time; for larger targets and longer distances, both hands performed about the same. Error rates did not differ significantly between hands. The authors conclude that the non-preferred hand is more than a poor approximation of the preferred hand. Rather, the hands are complementary; the non-preferred hand is capable of rough pointing or motion such as would be suitable in two-handed tasks.

3.2.2 Feedback

Feedback is the use of sensory information to change the course of action. When operating any pointing device, the human body and brain are constantly processing visual, auditory and haptic information to guide human performance. The discussion in section 2.3 highlighted the importance of feedback in motor movement from visual and haptic perception. Sensory perception is clearly involved in the initiation and termination of movement, although its role during motion is still not clear.

3.2.2.1 Haptic Feedback

Most pointing devices, because they are usually designed to be controlled by a limb, involve the haptic perception of pressure or spatial awareness. Control resistance, discussed in section 3.1.2.1, provides many types of pressure feedback. The movement of an isotonic pointing device such as a mouse provides kinaesthetic position and movement feedback. An isometric device, because it remains rigid, does not provide kinaesthetic position feedback.

Some earlier ergonomics research was done with force feedback for control sticks. Force feedback is feedback in which the control system reflects large inertial or viscous friction forces back to the operator through the control stick such as in-flight control, or non-powered gun-aiming systems. In experiments performed by Notterman and Page in 1962 (cited in Frost, 1972:239), participants performed tracking tasks in both mechanical and simulated electronic systems with both isotonic and isometric control under a variety of force conditions. The results of this study show that the isometric stick was superior to the isotonic when the control system has oscillatory position-control dynamics, but the differences become smaller with increasing natural frequency and increasing damping of the control system.

Another study by DiFranco in 1968 (also cited in Frost, 1972:239), shows that the dynamics of the control stick can seriously alter the controllability of an aircraft. As natural frequency and damping of the system 'feel' were reduced, pilot opinion degraded and the system became unflyable. Although neither of these experimental systems was computer-based, the results can provide valuable information on the importance of the role of force feedback during control to designers of some of the new computer pointing devices that provide force feedback to the user – see Chapter 8. It is clear from the development of recent technology, specifically force feedback and teleoperator systems, that there is a great need for research on haptic perception and its involvement in feedback during movement.

Using a mouse modified to provide tactile and force feedback controlled by software linked to the visual information of targets on the visual display, Motoyuki and Sato (1994) tested five participants with a pointing task. Results demonstrated that the addition of tactile and force feedback shortened the response time and widened the effective area of targets.

3.2.2.2 Visual Feedback

The visual perception of the position of the target and the cursor are critical feedback. Motion of the cursor is also important and the software system must be fast enough to display its motion without lag. Small lags in display response have been found to degrade human performance on Fitts' law tasks (Hoffman, 1992; MacKenzie and Ware, 1993). Visual perception of the position of a device and its trajectory during movement provides additional feedback about movement, even if it is available only as a part of the peripheral vision.

In a detailed study to test the hypotheses of the SOS model of human motion during mouse pointing movement (Walker, Meyer and Smelcer, 1993), it was discovered that pointing motion had three phases: *initiation*, *execution* and *verification*. Initiation time was constant at about 30ms regardless of width or distance of the target. Execution time was affected by width and distance and ranged from 331ms to 628ms. Verification time, the time duration between cessation of mouse motion and the clicking of the mouse button, ranged from 227ms to 157ms. Verification time was affected by target width but not target distance. Verification time was from 20% to 36% of the total pointing time. (Note that the overall pointing time ranges in this experiment are determined by the type of task the participants were given. See section 3.3 below.)

Thus, Walker *et al.* conclude that reducing verification time could have a significant effect on reducing pointing time with a mouse. They suggest that interface designers could reduce this verification time by providing dynamic visual feedback. One technique would be to highlight each target region with reverse video whenever the cursor entered it.

3.2.2.3 Auditory Feedback

Auditory feedback appears to be less important than haptic and visual perception during movement, but it may be critical for knowing whether a device has been activated or not or for interfaces where visual perception is not possible. 'Clicking' a mouse gives auditory feedback for the selection of interface objects in addition to highlighting or other visual change. Individuals who have vision deficits or tasks occurring in low- or no-light conditions can benefit from the substitution of visual cues with auditory. Gaver (1986) added sounds to the Macintosh Finder™ to convey both action and information, e.g. selecting a document made a sound that decreased in pitch with the size of the disk file. As another example, not mentioned by Gaver, increasing pitch can provide feedback of nearness to the target in aiding positioning accuracy. Monk (1986) investigated the use of auditory feedback to prevent mode errors. His study demonstrated that mode errors could be reduced by a factor of three by using a mode-contingent sound with each keystroke. The advantage of sound over visual feedback is that it does not require users to constantly look at the display.

3.2.2.4 Comparing Modalities of Feedback

In a study done by Sellen, Kurtenbach and Buxton (1992), the use of visual and kinaesthetic feedback in reducing mode errors was confirmed. Participants in this experiment performed a text-editing task where the key-based command language software, the *vi* editor, required the user to switch modes from moving in the text document to editing text. In the visual feedback condition, the whole screen turned a dark pink while the user was in edit mode after issuing the usual keyboard commands. In the kinaesthetic condition, participants entered and maintained the edit mode by holding down a foot pedal. Releasing the foot pedal returned them to moving mode. The results showed that there was a significant reduction in the number of mode errors for both visual and kinaesthetic feedback conditions. The authors argue that the magnitude of the foot pedal effect was greater by a factor of three than that of visual feedback.

In a second experiment, Sellen *et al.* tested the same sustained foot pedal as the first experiment against a latched version and standard keyboard commands. Using the latched foot-pedal, participants entered editing mode by depressing and releasing the pedal; exiting was accomplished by the same actions. The results of this second experiment were that the latching foot-pedal and keyboard had the same mode error rates; the sustained foot pedal, as in the first experiment, prevented mode errors by a factor of three. User preference was also surveyed and 11 of the 15 participants preferred the sustained foot-pedal over the keyboard or latched foot-pedal. Sellen *et al.* speculate that the use of a sustained foot-pedal provides kinaesthetic feedback through user-generated muscular tension that not only provides continuity of physical motion to bind transactions but also provides feedback on mode state. Conventional visual feedback as used in the first experiment is maintained by the system and does not confer these advantages.

A more extensive study by Akamatsu, MacKenzie, and Hasbroucq (1995) compared five different sensory feedback conditions – normal, auditory, color, tactile and combined – during pointing to a target. The within-subjects design had 10 participants and measured overall response times, error rates, final positioning time, and bandwidth. The normal condition was what is typically in use on a standard GUI system, namely visual observation of the cursor controlled by the pointing device. The auditory and color conditions provided sound and color change when the target was entered. Tactile feedback was provided by modifying a standard mouse to have a solenoid-driven pin projecting through a hole in the left mouse-button. The only significant difference was found in final positioning time; tactile feedback was the quickest and normal feedback was the slowest. Results show that tactile feedback allowed the participants to use a wider area of the target and to select targets more quickly once the cursor was inside the target.

3.3 Tasks

We have now reviewed two important factors, device operation and limb control, in determining human performance with pointing devices. In this section we turn

to a third factor, the type of task performed. A detailed understanding of the influence of task on performance is exceedingly important because all experiments or
empirical assessments require participants to do a task. In traditional experimental psychology, the task is usually invented just for the experiment and kept very
simple to provide experimental control. In applied psychology, or ergonomics, the
task may be defined more by the domain so that experimental results can be easily
transferred to real work environments, preserving ecological validity. On the other
hand, they cannot become too complex or else control is lost over variables in the
experimental design. It is very important that there be an agreement within the
ergonomics community about which tasks to study, and, if possible, the creation
of certain 'benchmark' tasks. Having such a set of tasks will allow more reliable
comparison between experimental research results. Currently such an agreement
does not exist, although the move toward standards such as ISO 9241 which do
define tasks (see section 8.2.1.2) will define them *de facto*.

In this section we will discuss the complexities of task from three different perspectives: tasks defined by graphical user interface actions, tasks defined by Fitts'
law experiments, and tasks in naturalistic work contexts.

3.3.1 GUI Primitives: Point and Select, Drag, Draw

A taxonomy, independent of a particular device, domain or application software,
can be developed. This approach to taxonomy was first developed by Foley and
van Dam (1982) in the first edition of their computer graphics text, *Fundamentals
of Interactive Computer Graphics*. Foley and van Dam define the notion of an
interaction task which is of four types: enter a position, enter text, select an object
on the screen, or enter a quantity. These tasks were determined by the data type of
the information entered by the user – (x, y) position, text string, object identifica-
tion, or number – respectively, for the above interaction tasks.

Following the same approach of independent description, we prefer another taxonomy based on GUI interaction primitives rather than software data types:
pointing and selecting, dragging, drawing, and device switching. This allows comparison independent of application domains. For example, pointing to text objects
such as a word or character is equivalent to pointing to graphic objects such as an
icon or pixel region. Both tasks can be subsumed under the more general concept
of pointing to a target.

3.3.1.1 Pointing and Selecting

The most common action done with a GUI is pointing, which, in its purest sense,
is the action of moving the cursor from one location on the screen to another.
Users point to an object by placing the cursor 'hot spot' on top of it.

In most GUIs, it is common to indicate the end of the pointing action by clicking
a button. This button is often located on the pointing device, such as the buttons

on a mouse or trackball. It can also be located on the keyboard or on a separate control device such as a foot pedal or separate hand control. Some devices such as touch tablet styluses will indicate a selection by a semantic action such as tapping. Most ergonomic studies involve a pointing task that is terminated by a selection, and have shown such tasks to follow Fitts' law (e.g. Card *et al.*, 1978; Epps, 1986; MacKenzie *et al.*, 1991; Walker *et al.*, 1993).

Not all GUIs require the button to be clicked in order to indicate the object selected. For example, in some settings of some window managers for the X Window interface, the active window is the one beneath the cursor. In contrast, the Macintosh interface requires users to first make the window active by pointing and clicking. Jagacinski *et al.* (1980a) showed that pointing movements that do not end in a click follow Fitts' law. In addition, if we can assume, as is done in the *keystroke level model*, that the button click takes constant time (Card, Moran, and Newell, 1980b; Card *et al.*, 1983), then, it seems reasonable that pure computer pointing action follows Fitts' law.

Chording occurs as a selection when a keyboard key and a pointing device button or multiple mouse buttons are concurrently pressed. For example, in Microsoft Word®, double-clicking a mouse button while pointing to a word selects it, while double-clicking a mouse button with the control key on the typing keyboard simultaneously depressed selects a sentence.

3.3.1.2 Dragging

Dragging is the task of moving an object on the screen to a target position. For most computer pointing devices, dragging is a pointing action with the selection button held down. On most GUIs, the object then follows the mouse, i.e. it is 'dragged'. When the object reaches the target location, the mouse button is released, i.e. it is 'dropped'. Dragging is a basic action in GUIs and is used to indicate operations such as moving an object to another location, and selecting a group of objects. An example of dragging in the Macintosh interface is the action of moving a document from one folder into another. It should be noted that there are many dragging actions in GUI use. On the Macintosh, for example, menu selection is also a dragging action, as is selecting a block of text.

MacKenzie showed dragging to follow Fitts' law (MacKenzie *et al.*, 1991). One of the devices he studied was the trackball; he noted that it performed poorly for dragging apparently because it was awkward to hold the button down and move the ball at the same time. This is probably the reason why some trackballs have a 'drag lock' feature. This requires two button-clicks: one to initiate dragging and one to terminate it, thus leaving the fingers free to move the ball.

Walker, Meyer and Smelcer did a study of the applicability of Meyer's stochastic optimized submovement model to mouse movement (Walker *et al.*, 1993). The pointing task they studied had the button down for the duration of movement, making it a dragging task, although the user did not get the visual feedback usually associated with a dragging action. The task had a high correlation to Fitts' law, and thus they indirectly showed that dragging is a Fitts' law task.

In addition to dragging, there are other cases where the pointer is moved with one or more buttons pressed. For example, 'option-drag' is used on the Macintosh interface to copy a file. Option-drag is a dragging action performed with the 'Option' key on the keyboard held down. There are numerous such 'chording' actions, none of which has been studied, though it is reasonable to assume that they all follow Fitts' law.

3.3.1.3 Drawing

In pointing and dragging, the path through which the cursor moves is not impor-tant. When that path becomes important, we have cases of drawing, such as drawing with a stylus on a touch tablet. (Note, that for a complete simulation of computer-based drawing by artists, we also need to capture velocity and pressure as the drawing instrument is applied to the surface.)

Drawing is an important computer-based task, particularly for graphics and CAD/CAM software. During drawing, the path of the pointing device is traced on the screen. Most pointing devices use the context of the task to determine drawing with the user executing a dragging operation. Note that although the operation of the device might be identical, the task is quite different. During dragging tasks, the path of the device is of no consequence. This is not the case for drawing.

If the device does not have a selection button, drawing is accomplished by changing modes on the device. For example, some graphics tablets have different modes for drawing (also called 'tracking') and pointing determined by the appli-cation software context.

Drawing has not been the subject of a Fitts' law analysis, but it has been sugges-ted that it would be similar to a time-constrained movement in that it has a linear relationship between time and distance (Meyer *et al.*, 1988; Schmidt *et al.*, 1978; 1979).

3.3.1.4 Device Switching

In general, we can think of *device switching* as the physical action and mental preparation that it takes a user to change from using one input device to another. Normally, device switching is only considered relevant if it involves a gross physi-cal movement, for example, taking one's hand off the keyboard to reach for the mouse. Pressing a button physically integrated into a mouse for selection would not be considered device switching. A few devices have multiple functions which allow *mode switching* and eliminate the need for device switching. For example, the Home Row J Mouse™ is a device that uses the same key for pointing and typing. Pointing mode is initiated when the key is depressed for longer than a threshold value.

Unidirectional device switching is sometimes called *homing* (Card *et al.*, 1978). Homing time is the time to remove one's hand from a pointing device and return it to the keyboard. Generally, homing time has been regarded as equal to reaching time, i.e. that the time to home to the keyboard is equivalent to the time to reach for the pointing device (Card *et al.*, 1980). Recent studies indicate that this is not an empirically valid assumption, since reaching motions can be considered Fitts' law tasks and target sizes differ between homing and reaching (Douglas and Mithal, 1994). In Chapter 5 we will examine this issue in depth.

3.3.2 Specialized Experimental Tasks for Pointing

While the basic tasks for a pointing device are often defined by the recognizable actions of the graphical user interface, more complex distinctions are often developed for experimental environments that test pointing using Fitts' law.

3.3.2.1 Discrete vs. Continuous Tasks

Pointing tasks can be discrete or continuous. Continuous tasks are performed one after another, without pauses between pointing actions, as in Fitts' first experiment (Fitts, 1954) described in section 2.1.2. The task in Fitts' second experiment was discrete, with pauses between each pointing action (Fitts and Peterson, 1964).

Actual computer use runs the gamut from discrete to continuous pointing actions, including what might be described as semi-continuous actions. When a user of a word processor moves the insertion point from one location to another, he or she has performed a discrete pointing action. Most pointing tasks, however, are made up of a series of pointing actions. For example, selecting an item from a menu requires two pointing actions: one to pull down the menu, and one to select an option from it. If this menu selection was preceded by an action which selected an object, then the command takes three continuous pointing movements. In this manner, pointing with a computer is typically made up of semi-continuous pointing actions. On the other hand, the use of arcade-type computer games typically requires continuous pointing movements.

Fitts showed that his equation was applicable to both continuous and discrete tasks (Fitts, 1954; Fitts and Peterson, 1964). When performed on a computer, both kinds of movement have been shown to follow Fitts' law. Discrete tasks have been the subject of most studies (Card *et al.*, 1978; Douglas and Mithal, 1994; Jagacinski and Monk, 1985; MacKenzie and Buxton, 1992). Continuous tasks have not often been studied, an exception being a study by MacKenzie *et al.* (1991), who replicated Fitts' original experiment on a computer.

3.3.2.2 1D, 2D, and 3D Fitts Tasks

We can characterize Fitts tasks as one- or two-dimensional on the computer screen depending on whether targets vary by angular position. In a one-dimensional task, targets vary only by size and distance and usually lie on a horizontal line. Fitts' original experiment used rectangular targets where the angle of approach never varied. (See Fitts original task in Figure 2.2, Chapter 2). This task can be directly replicated on a computer. (See Figure 6.5, Chapter 6.) In two-dimensional tasks, targets are positioned in the two-dimensional plane of the screen. (See Figure 5.4, Chapter 5, for an example.) Three-dimensional tasks incorporate depth as the third coordinate. Pointing, i.e. reaching, in a virtual reality environment would be three-dimensional. For purposes of computing a Fitts' law equation, attention must be paid to the type of targets in a two-dimensional task. If the targets become rectangles, as they typically are in textual targets such as words on a computer, then the effective width of the target depends on the angle of approach which may not be known during the experiment. Figure 3.3 illustrates that the variation in width depends on angle of approach.

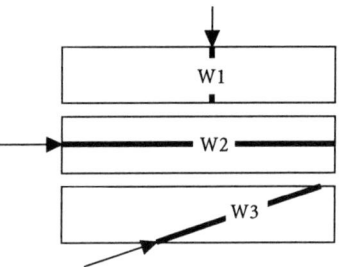

Figure 3.3: The effect of approach angle on the effective width of a target.

W1 represents the target size if the user approaches the word from above or below. *W2* represents the target size if the user approaches the word from the left or right. Finally, *W3* represents the target size if the user approaches the word at an angle. The differences can be illustrated mathematically:

$$W1 = h \tag{3.2}$$

where:

h is height of the rectangle

$$W2 = l \tag{3.3}$$

where:

l is length of the rectangle and $l > h$

$$W3 = \frac{h}{sin\theta} \tag{3.4}$$

where:

θ is the angle of approach and $W3$ intersects the top line of the rectangle

Previous experimental research on computer-based pointing devices has often failed to take this into account (Card, *et al.*, 1978; Gillan, *et al.*, 1990). Rather than using rectangular targets in a two-dimensional task we recommend the use of circles because their width remains constant no matter what the direction of approach is. (See also the research described later in this section by MacKenzie and Buxton, 1992, on the effect of width on Fitts' law formulation.)

It is important to distinguish the dimensionality of the computer task from three other concepts: motion of the limb, motion of the device, and dimensionality of the screen. Actions performed by the limbs are inherently three-dimensional. When a pointing device such as a mouse or touch tablet is used, the hand controlling the device moves in three-dimensional space. On the other hand, the mouse itself moves in a two dimensional plane, sensing displacement of position. When this is translated onto the screen, the movement occurs in two dimensions.

MacKenzie replicated the one-dimensional study by Fitts, showing that the one-dimensional task conformed to Fitts' law for a number of devices (MacKenzie *et al.*, 1991). Much of Jagacinski's work establishing Fitts' law for joysticks has been in one dimension (Jagacinski, Hartzell, Ward, and Bishop, 1978; Jagacinski *et al.*, 1980a; Jagacinski *et al.*, 1980b).

Most early studies that established Fitts' law for pointing devices were implicitly conducted in two dimensions since they involved text or menu selection, e.g., Card *et al.*, (1978). These studies show that Fitts' law holds in a two-dimensional task.

At least four studies explicitly looked at establishing Fitts' law in two dimensions (Boritz, Booth, and Cowan, 1991; Douglas and Mithal, 1994; Jagacinski and Monk, 1985; MacKenzie and Buxton, 1992). The studies by Jagacinski and Monk, and Boritz *et al.* established that the Fitts' *IP* appears to vary from angle to angle. Boritz *et al.* found that movements with the right hand moving from left to right were the fastest, and movements moving in towards the body were the slowest. The Jagacinski-and-Monk, and Douglas-and-Mithal studies both found variations in *IP*, but their results did not match those by Boritz. While it appears that *IP* varies with angle, the exact nature of this variation is unclear.

MacKenzie's work had a different focus: to determine the exact nature of the target width in the Fitts' law equation when the task takes place in two dimensions (MacKenzie and Buxton, 1992). In his experiment participants pointed to rectangular targets. In his analysis, MacKenzie used one of three widths. These were the 'canonical' width, which is the width of the target in the horizontal direction, the width of the target in the direction of movement, and the greater of the width and height. They found that when he used the canonical width as the width in the Fitts' law equation, they got a poor fit to the data. However, using either of the other two formulations, Fitts' law was a good predictor of movement time.

The issue of actual width of a target versus 'subjective' perception of width was addressed in the work of Meyer *et al.* (1988). They state that:

> ... subjects may act as if relatively narrow targets are wider than they really are and relatively wide targets are narrower than they really are. This would compress the range of subjective target widths compared with the range of objective widths, making changes in objective target width have less effect than they might otherwise.

Meyer et al., 1988:354

Using this concept of subjective target width Meyer *et al.* modified the computation of target width in the estimation of SOS model parameters for error rates and frequency of submovements.

Differences in movement kinematics due to differences in target width were the subject of a recent study by Graham and MacKenzie (1996). They investigated the differences in pointing between virtual pointing, where a 2D computer image representing the hand and targets was superimposed on the workspace, and physical pointing with vision of the hand and targets painted on the work surface. Using an Opototrak motion analysis system, no significant differences were found in the initial phase of movement. However, in the final phase of homing-in on smaller targets, significant differences were found in which movement time was longer for smaller widths in the virtual display. This increase in time occurred due to extra time in deceleration after reaching a peak velocity.

While current computer displays are two-dimensional, three-dimensional interface constructs are beginning to appear in a number of ways. First, virtual reality 'exists' in three dimensions; in simulations of three dimensions, Fitts' law takes on a new meaning. In addition, many computer games such as flight simulators and the ubiquitous 'shoot-em-up' games, present a two-dimensional perspective view of three dimensions (2½D). Another way in which three dimensions are beginning to appear is in layered interfaces, where a document can have layers, and there is a need to move along the z-axis. While a number of 3D input devices (mostly joysticks with a z-wheel) exist, we could find no published research that establishes Fitts' law for these types of devices or for pointing (in general) in 3D virtual reality environments.

3.3.3 Complex, Natural Environments

Up to this point in our discussion of tasks we have presented experimental work on tasks, such as pointing in one- and two-dimensional Fitts' task environments, which are relatively domain independent. They present targets which are rectangles, squares or circles of varying sizes located at various positions. The participant's activity is restricted to many trials of the same type of pointing movements. We will now briefly review studies which broaden the definition of the task environment.

3.3.3.1 Domain-specific Tasks: Target Acquisition, Text/Menu Selection, Text Editing, Tracking and Docking

In a review of the experimental literature, Greenstein and Arnaut (1988) describe types of domain tasks that have been used in studying input device performance: target acquisition tasks, text/menu selection tasks, text entering and editing tasks, and continuous tracking tasks. This taxonomy serves to unify the early human factors research of the 1950s to 1970s on non-computer-based control devices with the computer-based control devices of the 1980s and after. Target-acquisition tasks are those where the participant positions the display cursor at or inside a displayed stationary target. These tasks are equivalent to the previously described

two-dimensional Fitts' pointing tasks using squares or rectangles, although sometimes the target will be a graphic image of a real-world object such as an icon.

Menu and text selection presents the designated target, one of several, on the
display embedded in a larger text context; in target acquisition there is only one
target and it is presented in isolation on the screen. Fitts' law has been shown to
hold for text selection (Card *et al.*, 1978; Ewing *et al.*, 1986; Gillan, Holden, Adam,
Rudisill, and Magee, 1990; Gillan, Holden, Adam, Rudisill, and Magee, 1992). Karat
et al. (1986) and Whitfield *et al.* (1983) have studied menu-selection tasks. In text
entering and editing tasks, the target is first selected and then text is replaced by
typing. This type of task is actually a mixed-device task, similar to the device-
switching task described in section 3.3.1.4 and has been studied by Haller, Mutschler and Voss (1984).

Continuous-tracking tasks are tasks where the user matches a cursor's position
with a moving target with or without interception. Much of the early human factors work on input devices used tracking as a task due to its military usefulness.
Jagacinski (1980b) showed that tracking is not a Fitts' law task.

Studies are beginning to appear using three-dimensional pointing devices and
thus three-dimensional tasks specific to virtual reality domains. Zhai (1995, 1996)
in his dissertation work did an extensive performance evaluation of isometric,
isotonic and elastic input devices in 6 degree-of-freedom (DOF) tracking and
docking tasks. The docking task was a 6 DOF stereoscopic task that required the
participant to move a 3D cursor as quickly as possible to align it with a 3D target.
The cursor and the target were two tetrahedra of equal size (4.2cm).

3.3.3.2 Real-world Environments

Often, the criticism is raised that all experimental tasks present an impoverished
notion of task and do not resemble usual GUI environments nor users' real activities. The major reason for using very simple tasks is that in order to test and compare experimental results from one experiment to another, researchers need controlled and simplified task environments. Yet, researchers, who are ultimately
interested in applied science, walk a fine line between testing a task which is too
simplified and will have no transfer to a realistic situation, and one which is ecol-
ogically valid but too complex to test.

Underlying much of the experimental work in ergonomics is the assumption that
results from experimental tasks are valid when these tasks are incorporated within
a more complex task context. This is a compositional assumption – that more
complex tasks are composed of subtasks and that, for example, overall task time is
the sum of these individual subtasks. There is some evidence that complex task
environments may violate this assumption as based on the following personal
anecdote.

One of the authors was recently involved in testing a new foot-controlled pointing device. The pilot study consisted of three phases, each designed to have participants use the device in a variety of task environments, but all chosen for testing
pointing, dragging and pointing-typing performance. The first phase, which was

suggested by the developer, was the game of Solitaire, a simple card game that was bundled with Microsoft Windows 3.1. Participants played this game as a practice environment immediately after receiving basic instruction for pointing and dragging. The participants did well on the task and very quickly were able to use the pointing device to comfortably play the game of Solitaire. From basic impressions of the participants and the observer, the device appeared very usable.

After about 15–20 minutes of practice with the Solitaire game, participants were introduced to the second phase of the study and given a 2D Fitts' task environment. (Note, this environment is described in section 5.4.4 of this book.) Participants performed three tasks – pointing, dragging and pointing-typing – in this environment. Each task involved 192 different combinations of target size (3), distance (4) and angle of approach (16). The smallest target was approximately the size of a single character.

Within this environment major problems with device control appeared. In pointing or dragging small targets, participants would take a large amount of time and were frequently unable to exact the fine motor control over the cursor that is required to select when the cursor was within the target. This would cause the task to be categorized as an error and randomly presented again at a later time to the participant. Similarly, on long distances, participants would accidentally activate the selection mechanism before reaching the target, again causing an error condition. The observation from this segment of study was that the device had control problems related to the more difficult Fitts tasks, specifically with fine motor control and activation of the selection switch. Most participants spent approximately 45–60 minutes in this phase of the study and an analysis of the data showed they were well practiced with the device at the end.

The third and final phase tested participants with real application software. This phase was divided into five simple tasks each with Microsoft Word 6.0 and Excel 5.0. Participants did well with the Excel tasks and had great difficulty with the Word tasks with several participants unable to do them all. Upon later analysis, it was observed that the Excel tasks presented the spreadsheet cells as large targets. There were no penalties for selecting the wrong target.

On the other hand, the Word environment had very small targets requiring very fine motor control, such as positioning the 'I-beam' cursor between characters to insert text or dragging the cursor over several characters to select a text segment. Accidentally activating the device-selection mechanism before the target was reached would cause much confusion. If the Word drag-and-drop feature was activated, text would be deleted uncontrollably, and positioned in random locations. Needless to say, participants' and the observer's impression of the device was appropriately (i.e. negatively) affected by this experience.

This study reveals several complex issues regarding the design of tasks to evaluate pointing devices and suggests that one should exercise caution in applying the results of experimentally designed tasks to real-world environments. First, the importance of using an environment that is based on a wide range of Fitts tasks cannot be stressed enough. Device performance must cover a wide range of size, distance and angle of approach combinations. The size of the targets should reflect the size of targets within the real computing environment, including those of single characters. Second, the penalties for selecting an incorrect target may vary from environment to environment, something not often considered in experimental task design.

In the Solitaire game, targets were very large and there was no penalty for selecting the wrong target during a pointing or dragging operation. In the three Fitts tasks performed during the second phase of the pilot study, the targets and distances demanded a wide range of skill. The penalty for failure to select the correct target was annoying but not serious – i.e. the task had to be repeated. In the final phase of the study, the Excel task-environment, like the Solitaire game, was less demanding and more forgiving. However, the Word environment was the most exacting and demanding. Small targets and a high penalty for lack of control revealed a pointing device that could not be recommended for use and clearly needed more development.

This example illustrates the point that there are many complex issues relating experimental laboratory tasks to real-world work and entertainment environments. Current experimental research has tended to rely on the assessment of human performance using a Fitts' law task environment because it is the only well-understood and robustly reliable prediction of human movement time. A very important aspect of a Fitts' law task environment is the concept that target width and distance are related through an index of difficulty which contains a *log* term. Thus, a sufficient test of pointing time requires a broad range and combination of sizes and distances. Failure to understand this concept will often create an environment which insufficiently assesses performance. Testing environments are now available as public domain software over the Internet which present a standardized Fitts task while attempting to provide some flexibility in the task (Soukoreff and MacKenzie, 1995). This is an important step toward creating benchmarks. A similar standardization of tasks, although not explicitly built on the Fitts' law model, is implied in the ISO 9241 standard for pointing devices. (See section 8.2.1.2 for further details.)

Most researchers make the assumption that Fitts' law task findings will transfer to complex tasks incorporating pointing. We believe this is a reasonable assumption, but it must always be understood within the context of what is important in the overall performance measures for a particular pointing device and task environment. If pointing or dragging movement time are important in usability, then Fitts' law tasks are the best environment for assessment. However, as the earlier example illustrates, real work environments place equal emphasis on errors and they should be assessed as part of performance analysis. As we move into virtual reality 3D tasks, a much broader set of tasks and movements will need to be devised, evaluated and standardized.

3.4 Summary

We began this chapter with the point of view that, in addition to psychological factors such as skill level (learning) and basic aspects of human psychomotor behavior, ergonomic studies of pointing device performance must address three major factors: device operation and differences between types of devices, differences in limb control, and differences in tasks. We have approached this chapter as both a descriptive survey for readers less familiar with the details and findings, and as an analysis of these factors within empirical studies. In the next chapter we present a survey of ergonomic studies of particular types of pointing devices. We will also discuss human performance comparisons between devices.

4. *A Survey of Ergonomic Studies*

The following chapter is offered as a brief overview of the empirical studies that have been conducted on different devices and on the general issue of comparing performance between devices. In the first part of the chapter these studies will be presented by general categories of pointing devices:

- mouse;
- joystick;
- trackball;
- touch tablet and screen;
- lightpen and lightgun;
- head, hand and eye trackers, and datagloves;
- leg and foot controls.

A brief description of the history of the device, device operation, and sub-categories of device will be given, followed by a description of ergonomic research studies. Some of these studies limit their scope to a single device, anecdotal observations, and a general notion of ease of use. Other studies use an experimental evaluation of human performance comparing devices. These are usually studies of movement time, error rate and learning time using target acquisition tasks. (Readers interested in an excellent, in-depth, survey of studies prior to 1988 are referred to Greenstein and Arnaut, 1988.) In the second half of the chapter we will address the issue of comparing and predicting human performance by device type. This discussion will relate to the question: 'Which is the best pointing device?' and demonstrate the difficulties of providing a simple answer even when measuring human movement time for pointing.

4.1 Studies by Device

In this section we review the technology of each of the major pointing devices currently in use today. Table 4.1 gives a summary of device features in categories discussed in the previous chapter (see section 3.1). As we see from this summary, most devices that have been invented are hand-operated, relative mode, isotonic devices with position control.

Table 4.1: Summary of device features

Device	Absolute vs. relative mode	Isotonic vs. isometric input	Position vs. velocity control	Limb control
Mouse	Relative only	Isotonic only	Position	Hand and arm, or foot
Joystick	Both (usually relative)	Both	Both	Hand or finger
Trackball	Relative only	Isotonic only	Position	Hand and finger
Tablet	Both	Isotonic, possibly isometric with finger or stylus pressure	Position	Hand and arm, or finger
Touch screen	Absolute only	Isotonic	Position	Arm and finger
Lightpen and lightgun	Absolute only	Isotonic	Position	Hand and arm
Glove	Relative	Isotonic and isometric	Position and orientation	Hand and fingers
Eye tracker	Relative only	Isotonic	Position (gaze)	Eyes
3D head tracker	Absolute	Isotonic	Position and orientation	Head and neck

4.1.1 Mouse

Today, the mouse is the ubiquitous pointing device yet until the late 1980s it was relatively unknown. The mouse was developed in the 1960s by a research group led by Douglas Englebart at Stanford Research Institute. The purpose of the research was to study computer text retrieval for the National Library (English *et al.*, 1967). After the project terminated, William English, one of the project members, joined the Xerox Palo Alto Research Laboratory (PARC). He continued to study the mouse as a pointing device, and eventually it became an integral part of the Smalltalk and Alto graphical user interfaces invented at PARC in the 1970s.

The mouse did not achieve widespread commercial availability until it became the primary GUI pointing device for Apple Computer Co.'s Macintosh personal computer developed in the mid-1980s. The Macintosh development was led by Larry Tesler and several programmers hired from Xerox PARC's Smalltalk group. Their goal was to implement the PARC 'look and feel' in a personal computer GUI. The Macintosh development team transformed the mouse from the original three-button mouse into a one-button mouse. This design decision was based on results of empirical user testing. The users chosen for mouse testing were computer naïve – the target market for the Macintosh. During testing it was observed that users had difficulty remembering functions assigned to each of the three buttons. Consequently, Apple developed the Macintosh GUI for use with a one-button mouse.

This history demonstrates the tight coupling that sometimes occurs between physical design decisions and operating system software where double-clicking (even triple-clicking) supported as Macintosh Toolbox calls replaced the second and third mouse-button in GUI user interaction. The three-button mouse continues to survive as the pointing device for UNIX GUI systems, such as X Windows.

When Microsoft developed its Windows GUI for IBM PC-compatible computers, it chose to use a two-button mouse, although most of the windows operations and application software are based on single-button operation. The introduction of Windows 95 initiates more extensive use of the second mouse button.

The mouse is a hand-held device which is moved across a surface registering a relative displacement of the cursor. The mouse can be held in either hand, although there are ergonomically designed mice that are shaped to the palm of the hand and are therefore 'handed' devices. Mice usually have from one to three buttons for selection.

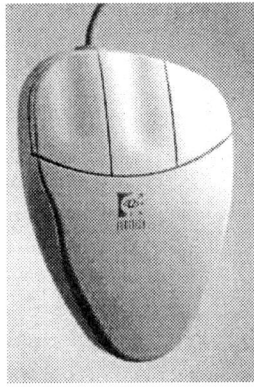

Figure 4.1: Ergonomically-shaped mouse: the MouseMan™ II. © 1993 Logitech Inc.

Current technologies for the mouse include mechanical and optical sensors. In the mechanical mouse, a small ball rolls along the surface and potentiometers sense the rotation of the ball to determine orientation. In optical mice the ball is replaced by an optical sensor. There are also wireless versions available, which, unlike mechanical and optical mice, do not have a cable connected to the computer.

Movement with a mouse is similar to movement with the hand, with two major differences. The first is that the focus of attention is the computer screen rather than the mouse. When pointing with a finger the focus of attention is the finger. The second is that the mouse moves in two dimensions while natural movement is in three dimensions.

Despite these differences, the mouse has been considered almost an optimum pointing device since the early ergonomic study of Card, English and Burr (1978) comparing the mouse with an isometric joystick, cursor and text keys. In that study, the mouse took significantly less time to learn, was faster and had fewer errors in practiced pointing tasks. Other experimental studies have tended to support the result that the mouse is a more usable device than the isometric joystick (e.g. Epps, 1986; Douglas and Mithal, 1994).

Among continuous devices, the mouse is probably the most highly studied, with a large ergonomic literature. Table 4.2 lists published ergonomic studies, devices used for comparison, the type of task tested, and what the performance measures were.

The Card *et al.* study was the first published study to analyze computer-based pointing as a Fitts' law phenomenon. There is now a large body of literature establishing that mouse movement time for both pointing and dragging follows Fitts' law (Boritz *et al.*, 1991; Card *et al.*, 1978; Douglas and Mithal, 1993; Douglas and Mithal, 1994; Epps, 1986; MacKenzie, 1992; MacKenzie *et al.*, 1991). Walker *et al.* (1993) established experimentally that the human control of the mouse is modeled by an SOS model of movement (see section 2.2.5). We delay a further comparison of the characteristics of the mouse with other devices until section 4.2.

Table 4.2: Ergonomic studies of the mouse

Study	Devices compared	Task	Performance measures
Boritz *et al.* (1991)	Mouse	Target acquisition	Time, Fitts
Card *et al.* (1978)	Mouse, isometric rate joystick, text keys, cursor keys	Text selection, device switching	Time, errors, leaning, Fitts
Douglas and Mithal (1994)	Mouse, isometric rate joystick (single finger)	Target acquisition (includes dragging), device switching	Time, errors, learning, Fitts
English *et al.* (1967)	Mouse, joystick (2 modes: rate and position), knee control, Grafcon, lightpen	Menu selection	Time
Epps (1986)	Two touch tablets (relative and absolute), trackball, isometric rate joystick, isotonic rate joystick, mouse	Target acquisition	Time, Fitts
Ewing *et al.* (1986)	Mouse, cursor keys	Text selection	Time, Fitts, preferred device
Gillan *et al.* (1990, 1992)	Mouse	Text selection (includes dragging)	Time, Fitts
Haller *et al.* (1984)	Lightpen, matrix tablet, mouse, trackball, cursor keys, voice	Text selection, text editing	Time, errors
Hodes and Akagi (1986)	Mouse		
Jellinek and Card (1990)	Mouse with differing values of acceleration	Target acquisition	Point time
Karat *et al.* (1986)	Touch screen, mouse, keyboard	Menu selection	Time, gain, preferred device
MacKenzie *et al.* (1991)	Mouse, trackball, touch tablet (absolute)	Target acquisition (includes dragging)	Time, Fitts
MacKenzie *et al.* (1990)	Mouse	Target acquisition	
Mithal (1995); Mithal and Douglas (1996)	Mouse, isometric rate joystick (single finger)	Target acquisition	Time, Fitts, SOS
Reinhart and Marken (1985)	Mouse, isometric rate joystick	Tracking	Error
Swierenga and Struckman-Johnson (1984)	Trackball, isotonic joystick (absolute, not spring-loaded), mouse	Tracking	Error, preferred device
Walker *et al.* (1993)	Mouse	Target acquisition	Time, SOS model

Undoubtedly, the learnability, fast pointing-speed and low error-rate of the mouse can be attributed to its simple mapping of displacement to cursor position, although the mapping is from the horizontal plane of the mouse's movement to the vertical plane of the screen. In addition, the advantages of the mouse include its ability to be used by either hand, fairly low fatigue factor due to resting on a desk surface, convenient location of selection buttons for finger use, and its physical robustness due to its technical simplicity. One of its disadvantages is that some novice users find it difficult to map the movement away and toward the self as the up and down motion of the cursor. Other disadvantages include the time to device switch between the keyboard and the mouse, *repetitive strain injury* (RSI) from unsupported overuse of the wrist, and the need for desktop space to operate. The mouse is excellent for pointing, dragging and tracking, but difficult to use for drawing.

Efforts have been made to improve pointing speed through the use of accelerated drivers for mice. Accelerated drivers have a non-linear mapping between input displacement and output displacement. The faster the mouse moves, the greater the gain. A study of such *power mice* concluded that accelerated drivers had no effect on pointing speed, and that any subjective gains were probably as a result of the reduced amount of desk space that the mice required to move on (Jellinek and Card, 1990).

4.1.2 Joysticks

Joysticks are one of the oldest types of modern control devices, originating in the early twentieth century to control airplanes and automobiles. Today, joysticks are used in military aircraft and in video games. They have been extensively studied. They are unusual among pointing devices in that there are many types of joysticks, as illustrated in Figure 4.2.

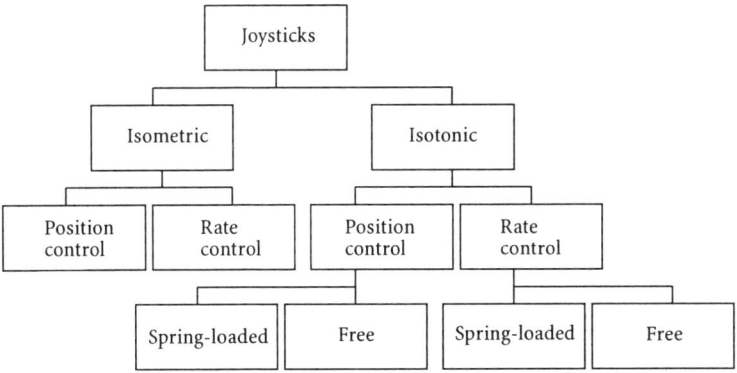

Figure 4.2: The different types of joystick.

Joysticks can be categorized in three ways, depending on whether they are isometric or isotonic, position-controlled or rate-controlled, and spring-loaded or free. Isometric joysticks do not move when pressure is applied to them, and use transducers such as strain gauges or varistors to sense the amount of force applied to them. The force sensed is turned into an output signal. Isotonic joysticks move when pressure is applied to them. Isotonic joysticks can be spring-loaded or free depending on whether a spring is utilized to return the joystick to the central position. Isotonic spring-loaded joysticks can measure either displacement or force, while free joysticks measure displacement. If the device driver maps the transducer output signal into a displacement on the screen, the joystick is position-controlled. The device driver can also map the transducer output signal into a velocity of movement of the cursor, in which case the joystick is rate or velocity-controlled. Selection is done by buttons positioned either on the top or front of the joystick. Occasionally selection will be done by a key located on the keyboard.

 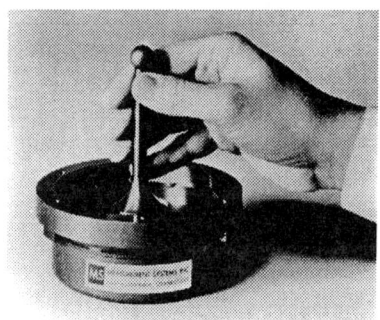

Figure 4.3: Joysticks. Courtesy of Measurement Systems Inc.

Joysticks have been as extensively studied due to their popularity as control devices in military applications. Table 4.3 describes these published studies in an abbreviated form.

Table 4.3: Ergonomic studies of joysticks

Study	Devices compared	Task	Performance measures
Albert (1982)	Touch screen, 2 joysticks (spring isotonic rate and isometric rate), trackball, matrix tablet (puck)	Target acquisition	Time, errors, preferred device
Card *et al.* (1978)	Mouse, isometric rate joystick, text keys, cursor keys	Text selection, device switching	Time, errors, leaning, Fitts
Douglas and Mithal (1994)	Mouse, isometric rate joystick (single finger)	Target acquisition (includes dragging), device switching	Time, errors, learning, Fitts
English *et al.* (1967)	Mouse, joystick (2 modes: rate and position), knee control, Grafcon, lightpen	Menu selection	Time
Epps (1986)	Two touch tablets (relative and absolute), trackball, isometric rate joystick, isotonic rate joystick, mouse	Target acquisition	Time, Fitts
Hottman (1981)	Eight position spring-centered joystick, matrix keyboard	Menu selection	
Jagacinski *et al.* (1978)	Joystick	Target acquisition	Time, Fitts
Jagacinski *et al.* (1980a)	Joystick	Target acquisition	Time, Fitts

Continued on the next page

Table 4.3 (continued)

Study	Devices compared	Task	Performance measures
Jagacinski *et al.* (1980b)	Two joysticks (isotonic position, isotonic rate)	Target acquisition	Time, Fitts
Jenkins and Karr (1954)	Isotonic joystick	Target acquisition	Gain
Kantowitz and Elvers (1988)	Two joysticks (isometric rate, isometric position)	Target acquisition	Time, Fitts
Mehr and Mehr (1972)	Joystick, trackball		
Mithal (1995)	Mouse, isometric rate joystick (single-finger)	Target acquisition	Time, Fitts, SOS
Reinhart and Marken (1985)	Mouse, isometric rate joystick	Tracking	Error
Rutledge and Selker (1990)	Isometric rate joystick (single-finger)	Target acquisition, device switching	Time, Fitts, acceleration curves
Swierenga and Struckman–Johnson (1984)	Trackball, isotonic joystick (absolute, not spring-loaded), mouse	Tracking	Error, preferred device

Since joysticks come in many varieties and with many different features, it is almost impossible to generalize their performance. It does appear to be the case that isometric rate-controlled joysticks are harder to learn, slower in pointing speed, and higher in errors than the mouse. Further discussion of evaluation across devices will be deferred until section 4.2.

Generally, joysticks are advantageous because they take up little space and are physically robust: standing up to heavy use during video-game play. Isometric joysticks are rigid allowing for situations where control without a moving part is desirable. There is evidence that velocity-controlled devices are faster and more stimulus–response compatible for tracking tasks (Jagacinski *et al.*, 1987). Unlike pointing, dragging and tracking, drawing is almost impossible with an isometric device due to the inability to regulate very fine motor-control and execute long, smooth motions. The early study by Card *et al.* (1978) cautiously suggested that isometric joystick performance might follow Fitts' law. Later studies confirmed that human performance with the following types of joysticks follow Fitts' law:

1. isometric rate control (Card *et al.*, 1978; Epps, 1986; Kantowitz and Elvers, 1988; Rutledge and Selker, 1990; Douglas and Mithal, 1993; Douglas and Mithal, 1994);
2. isometric position control (Kantowitz and Elvers, 1988);
3. isotonic position control (Epps, 1986; Jagacinski *et al.*, 1980b);
4. isotonic rate control (Epps, 1986; Jagacinski *et al.*, 1980b).

The literature does not consistently report whether the isotonic joysticks used were spring-loaded or not. While not all kinds of joysticks have been tested, it appears likely that Fitts' law will hold for all the kinds of joysticks listed above.

Jagacinski *et al.* (1980b) performed a series of studies on joysticks, contrasting conditions such as position control versus velocity control, endpoint conditions, and moving vs. stationary targets. Based on the studies by Jagacinski, Epps and Kantowitz, we can make two generalizations:

1. isotonic joysticks have a higher *IP* than isometric joysticks (Epps, 1986);

2. position-control joysticks have a higher *IP* than velocity-control joysticks (Jagacinski *et al.*, 1980a; Jagacinski *et al.*, 1980b; Kantowitz and Elvers, 1988; Jagacinski, 1989).

4.1.3 Trackball

Trackballs are used in air traffic control applications, medical equipment, CAD applications and in laptop and notebook computers. They are also quite popular among people who suffer from *repetitive strain injury* (RSI) caused by overuse of the wrist in mouse movement. Its technology is similar to a mechanical mouse turned upside down: the rolling ball of the mouse becomes a surface rotated by the fingers or palm of the hand. Because the trackball does not require a surface for movement, it is popular in applications such as laptop computers. Selection buttons are sometimes incorporated into the surface surrounding the ball and are operated by the thumb and fingers.

Figure 4.4: Trackball: the Turbo Mouse™ 5.0. Courtesy of Kensington Microware Ltd.

Trackballs are popular in situations where there is no desk space for moving a device such as a mouse. Movement times with the trackball are usually longer than the mouse in experimental tasks (e.g. MacKenzie *et al.*, 1991).

Table 4.4: Ergonomic studies of the trackball

Study	Devices compared	Task	Performance measures
Albert (1982)	Touch screen, 2 joysticks (spring isotonic rate and isometric rate), trackball, matrix tablet (puck)	Target acquisition	Time, errors, preferred device
Epps (1986)	Two touch tablets (relative and absolute), trackball, isometric rate joystick, isotonic rate joystick, mouse	Target acquisition	Time, Fitts
Gomez *et al.* (1982)	Trackball, touch tablet (absolute mode, finger or stylus)	Target acquisition	Time, errors
Haller *et al.* (1984)	Lightpen, matrix tablet, mouse, trackball, cursor keys, voice	Text selection	Time, errors
MacKenzie *et al.* (1991)	Mouse, trackball, touch tablet (absolute)	Target acquisition (includes dragging)	Time, Fitts
Mehr and Mehr (1972)	Joystick, trackball		

Differences in trackball design, particularly the size, weight, resistance and texture of the ball, will contribute to differences in 'feel.' Trackballs are quite usable for pointing, somewhat awkward for dragging tasks since the selection button must be held down while rolling the ball, and are extremely difficult to control during long movements in drawing. Studies by Epps and MacKenzie have shown trackballs to follow Fitts' law (Epps, 1986; MacKenzie *et al.*, 1991).

4.1.4 The Touch Tablet and Touch Screen

The touch, or digitizing, tablet is one of the earliest computer input devices dating from the 1970s. It has been used extensively in drawing systems such as for graphic art and CAD/CAM. The touch tablet has come into recent use in a reduced size as a touch pad, integrated into laptop computers and operated by the finger.

The touch, or digitizing, tablet is usually a fixed-size surface that provides positional information by measuring the position of a special pen called a *stylus*. On some tablets, the pressure of the stylus can be sensed as well. There are three different technologies for the tablet:

- The *resistive tablet* determines point contact between two separate conducting surfaces – it does not require a special stylus and can be operated with a finger.
- The *magnetic, capacitative* and *electrostatic field* tablets detect position using a specialized stylus which create changes in the field.
- The *sonic tablet* triangulates position by listening for an ultrasonic pulse emitted by a special stylus. It can work in three dimensions as well as two and does not require a special surface.

Figure 4.5: Digitizing tablet with pen and cursor: the SummaSketch™ III. Courtesy of Summagraphics Corp.

The touch tablet can be operated in two modes: *relative* and *absolute*. In an absolute-mode touch tablet, there is a one-to-one mapping of the surface of the touch tablet to the screen. For example, the top-left corner of the touch tablet corresponds to the top-left corner of the screen. Placing the pen in this corner immediately moves the cursor to that position. In relative mode, the user puts the pen down on the tablet and then moves it in the direction that the cursor should move. The cursor is displaced on the screen by an amount that is proportional to the displacement of the pen. This mapping is very similar to the mapping of the displacement of a mouse on a mouse pad to the displacement of the cursor on the screen. Tablet size is affected by display/control gain. For example, with a gain of 2.0 the surface area of the tablet can be one half the size of a gain of 1.0. Although most tablets require a large amount of desk space, small, relative mode touch tablets for use with a single finger started appearing in notebook computers in the middle of 1994, when they were introduced by Apple in their PowerBook™ computers.

Figure 4.6: Finger-controlled tablet: the PowerBook™ 2300C. Courtesy of Apple Computer Inc.

Touch screens are touch-sensitive computer display screens. They can be used with either the finger or with a stylus. Touch screen technology is similar to that of tablets. They work by the interruption of a matrix of light sources, by capacitance changes on a grid overlaying the screen, or by ultrasonic reflection. They are absolute mode devices because there is no mapping from another surface to the screen.

The touch tablet is similar to pen usage and therefore requires little learning. Direct mode tablets are especially easy although users must learn that movement away from and toward the self in the horizontal plane is up and down on the screen. Tablets are very fast and very accurate devices with movement times as fast, or faster than, the mouse, e.g. MacKenzie et al., 1991. They are a particularly good device for drawing and handwriting since it can be as accurate as the point of stylus and is as easy to control as any pen. However, it is awkward to use if displaced to one side and holding the pen upright can be quite fatiguing over several hours. It is also easy to lose one's position if the tablet is a relative mode device since lifting the pen loses the mapping to the screen.

The touch screen is the easiest device to learn because of its direct mode in which there is no spatial mapping between input device and the screen. Pointing, dragging and tracking are very fast and accurate, although drawing is not feasible. Because the surface of finger is large, the touch screen is not useful for small targets, and the finger may cover up screen objects during a task. Using the screen as a pointing surface will leave greasy marks. Finally, continuous lifting of the arm to the screen is very fatiguing. Thus touch screens are best for situations where use is infrequent, where users are novices, or where a keyboard or mouse cannot be placed, such as a kiosk.

Epps and MacKenzie *et al.*, studied the touch tablet as an input device and showed it to follow Fitts' law (Epps, 1986; MacKenzie *et al.*, 1991). The Epps study included both a relative mode tablet, as well as absolute mode tablet, and showed the relative mode tablet to have a higher *IP* than the absolute mode tablet. This might have been because of the tablet technology available at the time. It is possible that for modern tablets with cordless pens, absolute mode tablets will be faster than relative mode tablets.

Table 4.5: Ergonomic studies of touch screens and tablets

Study	Devices compared	Task	Performance measures
Albert (1982)	Touch screen, 2 joysticks (spring isotonic rate and isometric rate), trackball, matrix tablet (puck)	Target acquisition	Time, errors, preferred device
Arnaut and Greenstein (1986)	Two touch-sensitive tablets (finger relative and finger absolute)	Target acquisition	Time, gain
Baggen (1987)	Touch screens (6 types)	Various tasks	
Becker and Greenstein (1986)	Two touch tablets (position and position–velocity)	Target acquisition	Time, errors, gain
Beringer and Peterson (1985)	Touch screen	Target acquisition	Errors
Buxton *et al.* (1985)	Touch sensitive tablet (finger)		
Cakir *et al.* (1995)	Touch tablet (relative)		
Ellingstad *et al.* (1985)	Two touch tablets (finger and stylus)	Target acquisition, tracking, menu selection	Time, errors
Epps (1986)	Two touch tablets (relative and absolute), trackball, isometric rate joystick, isotonic rate joystick, mouse	Target acquisition	Time, Fitts
Gaertner and Hozhausen (1980)	Touch screen		
Gomez *et al.* (1982)	Trackball, touch tablet (absolute mode, finger or stylus)	Target acquisition	Time, errors
Haller *et al.* (1984)	lightpen, matrix tablet, mouse, trackball, cursor keys, voice	Text selection	Time, errors
Karat *et al.* (1986)	Touch screen, mouse, keyboard	Menu selection	Time, gain, preferred device
MacKenzie *et al.* (1991)	Mouse, trackball, touch tablet (absolute)	Target acquisition (includes dragging)	Time, Fitts
Pfauth and Priest (1981)	Touch screen		
Rosenberg and Martin (1988)	Matrix tablet (digitizer puck)		
Stammers and Bird (1980)	Touch screen		
Whitfield *et al.* (1983)	Touch screen, touch tablets	Menu selection	

4.1.5 Lightpen and Lightgun

The lightpen is one of the earliest pointing devices invented. During the 1950s the SAGE air-defense system developed the use of the lightpen to identify targets on a CRT screen. Later, in 1963, Sutherland used the lightpen and keyboard as the primary sources of input for the first interactive graphics program called *Sketchpad*. Lightpens and lightguns are still in use in CAD/CAM and interactive control systems such as air traffic control.

The lightpen and lightgun differ only in how they are held by the hand: one is grasped by the fingers; the other is grasped by the whole hand. Operation is similar to the touch screen since the user points directly to the computer display screen. The lightpen or lightgun has a cable which connects it to the computer. During operation the lightpen or lightgun detects a burst of light from the cathode ray phosphor of the screen during the scanning of the monitor. It is highly accurate and can detect individual pixels, unlike the touch screen. It is obviously an absolute mode device. The lightpen and lightgun are more accurate than the touch screen for fine selection since they use a 'stylus' type of pointer which has a smaller surface than the finger. However, the act of pointing may still obscure the screen if the device is placed between the screen and the eyes. They are tiring on the arm if used during frequent or long operations. They are also fragile devices.

Three kinds of continuous devices, lightpen, lightgun, and digitizer pucks were studied to determine their pointing speed, but a Fitts' law analysis was not done on them (Goodwin, 1975; Rosenberg and Martin, 1988). However, it seems likely that Fitts' law holds for them because pointing with them is continuous, and is similar to pointing with a finger. Table 4.6 briefly describes the few ergonomic studies.

Table 4.6: Ergonomic studies of the lightpen and lightgun

Study	Devices compared	Task	Performance measures
Avons *et al.* (1983)	Lightpen	Target acquisition (children)	Error, fatigue
Beringer and Scott (1985)	Lightpen on head		Fatigue
English *et al.* (1967)	Mouse, joystick (2 modes: rate and position), knee control, Grafcon, lightpen	Menu selection	Time
Goodwin (1975)	Lightpen, lightgun, keyboard	Text selection	Time
Haller *et al.* (1984)	Lightpen, matrix tablet, mouse, trackball, cursor keys, voice	Text selection	Time, errors

4.1.6 Head, Hand and Eye Trackers, and Datagloves

A number of devices have been invented within the past 10 years to extend pointing into three dimensions. The Polhemus cube is a three-dimensional tracker that uses magnetic fields to measure the absolute location and rotational orientation of a cube that can be either held or attached to some other object such as a glove or helmet. It is an absolute device.

The dataglove has transducers that detect light leaking from optical fibers stretched along the fingers of the glove. Thus, joint angles of the fingers and thumb are measured with flexing of the fingers within a three-dimensional space that senses hand orientation. The dataglove can be combined with a Polhemus cube to give absolute location and orientation of the hand (wrist rotation). Virtual reality systems may use either or both these devices to create a three-dimensional input space. These devices are still very expensive.

Another 3D hand device called the *Owl* in European markets and the *RingMouse* in the United States, consists of an ultrasonic transmitter that wraps around the index finger with Velcro straps and has two buttons accessible to the thumb for selection. A unit containing three receivers is mounted on the computer display and connected via the serial port to the computer. This computes position of the transmitter in two or three dimensions. Accuracy is reported to be better than 0.5mm on each axis. The device can be used for cursor control in traditional two-dimensional GUI software as well as 3D virtual reality and takes advantage of the naturalness of gesture. Device switching between pointing and typing are advertised to be effortless. Preliminary tests done within the senior author's lab have not tended to support the usability of this device, and suggest that it is very difficult to control.

The eye tracker has been used as a laboratory device for at least 30 years. Early eye trackers used three technologies to measure the direction of eye gaze:

1. a light beam reflected from the cornea;

2. an electrical potential across the eye;

3. electrical signals generated in eye muscles.

Modern eye-trackers use a low-power laser which is shone into the eye and reflected off the retina. Eye gaze can then be used to direct a cursor. Again, this device is still quite expensive.

Very few ergonomic studies have been done on the use of head controls, eye trackers, or the glove. Most of the studies of head controls and eye trackers are for two-dimensional control of a screen cursor. Table 4.7 lists the few that have been done. The Beringer *et al.* study is of head controls for the disabled. The Glenn *et al.* study compares various feedback methods. Calhoun *et al.* recommends a physical button to confirm target selection once the eye has fixated. Ware and Mikaelian recommend that target sizes should subtend at least one degree of visual angle.

Three-dimensional use of head controls – such as the Polhemus head tracker – has not been extensively studied in an experimental format. One study is that of Jacob *et al.* (1994) which compared two perceptually different matching tasks by participants using either a Polhemus 3D head tracker or a mouse with a mode for the z-direction. Participants were given two tasks: one required matching the size and location of a square with that of a target (spatial task); the second required matching the greyscale values of a square with that of a target (color task). Participants' performance was measured by time to match and accuracy of match. The Polhemus participants performed better in both speed and accuracy on the spatial task and the mouse participants on the color task. The authors conclude that performance can be greatly affected by perceptual qualities of task differences and how compatible those are with the device.

Table 4.7: Ergonomic studies of head control, eye tracker and glove

Study	Devices compared	Task	Performance measures
Beringer and Scott (1985)	Lightpen on head		Fatigue
Boyd (1995)	Virtual reality	Way finding	Ease of use
Calhoun et al. (1986)	Eye tracker	Target acquisition	Ease of use
Glenn et al. (1986)	Eye tracker	Target acquisition	Time, errors
Jagacinski and Monk (1985)	Head control	Target acquisition	Time, Fitts
Jacob et al. (1994)	Polhemus 3D head tracker, mouse with mode for z-direction	Size and grayscale matching	Time, accuracy
Kessler et al. (1995)	CyberGlove	Hand positioning	Sensory characteristics
Lin et al. (1992)	Head control	Target acquisition	Time, Fitts
Ware and Mikaelian (1987)	Eye tracker	Target acquisition	Time, Fitts
Zhai (1995, 1996)	6 DOF hand- and finger-controlled devices	3D tracking, docking	Time
Zimmerman et al. (1987)	Glove	Hand positioning	Ease of use

Unlike the typical head-control unit, the dataglove is comfortable to wear. Because the dataglove is fitted to the hand and naturally captures limb movement, we can assume it will be easy to use and require no learning. Gloves can be fitted with force-feedback to simulate the effect of grasping different materials. The dataglove prevents typing, which limits it in some applications.

The increasing use of virtual reality systems and other three-dimensional computer-based environments underscores the need for experimental ergonomic research in these environments.

4.1.7   Leg and Foot Controls

Although lower-limb controls are used in situations such as automobiles, airplanes, organs, and sewing machines, very few devices have been designed for pointing control by the foot and leg. Knee controls were developed in the mid-1960s by Douglas Englebart's research group at SRI (English *et al.*, 1967). Foot-controlled devices, called *moles*, were designed by Pearson (Anderson *et al.*, 1993; Pearson and Weiser, 1986, 1988). The mole is a discrete pointing device somewhat similar to cursor control keys. The cursor is controlled by exerting pressure from the foot onto the surface of the pedal. Pressure on the left or right side moves the cursor horizontally; pressure on the top or bottom moves it vertically. Similarly, the *Versatron footmouse* is a stationary-pedal discrete device developed in the early 1980s. In mid-1996, a continuous foot-controlled isometric joystick is currently being marketed under the name 'Footmouse' by Hunter Digital.[1] One pedal controls the joystick and a separate pedal controls selection.

Although lower limbs are difficult to use for fine motor control, they can be successfully used for gross muscle movement. They are advantageous in situations where the user does not have the ability to use the hands, or where concurrent use of hand and feet may be desired.

Table 4.8 describes the few studies of foot controls that have been published. The earliest study by English *et al.* (1967) used a knee control which had the fastest selection time and modest error rate among devices, including the mouse, tested for inexperienced users. Studies by Drury (1975) showed that Fitts' law holds for a foot-controlled device.

Table 4.8: Ergonomic studies of leg and foot controls

Study	Devices compared	Task	Performance measures
Drury (1975)	Foot control	Target acquisition	Time, Fitts
English *et al.* (1967)	Mouse, joystick (2 modes: rate and position), knee control, Grafcon, lightpen	Menu selection	Time, errors
Harriman (1985)	Footmouse (discrete device)		
Pearson and Weiser (1986, 1988)	Mole	Target acquisition	Time, Fitts
Anderson *et al.* (1993)	Mole II	Pointing, tracking	Time

4.2 Comparison Between Devices

This chapter has described many studies with variations in device characteristics, limbs, types of tasks, and types of participants. Within a particular, well-conducted study it is reasonable to measure performance experimentally between devices, since the task remains the same for all participants. Thus, task-dependent evaluation is well understood and widely accepted as an evaluation method for comparing devices. Can we not extend our evaluation to be task independent?

4.2.1 Buxton and Mackinlay–Card–Robertson Device Taxonomies

There has been recent work within the HCI field to analytically categorize devices by their features and then to make predictions about their human performance attributes. To understand that effort, first we must review the project of creating these taxonomies of devices to describe the *expressiveness* of an input device or the range of actions it can perform, then see how this same taxonomical approach can be applied to predicting *effectiveness* of human performance.

Buxton suggested that there are lexical and pragmatic factors to be considered regarding input devices (Buxton, 1983). He suggested that devices can be categorized along three dimensions: the property sensed, the number of degrees of freedom, and a third dimension which captures whether the device moved or was touch sensitive. For example, a touch tablet senses position in two dimensions by touch, while a lightpen senses position in two dimensions by non-touch-sensitive means (electronic in this case). A mouse senses motion in two dimensions by measuring mechanical movement.

More recently, Mackinlay, Card and Robertson (1990), in work inspired by a language of graphical primitives developed by a cartographer, developed a similar taxonomy for input devices that could be used to categorize all existing input devices, as well as to predict novel input devices. In this approach, they demonstrate the usefulness of the taxonomy to analyze the *expressiveness* of devices. Expressiveness is defined as the ways in which physical manipulation can communicate meanings, i.e. parameter values, to an application. In a companion paper, the taxonomy is used to analyze the *effectiveness* of devices (Card, Mackinlay, and Robertson, 1990, 1991). Effectiveness is defined implicitly as the value of the device, for example, its pointing speed, errors, time to learn, user preferred device, desk footprint, and cost.

Like Buxton, Mackinlay *et al.* use three dimensions in their taxonomy. The first dimension was the property sensed, which was either force, difference in force, position, or difference in position. The second dimension was the number of dimensions of the property that were sensed, and the third dimension was whether a rotary or linear movement was detected. For instance, a trackball measures a difference in position in two spherical coordinates. After developing this taxonomy, and analyzing the expressiveness of existing devices, Mackinlay *et al.* use it to design a new device, a mouse-based egocentric motion controller for virtual 3D worlds.

While the Buxton and Mackinlay taxonomies are useful for categorizing and understanding the expressiveness of devices, and even for inventing new devices, we find that the taxonomy is not particularly useful in predicting effectiveness, particularly human performance aspects. For example, in Card *et al.* (1990) they make the assumption that knowing the Fitts' *index of performance* (bandwidth) for different limbs will allow prediction of performance independent of the task, the device and the person. For example, based on Langolf *et al.* (1976) the finger has a higher *IP* than the wrist. This would lead us to predict that all finger-controlled devices would be faster in movement time than wrist-controlled devices. As we will show later in this chapter, and again in Chapters 5 and 6, this is not supported by experimental evidence. The factor of limb control cannot be isolated from aspects of device operation or type of task. These variables interact with each other in complex ways that are poorly understood and cannot be used analytically to predict behavior.

4.2.2 Comparison by Experimental Measures and Fitts' Law

The failure of analytical methods such as taxonomies to predict device performance necessarily restricts comparisons between devices to experimental studies. We will first examine experimentally derived means for movement time from four studies to see how devices differ across studies and then analyze these results with the goal of deriving some sort of absolute performance measure.

4.2.2.1   A Comparison of Performance From Four Studies

Table 4.9 lists the ranking of devices by pointing speed for skilled users within four studies: Card *et al.* (1978), MacKenzie *et al.* (1991), Rutledge and Selker (1990), and Douglas and Mithal (1993, 1994; also Chapter 5). The joysticks in these studies are all isometric, velocity-controlled devices. The joysticks in the Rutledge and Selker, and Douglas and Mithal studies are controlled by a single index finger; the others are controlled by either multiple fingers or the whole hand (gripping).

Table 4.9: Comparison of different devices

Study	Device	Pointing		Dragging		Homing to keyboard	Homing to pointing device
		Time (ms)	Error rate	Time (ms)	Error rate	Time (ms)	Tim (ms)
Card *et al.* (1978)	Mouse	1290	5%				360
	Joystick	1570	11%				260
	Text teys	1950	9%				320
	Step teys	2310	13%				210
MacKenzie *et al.* (1991)	Tablet	665	4.0%	802	13.6%		
	Mouse	674	3.5%	916	10.8%		
	Trackball	1101	3.9%	1284	17.3%		
Rutledge and Selker (1990)	Mouse	760					
	Pointing Stick	1180					
Douglas and Mithal (Chapter 5)	Mouse	1123	6.9%	966	3.7%	667	
	Key joystick	1779	10.3%	1407	6.2%	438[†]	

[†]Homing time for key joystick is mode switching the keyboard

As we would expect, the tablet is the top performer because it most directly translates finger, hand and arm control. The mouse is the next top performer in all four studies for both pointing and dragging. For pointing, if we examine the proportional difference between the mouse and the other devices, the key joystick seems to fall in the middle of the devices along with the trackball and standard joystick. Also shown in Table 4.9 are the values obtained by Rutledge and Selker (1990) in their study of the Pointing Stick, also known as the Trackpoint™, which is another finger-controlled isometric joystick. For the dragging task, the key joystick appears to be slower than the trackball and mouse, but had fewer problems of control than the trackball.

4.2.2.2   Difficulties in Comparing Means of Movement Time and Error Rate Across Studies

The difficulty with this comparison is that these experimental studies do not allow us to draw firm conclusions about the overall performance of one device compared with another. For example, the Douglas and Mithal study that compared an isometric joystick with a mouse found that the joystick was approximately 50% slower than the mouse. This is surprising because in the Card *et al.* study (1978), the joystick was only 22% slower than the mouse.

MacKenzie (1992) provides a framework to understand this. He lists eight factors that can affect the average movement time and *IP* obtained in a study:

1. the task;
2. the selection technique;
3. the range of conditions;
4. the choice of model;
5. the approach angle and target width;
6. learning effects;
7. error handling;
8. the device.

Most of these factors, except for choice of model, we have anticipated in our earlier discussions. As we have readily illustrated in this chapter, the same 'type' of device can differ enormously depending on limb control, whether it is an absolute or relative mode device, its control/display gain, its transfer function, whether it is isometric or isotonic, and whether it controls position or velocity of the cursor. Likewise, we have discussed the critical difference the task plays in performance testing, whether it is a one-, two- or three-dimensional Fitts' task; the activities incorporated into the task; the range of trial conditions tested; the approach angle; the definition of target width; or the selection technique. Learning effects have also been discussed as having a significant role in determining performance. We have not previously discussed the effect of the experimental model, but will address that shortly.

The four studies listed in Table 4.9 differ in all these ways. There are differences between device characteristics that may contribute to differences in performance. For example, two of the isometric joysticks are controlled by single index fingers and the rest by multiple fingers or even the whole hand, and Fitts' task studies lead us to expect differences in performance because of differences in limbs – see section 2.1.4. Differences in non-linear transfer functions (control/display gain – see section 3.1.1.3) for these joysticks also might tend to affect performance. For example, Karat *et al.* (1986) compared a touch screen, mouse and keyboard using three tasks: target acquisition, menu selection and menu selection with typing tasks. The mouse appeared to be a relatively poor performer when compared to the keyboard. After making several changes to the design of the experiment, including setting the control/display gain equal that of the Card *et al.* study (from 1.0 to 0.5), mouse performance improved from the first study.

Although they all used a Fitts target-acquisition format, no study used exactly the same task environment. Pointing tasks differed greatly in overall movement time. For example, the Card *et al.* study used real text targets embedded in a two-dimensional document; the Epps and MacKenzie *et al.* studies used the traditional Fitts one-dimensional task environment (see Figure 6.5), the Douglas and Mithal study used a two-dimensional environment with circular targets (see Figure 5.4), and the Rutledge and Selker environment was not reported. Repetitive one-dimensional tasks are frequently faster than two-dimensional since practice effects are sometimes greater when the task environment is simpler. All four studies used different sizes and distances for targets and thus may vary in the range of index of difficulty tested. For example, the MacKenzie *et al.* study has a lower maximum index of difficulty than the Douglas and Mithal and the Card *et al.* study. This may account for the fact that the MacKenzie study reports a much faster mouse pointing speed of 665ms versus 1123ms for that of Douglas and Mithal and 1100ms for the Card *et al.* study.

As discussed earlier in section 3.3.2.2, tasks can be serial or discrete, and discrete tasks are faster. The MacKenzie *et al.* study used a serial task; the Douglas and Mithal study used a discrete one. The selection technique used to indicate the end of a trial also makes a difference. In some studies, the end of the trial was indicated by a button press, e.g. the space bar (Card *et al.*, 1978), and the mouse button (Douglas and Mithal, 1993). In one joystick study (Jagacinski *et al.*, 1980a), the termination criteria required the participants to hold the cursor steady over the target. There is some evidence that two-handed input might speed performance (Buxton and Myers, 1986). Some of the tasks have been two-handed, e.g. the Douglas and Mithal study of the key joystick and the Card *et al.* study where selection is done with the opposite hand, while others have been one-handed.

All four studies used different analysis-of-variance models. Some tested devices as a within-subject variable: e.g. Card *et al.* and MacKenzie *et al.*, others tested devices as a between-subject variable, e.g. Douglas and Mithal. The Card *et al.* and the Douglas *et al.* study used participants who had never used the devices before. The MacKenzie study does not appear to have screened for that. The studies also varied in how they determined practiced performance. The Card *et al.* and Douglas and Mithal studies used a statistical test for non-significance between means of blocks of movement times and then averaged the times for blocks after the learning phase. The MacKenzie *et al.* study used a fixed number of blocks and averaged performance for all of them.

4.2.2.3 Difficulties in Comparing Fitts' Law Coefficients Across Studies

This evidence will convince the reader that we cannot automatically draw conclusions about which device is faster or easier to learn or has a lower error rate independently of experimental details. On the other hand, moving away from simple comparisons of pointing 'speed' across experiments, Fitts' equation makes it seem possible to compare devices independently of an experiment. All we need do is use the experimentally derived coefficients for the equation as an index of performance (see Equation 2.3, section 2.1.1) for a particular device. This allows us to compare movement times between devices on an absolute basis for any task. Card *et al.* (1983) use this assumption in their *keystroke level model* (see section 7.3), and it is commonly repeated in HCI textbooks. For example, Dix, Finlay, Abowd and Beale, in their popular text *Human–Computer Interaction* (1993, pp. 211; 213–214) use for the mouse the Fitts' equation coefficients computed by Card *et al.* (1978) and for the trackball those of MacKenzie *et al.* (1991) for predicting pointing time in any task given distance and size of the target. Unfortunately, the same issues that arise in comparing average (mean) performance-time and error rates across experiments, such as in Table 4.9, are repeated with using Fitts *IP* parameters. MacKenzie (1992) compared the *IP*s from six different Fitts law studies. Table 4.10 compares Fitts parameters for the mouse and the same type of joystick (isometric, velocity control) from four different studies. Comparing the Card *et al.* *IP* for the mouse (10.4 bits/second) with that of Epps (2.6 bits/second) shows a difference of a factor of 4.

Table 4.10: Comparison of Fitts' parameters from four studies (adapted from MacKenzie, 1992:124)

Device	Study	Regression coefficient[†]			Comments
		Intercept, a (ms)	Slope, b (ms/bit)	IP (bits/s)	
Mouse	Card *et al.* (1978)	1030	96	10.4	
	Epps (1986)	108	392	2.6	
	Douglas and Mithal (1994, Chapter 4)	480	241	4.2	
Joystick	Card *et al.* (1978)	990	220	4.5	Isometric, velocity control
	Epps (1986)	-587	861	1.2	Isometric, velocity control
	Kantowitz and Elvers (1988)	-846	449	2.2	Isometric, velocity control, high gain
	Kantowitz and Elvers (1988)	-880	449	2.2	Isometric, velocity control, low gain
	Douglas and Mithal (1994, Chapter 4)	468	507	2.0	Isometric, velocity control, single-finger

[†]$MT = a + bID$; $IP = 1/b$

Again, differences in tasks, characteristics of devices, limbs, experimental design, and Fitts' equation computation have an effect on the *IP* and negate our ability to form cross-experimental, absolute comparisons of devices. In his excellent analysis of the situation, MacKenzie states:

> If the research goal is to establish a Fitts' law (or other) performance model for two or more input devices, then the only source of variation that is desirable is the between-device differences. This is what the investigations are attempting to measure. Accomplishing this assumes, somewhat unrealistically, that all other sources of variation are removed or are controlled for. Of course, very few studies are solely interested in device differences. *Sources of variation* become *factors* in many studies equally as important to the research as model fitting across devices.
>
> *MacKenzie, 1992:125*

4.2.2.4   A Final Possibility: Comparing Ratios of IP Across Studies

MacKenzie suggested that while it is not possible to compare devices using *IP*s across experiments, the ratio of *IP*s within a study can be compared across studies.

Based on this, Table 4.11 gives the *IP* ratios for five studies which compared a mouse with an isometric, velocity-control joystick. The Card *et al.* (1978) and Epps (1986) studies used a hand-controlled joystick made by two different manufacturers; the Douglas and Mithal (1994), Mithal (1995), and Rutledge and Selker (1990) studies use a single-finger joystick. The Mithal and the Rutledge and Selker studies use a joystick made by the same manufacturer. We can assume that the mouse in each of these studies was also made by different manufacturers. All of these devices may also differ in control/display gain, which may or may not have affected performance.

Table 4.11: The IPs for mouse and joystick from five studies, and their ratios (in bits/second)

	Card *et al.* (1978)	Epps (1986)	Rutledge and Selker (1990)	Douglas and Mithal (1994, Chapter 4)	Mithal (1995, Chapter 5)
IP mouse	10.4	2.6	8.33	4.15	8.13
IP joystick	4.5	1.2	4.35	1.97	5.75
Mouse:joystick	2.31	2.16	1.91	2.10	1.41

Note: values for the Epps and Card *et al.* studies are taken from MacKenzie (1992).

As the table demonstrates, while *IP*s for a device may differ considerably between experiments, the ratios are approximately 2. It is also important to note that this ratio is still not an absolute measure. What we see from these ratios is a clearer picture of relative performance: the mouse is a faster device than the joystick.

To summarize, cross-study comparison of devices must always be approached cautiously. Experiments differ greatly in their design and the devices they use. As MacKenzie pointed out, it is simply not practical to restrict research to a single experimental design. However, valid experimental replication is critical to the formation of an understanding of human performance with these devices. One approach is to begin to develop a database of experimental results using the same experimental paradigm. MacKenzie has recently made available to the ergonomics research community a software program for designing Fitts' law experiments (Soukoreff and MacKenzie, 1995). This is a step in the right direction although, in our opinion, the research community needs to agree on what constitutes a benchmark task environment and experimental design rather than provide for more variation. Testing of different devices could then be conducted with the aim of overall evaluation.

4.3 Summary

The first half of this chapter has functioned as a brief description of each type of pointing device and the major ergonomic studies that have been done by device.

By necessity this has been a survey, forcing us to ignore the complexity of individual studies and experiments. As this review demonstrates, most of the attention in the experimental studies of human performance has been on Fitts' law tasks of pointing. A few studies compare performance between devices within the same experiment.

In the second half of the chapter we posed the problem of comparing device performance independent of a particular experiment. We described the attempt to predict human performance analytically by device characteristics based on a taxonomy. We found the approach limited because of the fact that device features interact with other complex factors in device use. Not enough is known about these factors and their interaction to make reliable predictions. We then turned to the possibility of comparing device performance, specifically pointing time, across experimental studies. At least twenty years ago, the discovery that Fitts' law could hold for computer-mediated pointing, offered the promise that each type of device would have its own unique index of performance, allowing some sort of absolute performance measure. Again, we found that this approach ignores many differences between experiments such as different tasks, levels of skill, etc. We caution drawing cross-study comparisons between devices, although using the ratios of IPs is a promising possibility.

The inability to compare device performance across studies leaves only one reliable approach: the comparison of performance between devices within a single study. In the next chapter we demonstrate this approach with a case study illustrating how such an experimental evaluation is done in detail.

4.4 Endnotes

[1]   Hunter Digital, 11999 San Vicente Blvd, Suite 440, Los Angeles, CA 90019. They can be contacted at http://www.footmouse.com

5. Evaluating New Devices: A Case Study

In the previous chapters we surveyed the extensive psychological and HCI literature that forms the basis for empirical studies of human performance with computer pointing devices. As we have seen, human performance results from the interrelationships between many complex factors: fundamental psychomotor behavior, the user's experience level, the characteristics of the device, the limb used, and the type of task. Deciding whether one device is *better* than another must take these issues into account. In addition, the notion of 'better' must be defined in terms of one or a set of particular performance variables, that is, learning time, practiced performance time, error rates, user-preferred device, etc. There is no context-free notion of the *best* device for pointing. For these reasons, we have advocated an experimental approach to evaluation of a device and comparing it to the performance of another type of device.

This chapter presents a comprehensive evaluation of the human performance of a pointing device, the key joystick, conducted by the authors in 1992 (Douglas and Mithal, 1993, 1994). The study was originally done to help the developers improve their device by providing a baseline comparison with the mouse. Since that time, similar devices have become quite popular in laptop and notebook computers. For example, IBM recently developed a miniature isometric joystick, called the Trackpoint™[1], which is built into the center of a standard keyboard between the G, H and B keys and is controlled by the finger. The joystick protrudes only 2mm above the keys so as not to interfere with typing. Mouse buttons are replaced by keys located on either side of the keyboard's space-bar. These keyboard-based joysticks present some unique challenges to the evaluation of the device.

We present this study with several purposes in mind. Firstly, it will provide readers with a very concrete example of the experimental studies which have been cited and reviewed in the previous chapters. Secondly, it demonstrates the usefulness of experimentation during design if a baseline comparison to another device is made. Thirdly, it illustrates the necessity to carefully assess how aspects of tasks interact with performance and to incorporate those into the design of the experimental evaluation. Finally, the design and results from this study provide an analysis of similar devices such as the IBM Trackpoint™ and contribute to the experimental literature on pointing devices.

5.1 Overview

A keyboard with an integrated isometric velocity-controlled joystick located under the 'J' key, called a key joystick, was compared in learning and skilled human performance with a standard mouse. To support a broad study of human performance using these two devices, data was collected via: videotape, computer-generated data collection and questionnaire on performance time, errors, and subjective experience during learning and practicing with the experimental devices. This presents a fairly comprehensive picture of the evolution of a learner into a competent experienced user and allows us to compare human performance on the key joystick with a standard mouse.

Participants performed three tasks: pointing, dragging and device/mode switching between typing and pointing. The experimental procedure tested Fitts tasks in a two-dimensional (i.e. motion in a plane) environment. Skilled key-joystick performance was comparable to that reported in the literature for other isometric velocity-control joysticks. The key joystick was significantly slower for pointing and dragging in both learning and skilled performance, and had more errors. For practiced performance the pointing task time for the key joystick was approximately 58% slower than the mouse; the dragging task time was approximately 46% slower. For the mode-switching task, the key joystick had a significantly faster homing time, but it was not enough to compensate in overall task time for the significantly longer pointing time and non-significant difference in typing time. Both devices were shown to obey Fitts' law for pointing tasks. This result suggests that Fitts' law does accurately describe motion of finger-operated, isometric velocity-controlled devices. Finally, a comparison of index-of-performance (IP) ratios within the experimental literature places the finger-controlled isometric joystick at the same performance level as a hand-operated isometric joystick. This leads to our theoretical conclusion that continuing to reduce mode-switching or homing time will have little effect on the overall performance time of this device, and that *IP* is still a better indicator of pointing device performance than mode-switching time. In other words, in order to make this device faster, it is more fruitful to concentrate on improving the pointing speed than on the mode-switching speed.

5.2 Introduction

While numerous studies have shown the mouse to be a superior pointing device when compared to other devices such as trackballs and joysticks (Card *et al.*, 1978; Epps, 1986; MacKenzie *et al.*, 1991), the research literature has described drawbacks in the use of mice from a very early stage. Card, English and Burr (1978) described a homing time, which was the time a user takes to move his or her hand from one input device to another. In their study this was from the keyboard to the mouse and was 360ms. (See Table 4.9 in the previous chapter.) This time was so significant that Card, Moran and Newell subsequently incorporated it into the *keystroke level model* (Card *et al.*, 1980; Card *et al.*, 1983). In this model, a typical pointing task incorporates a pointing action (1.1s), and two homing actions (0.4s each). Note that the original empirical data were rounded to the nearest tenth of a second. Moving from the keyboard to the mouse and back therefore takes approximately 40% of the total time it takes to point to an object on a computer screen.

In general, we can think of a homing time as a device-switching time. It is the time that encompasses the physical action and mental preparation that it takes a user to change from using one input device to another. For a keyboard and mouse combination, therefore, there are two device switches, one when the user goes from the keyboard to the mouse, and one when the user goes from the mouse to the keyboard.

The key joystick was designed to reduce this device-switching time. It incorporates an isometric, rate-controlled joystick placed under the 'J' key of a standard keyboard. An isometric device is one that does not change shape when force is applied to it, so there is no discernible movement when pointing with the key joystick. Holding the 'J' key down activates the joystick, and the user can move the cursor around the computer screen. Releasing the 'J' key returns the keyboard to typing mode. A second drawback of the mouse is the additional desktop space that it requires. It requires a surface to operate on, and a cable for connection. Various approaches have addressed these issues, such as cordless mice, trackballs, and trackballs integrated into the keyboard. A side effect of the design of key joystick is that it eliminates the need for additional space and cables, making it ideal for situations where space is at a premium – such as in notebook computers.

Although the key joystick appears to provide the user with a faster overall task time through the reduction of device-switching time and therefore better usability, that is a hypothesis which can, and should, be evaluated empirically. Caution should be given to accepting it since research data substantiates the superior efficiency of the mouse as a pointing device over the isometric joystick (Card *et al.*, 1978; MacKenzie *et al.*, 1991) and may account for its widespread popularity. For these reasons our experiment uses the mouse as the baseline performance device. In addition, replication of the findings of other independent mouse performance experiments develop confidence in results of the present experiment and its findings concerning the key joystick.

5.3 Previous Research

While there is a broad range of studies examining Fitts' law and the applicability of Fitts' law to pointing devices (see MacKenzie, 1992, for an overview), two aspects of the literature on pointing devices were of particular interest to our study. We were interested in studies of the mouse and joystick to provide us with clues about how the devices would compare. We were also interested in studies of the finger in a pointing task.

Card *et al.* (1978), studied the mouse and isometric velocity-controlled joystick, and measured homing time. Numerous other studies (cf. Epps, 1986; MacKenzie, Sellen and Buxton, 1991; Rutledge and Selker, 1990) have studied the mouse. Jagacinski *et al.* (1980); Jagacinski and Monk, (1985); Epps, (1986); and Kantowitz and Elvers, (1988) have studied wrist- and finger-controlled isometric velocity-controlled joysticks; Rutledge and Selker (1990) a single-finger controlled joystick similar to the key joystick. While it is difficult to compare devices across studies, MacKenzie (1992) suggests the use of the Fitts' *index of performance* (IP) to compare devices within experiments such as the Card *et al.* (1978) and the Epps (1986) studies which compared both mice and joysticks.

Fitts' law (1954) relates the size and distance of a target to the time it takes to point to it. The Welford version (cf. Card *et al.*, 1978) of this relationship is described by the equation:

$$MovementTime = a + \frac{1}{IP}log_2\left(\frac{distance}{width} + 0.5\right) \qquad (5.1)$$

MovementTime is the time it takes to point to a target; *distance* is from the starting location to the target center, and *width* is of the target in the direction of movement. The constants a and IP (*index of performance*) are derived empirically. The *log* term is referred to as the *index of difficulty* (ID), giving us the equation:

$$MovementTime = a + \frac{ID}{IP} \qquad (5.2)$$

Thus, given a pointing task, its *ID* can be measured, and given the *IP* of a pointing device, we can estimate the time it would take to perform the pointing task with that device. In general, the larger the value of *IP* for a given device, the faster it will perform. If devices are known to follow Fitts' law, their *IPs* can be used to compare them within the same experiment. The *IPs* obtained from the Card *et al.* (1978) and Epps (1986) studies predict that the mouse would perform better than the isometric joystick based on differences in device alone. (See Table 4.11, Chapter 4). On the other hand, the Langolf *et al.* (1976) limb study found that the *IP* for the finger (38.4 bits/second) was higher than that for the wrist (23.3 bits/second), predicting that the key joystick, a finger-controlled device, would outperform the mouse, a wrist-controlled device. Based on these studies we hypothesized that the key joystick would be slower than the mouse, but faster than the multiple-finger, wrist-controlled joysticks studied by Card *et al.* and Epps.

5.4 Method

5.4.1 Participants

The sample consisted of 23 participants recruited using the following method. Requests for participants for the experiment were advertised through flyers posted around the University of Oregon campus. An additional request for participants was also made in two classes on introductory computer science for non-majors (class size 250 students each). Thirty-six people responded to these advertisements. The candidates were asked to fill out a form describing their computer experience. Candidates indicating that they had experience with a mouse or joystick were eliminated from further participation in the experiment.

This left a final participant pool of 23 individuals – all were undergraduates. Seven participants were male and 16 were female. One participant (male) was left-handed, while the rest were right-handed. The participants were randomly assigned to one of the two pointing devices, with 11 participants using the mouse and keyboard combination, while 12 participants (including the left-handed participant) used the key joystick. Participants were paid $5 per one-hour session for their participation in the experiment.

5.4.2 Experimental Equipment

All experimental tasks were computer-based. The hardware used for the experiment was an IBM-PC compatible made by Austin Computers, using a 386SX CPU, operating at 16Mhz, with 4MB of memory. The operating environment was Microsoft Windows 3.0 and Microsoft MS-DOS version 4.0. The display adapter was a Tseng 3000 VGA card. The screen was a 16-color SVGA with a resolution of 800 × 600 pixels. The point size was .28mm per pixel. Experimental materials were presented to the participants using this display.

One pointing device was a Microsoft Mouse. The other pointing device was a Keytronic keyboard fitted with an isometric velocity-controlled joystick under the 'J' key. Outwardly, there is no apparent difference between the key joystick keyboard and a standard keyboard apart from visual cues such as additional legends on the 'J' key, or a different color for the key cap. In order to point, a user presses down on the 'J' key. After the key is held down for more than a threshold of time, the keyboard behaves like a pointing device. At normal typing speeds, pressing and releasing the 'J' key would produce a character on the screen, though errors did occur. The magnitude and direction of pointer movement was controlled by the magnitude and direction, respectively, of the lateral force on the 'J' key. Clicking was done with the 'F' key in a manner analogous to clicking with a mouse.

Since both devices were used for the tasks of pointing, dragging and device/mode switching, the following is a description of the definition of these tasks for the experiment and how these are accomplished on the equipment. (*Note*: all actions with a pointing device relate to the cursor on the computer screen. This cursor is controlled by the actions of the user on the pointing device.)

1. *Pointing* is the task of moving the cursor to a specific location on the screen. For the mouse, pointing is accomplished by moving the device across a surface. The displacement of the mouse causes a corresponding displacement of the cursor on the screen. For the key joystick, pointing is accomplished by pressing and holding down the 'J' key on the keyboard. When the duration that the key is held down exceeds a threshold, estimated at 200ms, the keyboard automatically switches from typing mode to pointing mode. This activates the joystick, which then senses the direction of lateral force on the key, and moves the cursor in the corresponding direction, the velocity of movement being controlled by the force on the joystick. If there is no lateral force on the 'J' key, the cursor does not move. When the 'J' key is released, the keyboard returns to typing mode. On many GUIs, the final selection of a location or object through the cursor is accomplished by clicking. On the mouse, this means pressing and quickly releasing one of the buttons on the mouse. Final selection of location on the key joystick is made by clicking the 'F' key while remaining in pointing mode, i.e. keeping the 'J' key pressed down.

2. *Dragging* is the task of moving an object on the screen to a target position. On the mouse this is accomplished by pointing the cursor at a target on the screen, depressing a mouse button without releasing it, and then moving the mouse. On most GUIs, the object then follows the mouse (i.e. it is dragged). When the object reaches the target location, the mouse button is released. On the key joystick, dragging is performed in an analogous fashion to mouse operation except the 'F' key is held down instead of a mouse button.

3. *Device/mode-switching*. A device- or mode-switch occurs when a user changes between a pointing task and a typing task. For a mouse and keyboard combination, this is equivalent to a pointing task, homing the hand back to the keyboard, and then a typing task, or vice versa. For the key joystick, this is equivalent to entering and leaving pointing mode from typing mode.

It is helpful to understand these devices in terms of a transition diagram describing the states that the device goes through during pointing, dragging and mode-switching.

Buxton (1990) suggests the state transition diagram shown in Figure 5.1 as a model for describing pointing and dragging with a device such as a mouse or trackball. In our attempt to use this model for our experimental design, we found it inadequate, and substituted it with the more elaborate diagram found in Figure 5.2.

The state transition diagram in Figure 5.2 is closer to representing the state of the system than Buxton's diagram. It is also more useful for the programmer trying to implement code for dragging.

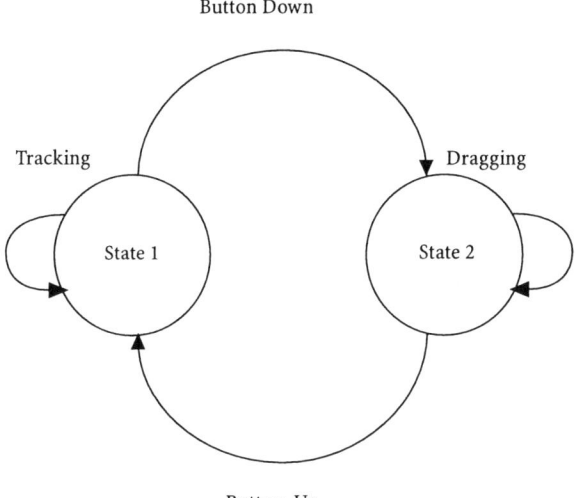

Figure 5.1: Buxton's state transition diagram for tracking and dragging.

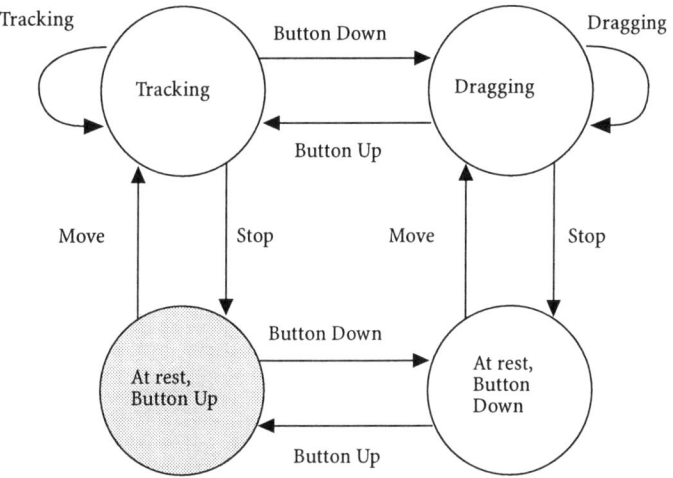

Figure 5.2: Modified state transition diagram for tracking and dragging with mouse or trackball.

While this state transition diagram is sufficient for separate pointing devices like mice and trackballs, it is inadequate for the key joystick because the key joystick needs additional states to represent the states of the keys on the keyboard. The state transition diagram for the key joystick is shown in Figure 5.3. This figure illustrates the complex interaction between the modes of the key joystick for typing and pointing, since the 'J' key and 'F' key can be used in both modes.

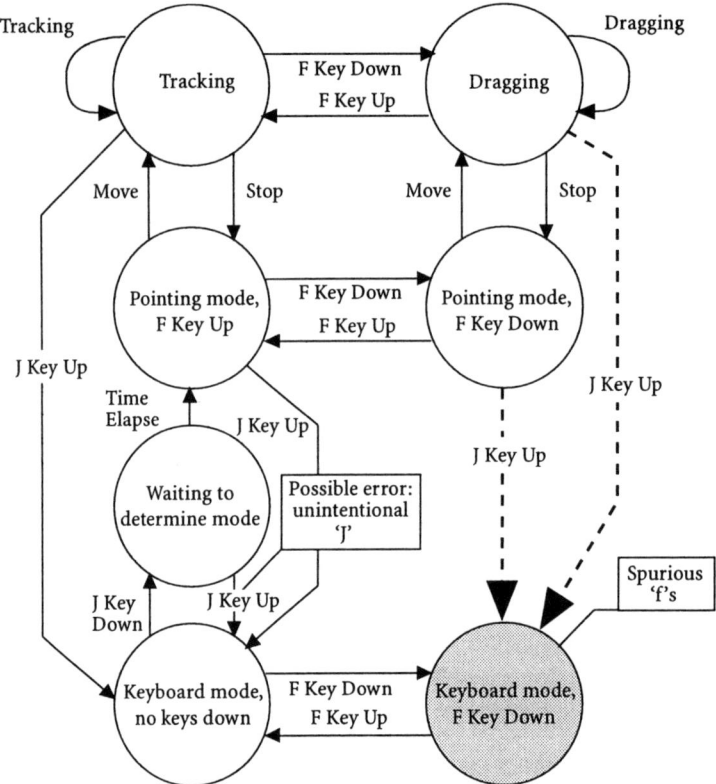

Dotted arcs represent error transitions leading to the shaded state where
the keyboard starts to send out a stream of spurious 'f's. The J key is
used for pointing and typing the letter 'J'; the F key for selection.

Figure 5.3: State transition diagram for the key joystick.

5.4.3 Experimental Procedure

Participants were seated in front of the computer system and provided with a chair
adjustable for height and angle, as well as a foot rest. Thus, they could choose as
comfortable a posture as possible. All participants assigned to the key joystick, including the left-handed person, placed their hands on the keyboard in the standard touch-typing position, so that the 'J' key came under the index finger of their
right hand, and the 'F' key came under the index finger of their left hand.

At the beginning of the experiment, each participant received brief instruction on
use of the experimental device. The instruction period lasted approximately five
minutes and included demonstration by the experimenter and spontaneous practice by the participant. Participants then continued on to an experimental session
of the three tasks. The session was composed of a block of pointing trials, followed

by a block of mode-switching trials and, finally, a block of dragging tasks. During this first session, the experimenter explained each type of task and demonstrated it. The participant then performed 10 warm-up trials which were discarded from the recorded data. The task block was then restarted, and the participant completed the assigned block. The first session for all participants learning a device was videotaped for later analysis of learning difficulties.

Participants returned for more experimental sessions until five sessions had been completed. When participants returned to the experiment for a session, the first 10 trials of each task type were considered warm-up. The warm-up trials were discarded and the presentation restarted.

For the whole experiment participants had an average session length of one hour and, on the average, returned for a session once a week. After completion of the entire learning experiment, participants were interviewed using a questionnaire to gather more insights into their subjective experience with the device.

5.4.4 Experimental Tasks

5.4.4.1 Pointing Task

During the pointing tasks, participants were shown the screen depicted in Figure 5.4 with varying sizes and positions of targets. They were instructed to move the cursor to the home square, select it by clicking the pointing device button, then to move the cursor to the target circle and select it. They were instructed to do this as fast as possible, while maintaining accuracy. The status bars, described below, provided motivational information. At the start of a trial, the home square was displayed in red, with the target circle in gray, on a white background. The trial started when the participant clicked in the home square. All other clicks prior to the click in the home square were ignored. When the participant clicked in the home square, it became gray, and the target circle became red. This provided participants with feedback, to let them know that their click was successful, and that the trial had started. The participants then clicked in the target circle, ending the trial. The time from the first click to the second click was measured.

After the click in the target, the trial ended, and the home and target were redrawn. The home square was always drawn in the same place, in the center of the window. The target circle was positioned randomly as described later. The cursor was automatically positioned in the middle of the home square after the end of each trial in readiness for the beginning of a new trial. This was done to prevent participants from lengthening the experiment unnecessarily. If they had to reposition the cursor themselves, they would have made two positioning movements for each measurement made.

There were two status bars at the bottom of the screen. The first (top) one displayed the 'score', which was a running average of the time taken for the last 20 trials, as well as the number of error-free trials completed. The lower status-bar alternated between displaying the score on the last trial, and displaying informational messages such as where the participant should click next.

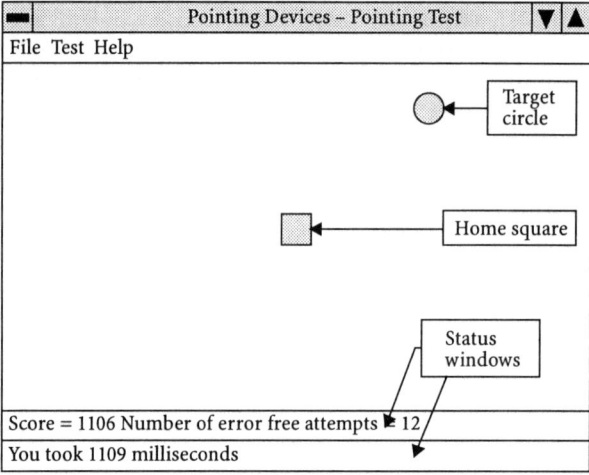

Figure 5.4: Pointing task screen.

When participants missed the target and clicked outside it, the machine beeped and a message flashed in the second status window indicating that they had made an error. Participants were then required to complete the trial.

5.4.4.2 Device/Mode-switching Task

The mode-switching tasks started with a screen similar to that in the pointing experiment (see Figure 5.4). The participant started the trial by clicking in the home square.

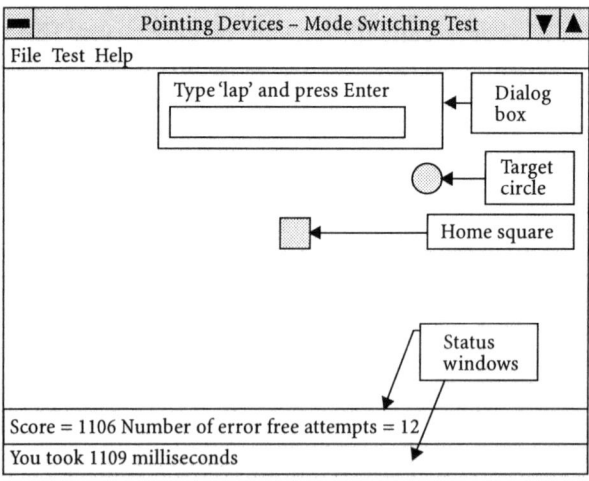

Figure 5.5: Device/mode-switching task screen.

The next action required was to point to the target circle and click to select it. At this point, a dialog box appeared and asked the user to type in a word: either 'lap' or 'fur'. The participant typed the requested word and pressed the 'Enter' key. (See Figure 5.5). The trial ended when the participant pressed the Enter key. The words 'lap' and 'fur' were chosen to balance tasks between fingers. The word 'fur' uses the index fingers for typing which are also used for pointing and selecting on the key joystick; 'lap' does not.

Error trials were treated in a manner similar to the pointing experiment: participants repeated the trial until they got both parts of the trial; selecting the target and typing in the word correctly

5.4.4.3 Dragging Task

In the dragging tasks, participants were asked to drag the home square into the target circle. The experimental materials, presentation and data collection were identical to that of the pointing and mode switching tasks except that the size of the target circle was not varied. (The reason for not varying the size of the target was that dragging had not been shown to be a Fitts' law task and we wanted to reduce the overall number of trials the participants performed.)

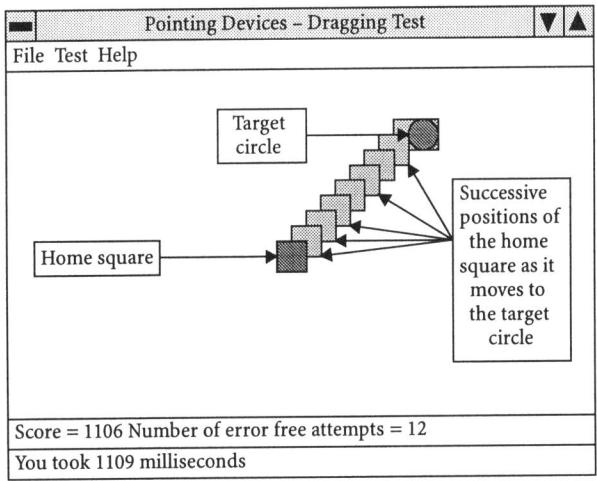

Figure 5.6: Dragging task screen.

The trial started when the participant selected the home square. The home square then followed the cursor as long as the pointing device button was held down (i.e. dragging). (See Figure 5.6 for a depiction.) Upon reaching the target circle, the participant released the button and ended the trial. The data recorded was the same as in the pointing experiment. The criterion for a successful drag was that the tip of the cursor (the hot spot) should be in the target circle.[2]

Errors occurred when the button was released before the cursor was in the target circle. Participants were informed that they had made an error by a beep and a message in the lower-status window, and were asked to complete the trial.

5.4.5 Experimental Design

The experiment comprised of a three-factor-mixed design:

- one *between-subjects* factor: device type (mouse vs. key joystick);
- two *within-subject* factors: task type (pointing vs. mode-switching vs. dragging) and time (in blocks of trials).

That is, participants learned and used only one of the two devices but repeatedly practiced all three task types over a period of time.

Each participant was required to complete a total of 19 blocks (7 pointing, 7 dragging and 5 mode-switching) of experimental trials. Each pointing and mode-switching block was 192 trials and each dragging block was 64, giving a total number of trials completed by each participant equal to 2752. Participants performed a pointing block followed by a mode-switching block followed by a dragging block. We presented only 5 blocks of mode-switching to reduce the overall experiment time.

5.4.5.1 Pointing Task Design

Because most of the studies of pointing relate time-of-performance to Fitts' law, the participant was presented with a variety of targets which differed in target size and distance to the target. We also varied the targets by angle-of-approach to verify that both devices were fully functional in all directions. Time to perform each trial as well as percentage of errors were measured as dependent variables. Longitudinal change in performance time as a function of practice was computed to measure learning. Finally, the data was computed as a Fitts' law equation to determine the relevant parameters.

The size, distance from home, and angle of the target circle were varied. For this experiment, there were 3 sizes (8, 16 and 32 pixels), 4 distances (31, 62, 124 to 248 pixels) and 16 angles (in 22.5-degree increments where 0.0 is directly above the home square, negative angles go counter-clockwise, positive angles go clockwise), giving 192 possible combinations. Both size and distance were varied by powers of 2 to facilitate Fitts' law analysis. Each width/distance combination creates one of the Fitts' law *index of difficulty* values from 0.5 to 5. This allows comprehensive testing of Fitts' law behavior.

These combinations were sequenced randomly within the first block and repeated in this sequence for the remaining blocks. All participants received identical presentations. The time at the start of the trial, the time at the end of the trial, the position of the click in the home square, the position of the click in the target circle, and the position and size of the target circle were computer-generated and saved at the end of each trial.

The size of the target circle varied between 8, 16 and 32 pixels (0.224cm, 0.448cm, and 0.896cm respectively). These pixel sizes were chosen to approximate the sizes of objects that a person using a windowing environment would encounter. The size of an icon in Microsoft Windows is 32 × 32 pixels. It is also the approximate size of a word (using 12-point Helvetica font), when approached from the side. The size of the average word when approached from the top or bottom is approximately 16 pixels. This is also the size of a character when approached from the top or bottom, and 8 pixels is approximately the width of a character when approached from the side.

Circles were chosen as targets to eliminate possible bias in Fitts' law computation caused by the angle of approach. Fitts' law computes the time to point to a target object as a function of object size which is effectively its width. A circle's radius presents a constant width from different approach angles. (See Chapter 3, section 3.3.2.2.)

The distance between the home square and the target circle varied from 31, 62, 124 to 248 pixels (0.868cm, 1.736cm, 3.472cm and 6.944cm respectively). These distances were chosen based on the available screen size, and we wanted to fit in as many distances as possible while increasing them by powers of 2.

In order to determine whether the angle of approach to the target made any difference, the angular position between home square and target was varied in 22.5-degree increments, thus giving 16 different angular positions.

We required participants to complete all trials error-free to ensure that they could not ignore the (more difficult) small targets. Trials were repeated until correctly completed. An error trial was any trial where the participant selected outside the area of the target circle. Data from the error trial was recorded, but ignored when calculating performance time.

5.4.5.2 Device/Mode-switching Task Design

A significant amount of time, called *homing time*, is necessary for a user to move her or his hand from the keyboard to the mouse and back again. Elimination of these two instances of homing time was one of the motivations for development of the key joystick. The second experimental task, an extension of the first, was designed to measure this time by combining a pointing action with a typing action.

The first part of this task repeated the design of the previous pointing-task design. Participants pointed to a target circle as in the pointing task. However, upon selecting the target circle, a dialog box appeared and asked the participant to type in one of two words: either 'lap' or 'fur.' Participants were randomly assigned one of the words and repeatedly used that word for all trials within a block. The next block for the participant presented the alternate word. The rationale behind this protocol is as follows. Because we wanted to measure the physical time of homing the mouse, i.e. the time between the end of selecting the target and the initiation of typing, we did not want it inflated with 'thinking' time caused by response to a random presentation of either word.

The words 'fur' and 'lap' were chosen with the placement of the key joystick in mind. The joystick uses both index fingers to activate normal mouse functions, one to press the 'J' key to move the cursor, and one to click (the mouse button) using the 'F' key. When a person is touch-typing, the word 'lap' does not require the use of the index fingers, while the word 'fur' requires exclusive use of the index fingers. We assumed that participants using the key joystick would find it harder to type 'fur'. They would first use the 'J' and 'F' keys to point and click in the target. Immediately after this, they would have to release the keys to start typing, and then they would have to use those fingers again, this time to type. Similarly, they would find it easier to type 'lap'. This would counterbalance the difficulty for key joystick users giving us a better average performance. Four time-points were recorded during a trial; the times at which the participant:

1. clicked in the home square;
2. clicked in the target circle;
3. started typing
4. pressed Enter to signal the termination of typing.

Because of the sequence of physical actions within a trial, mouse-homing time is measured as the duration between times (2) and (3), or the time it takes to move the hand from the mouse to the keyboard.

Error trials were treated in a manner similar to the pointing experiment: participants repeated the trial until they both selected the target and typed in the word correctly. For this experiment, errors were recorded and classified in three possible categories: the participant selected a point outside the target, the participant typed the word incorrectly, or the participant made both errors. As in the pointing experiment, only error-free trials were used for computing performance time.

5.4.5.3 Dragging Task Design

The third experiment was designed to determine performance on dragging. The size of the target circle was not varied because at the time we conceived the experiment we had not thought of dragging as a Fitts' law task and therefore subject to the same size–distance interaction. We therefore fully crossed 4 distances with 16 angles giving 64 trials rather than 192 in the previous tasks. The home square and the target circle for all trials were 32 pixels in diameter which is the size of an icon – a common target for dragging operations.

5.5 Results

5.5.1 Effect of Learning on Performance Time

Learning can be characterized as the improvement of performance time when repeating a task. Table 5.1 shows the differences in mean trial time for each block of tasks varied by task type.

Table 5.1: Change in mean trial time as a result of practice

Task	Device	Mean trial time in ms and (standard deviation) by block number within task type						
		1	2	3	4	5	6	7
Point	Mouse	1473	1301	1208	1126	1117	1105	1111
		(242)	(215)	(158)	(144)	(149)	(169)	(176)
	Key joystick	2687	2056	1888	1879	1796	1729	1723
		(586)	(450)	(360)	(350)	(288)	(238)	(199)
	Key joystick: mouse	+82%	+58%	+56%	+67%	+61%	+56%	+55%
Mode-switch	Mouse	3112	2569	2464	2361	2283		
		(527)	(290)	(397)	(247)	(288)		
	Key joystick	4002	3340	3118	2870	2662		
		(969)	(732)	(708)	(487)	(415)		
	Key joystick: mouse	ns	ns	ns	ns	ns		
Drag	Mouse	1214	1088	1016	1012	982	955	928
		(206)	(126)	(113)	(107)	(153)	(138)	(201)
	Key joystick	1928	1744	1632	1516	1496	1432	1417
		(385)	(348)	(306)	(228)	(196)	(194)	(247)
	Key joystick: mouse	+59%	+60%	+61%	+50%	+52%	+50%	+53%

Note: all differences between devices are significant at $p \le .05$; ns = 'not significant'.

As one can see, the time to perform a trial decreases with practice for all tasks. It also differs between the two devices. For pointing tasks, on the first block the average trial for the key joystick takes 82% more time than the mouse, however by the seventh block, the key joystick takes only 55% more. This suggests that key joystick users are improving at a faster rate. There is also a difference between tasks in that the advantage for mouse users was not as great in the mode-switching tasks. There is a faster mean task-time on dragging tasks than pointing tasks because the size of the target did not vary from 32 pixels (0.896cm) which was the largest target. According to Fitts' law, positioning time should be fastest on the largest targets. Since smaller targets were included in the pointing tasks, the overall mean time is greater. The mode-switching tasks are longer not only because they include all the pointing tasks, but also an extra typing step.

Repeated measures of analysis of variance for the first four blocks with one between-subjects factor (device) and two within-factors (task and trial block) were performed to verify whether the apparent distinction between the two devices was statistically significant. There is a main effect of device ($F_{1,20} = 26.54$, $p \leq 0.0001$); performance also differed by tasks ($F_{2,40} = 297.01$, $p \leq 0.0001$); as well as trial block ($F_{3,60} = 44.5$, $p \leq 0.0001$). There was no significant difference in task-by-device. The lack of significant difference for task-by-device can be seen in Figure 5.7. The means for dragging and pointing tasks are very close to one another and given the variance do not show significant difference by task. There is an effect of task by trial block by device ($F_{6,120} = 2.27$, $p \leq 0.05$).

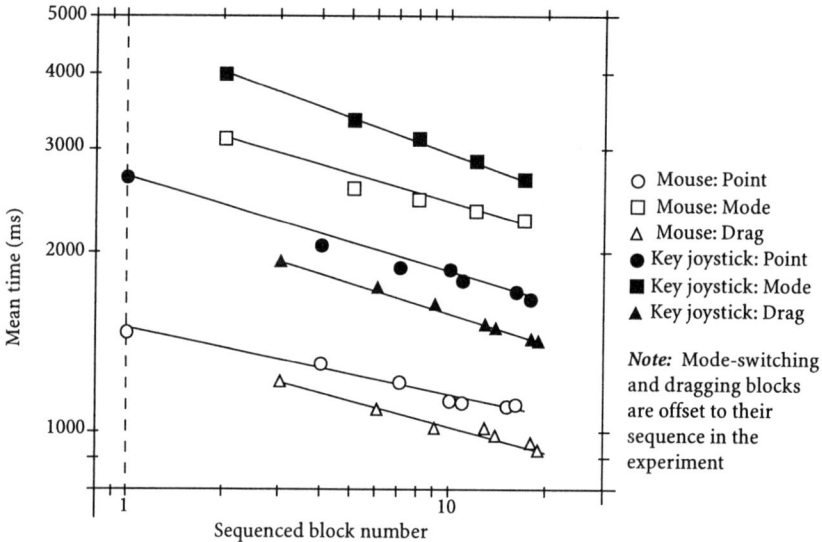

Figure 5.7: Change in mean trial time as a result of practice.

Analyzing each type of task separately for all seven blocks using repeated measures shows that for pointing tasks there is a main effect by device ($F_{1,17} = 37.8$, $p \leq 0.0001$), trial block ($F_{6,102} = 33.9$, $p \leq 0.0001$), and an interaction effect of trial block and device ($F_{6,102} = 6.2$, $p \leq 0.0001$). We find a similar result for dragging with main effect by device ($F_{1,17} = 71.7$, $p \leq 0.0001$), trial block ($F_{6,102} = 16.5$, $p \leq 0.0001$), and an interaction effect of trial block and device ($F_{6,102} = 2.3$, $p \leq 0.05$). For mode-switching the results are slightly mixed. There is a main effect by device ($F_{1,20} = 10.7$, $p \leq 0.05$), trial block ($F_{4,80} = 19.7$, $p \leq 0.0001$), but no interaction effect of trial block and device.

The decrease in performance time as a result of practice can be quantified as the *Power Law of Practice* (Card et al., 1983). This equation can be plotted as the *log* of the mean trial time for participants (*y*-axis) vs. the *log* of the trial block number (*x*-axis) and will yield a straight line if the data are well-behaved. Figure 5.7 displays the data for the experiment for all three task types with the *log* of the mean trial time for participants (*y*-axis) plotted vs. the *log* of the block number (*x*-axis).

The resulting plot shows an excellent fit to a straight line. The regression equations for these data are shown in Table 5.2.

Table 5.2: Regression equations as a result of practice

	Regression equation	Correlation	F-statistic	Probability
Mouse pointing	$\log 1483\,ms - 0.110 \log(n)$ $[3.17s - 0.11 \log(n)]$	$r^2 = 0.975$	$F_{1,5} = 196.41$	$p = 0.0001$
Key joystick pointing	$\log 2636\,ms - 0.158 \log(n)$ $[3.42s - 16 \log(n)]$	$r^2 = 0.981$	$F_{1,5} = 254.10$	$p = 0.0001$
Mouse mode-switch	$\log 3350\,ms - 0.143 \log(n)$ $[3.52s - 14 \log(n)]$	$r^2 = 0.958$	$F_{1,3} = 68.38$	$p = 0.0037$
Key joystick mode-switch	$\log 4560\,ms - 0.187 \log(n)$ $[3.66s - 19 \log(n)]$	$r^2 = 0.998$	$F_{1,3} = 1220.62$	$p = 0.0001$
Mouse dragging	$\log 1393\,ms - 0.134 \log(n)$ $[3.14s - 0.13 \log(n)]$	$r^2 = 0.972$	$F_{1,5} = 171.96$	$p = 0.0001$
Key joystick dragging	$\log 2344\,ms - 0.169 \log(n)$ $[3.34s - 17 \log(n)]$	$r^2 = 0.996$	$F_{1,5} = 1266.36$	$p = 0.0001$

5.5.2 Practiced Performance Time

At the end of the experimental sessions, we are able to assess the relative difference in performance speed by examining the last block of a task type. A Bonferroni t-test was applied to determine if significant improvement, i.e. learning, was still occurring by these last blocks of tasks. For all three task types, significant improvement ($p \leq 0.05$) in performance time did not occur after the third block of each type of task.

Table 5.3: Practiced task times

		Mean trial time (ms)
Point	Mouse	1123
	Key joystick	1779
	Key joystick: mouse	+58%
Mode-switch	Mouse	2357
	Key joystick	2823
	Key joystick: mouse	+20%
Drag	Mouse	966
	Key joystick	1407
	Key joystick: mouse	+46%

Note: these times are the means for all trials in blocks occurring after block 3. All differences between devices are significant at $p \leq 0.05$.

We can safely conclude that data analyzed from the last four blocks of pointing and dragging and the final two blocks of mode switching is that of well-practiced performance. Thus, for the remainder of this study when referring to practiced performance time, we shall use the means computed from trials occurring after block three.

Practiced means (i.e. averages) for all task times and devices are shown in Table 5.3 (Figure 5.8 plots these times). There was a significant main effect for device ($F_{1,20} = 27.0$, $p \leq 0.0001$) with the mouse faster than the key joystick. Likewise, there was a difference in performance time by task ($F_{2,40} = 498.1$, $p \leq 0.0001$) with dragging faster than pointing which was faster than mode switching. This is not a very interesting effect in that these three tasks are quite dissimilar from one another.

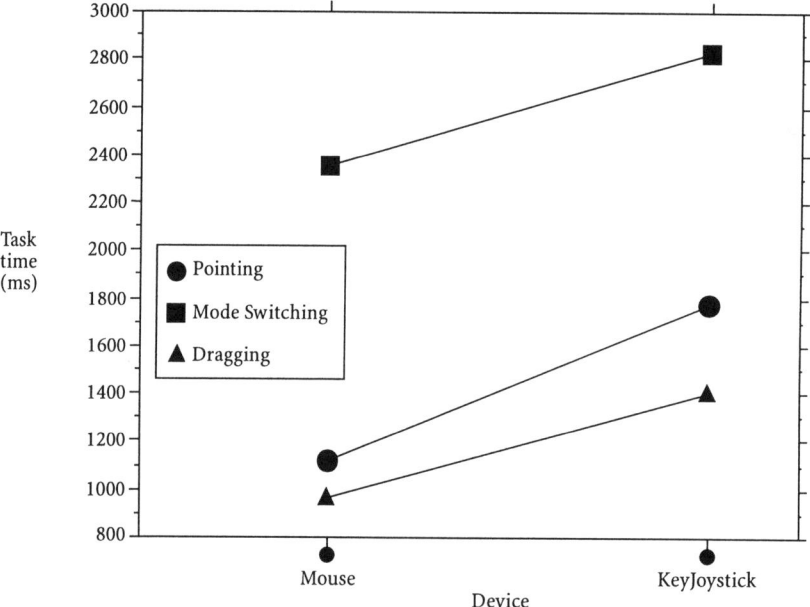

Figure 5.8: Interaction plot of device × tasks.

Unlike pointing and mode-switching, dragging did not vary the size of the target. Similarly, mode-switching was slowest because of the multiple subtasks of point, home and type. There was also a task by device interaction ($F_{2,40} = 3.2$, $p \leq 0.05$). These are all within the acceptable level and thus we will accept the hypothesis that the users of the mouse and the users of the key joystick do differ significantly in performance.

As we see in Table 5.3, for practiced performance the key joystick users are 58% slower in pointing tasks, 20% slower in mode-switching tasks, and 46% slower in dragging. These data suggest that the key joystick does save performance time by reducing homing time, but is slower as a pointing device both for basic pointing and for dragging. We did further analysis of the mode-switching tasks on the savings due to homing-time reduction. Figure 5.9 displays an interaction plot of device by mode-switching subtasks. The mode-switching task data for the last block is shown in Table 5.4.

Table 5.4: Mode-switching subtask times

Device	Mean trial time (ms) for mode-switching subtasks		
	Pointing	Homing	Typing
Mouse	1158	667	531
Key joystick	1746	438	639
Key joystick: mouse	1.51[†]	0.66[†]	not significant

[†] Is significant at $p \leq 0.001$.

There is a main effect by device ($F_{1,20} = 8.0$, $p \leq 0.01$), and also an effect by subtasks ($F_{2,40} = 236.7$, $p \leq 0.0001$). The major cause of this subtask effect is that the mouse greatly outpaces the joystick in pointing ($F_{1,20} = 38.3$, $p \leq 0.0001$). This effect occurs despite the fact that there is no significant difference in typing time and a significant difference in homing time in favor of the key joystick ($F_{1,20} = 19.2$, $p \leq 0.0003$). Faster homing on the key joystick saves approximately 229ms but the difference in pointing speed between mouse and key joystick is 588ms, not enough to catch up to the mouse.

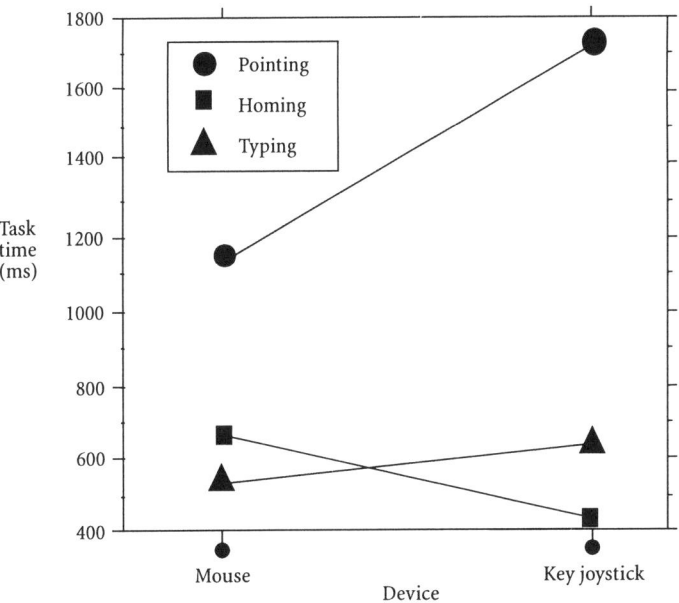

Figure 5.9: Interaction plot of device × mode-switching subtasks.

5.5.3 Fitts' Law Analysis

To test whether the key joystick could be characterized as a Fitts' law device, we analyzed the final task block of pointing tasks to determine the effect of target distance, target width and angle of approach on pointing time using the Welford formulation (see Equations 5.1 and 5.2).

The final block of the pointing tasks was analyzed to determine how well the devices fit the Fitts' law equation. In Figure 5.10 we plot pointing time as a function of the index of difficulty. The regression equation derived for the mouse was:

$$MT = 480 + 241ID \text{ with } r^2 = 0.992 \text{ and } p \leq 0.001 \qquad (5.3)$$

The regression equation for the key joystick was:

$$MT = 468 + 507ID \text{ with } r^2 = 0.987 \text{ and } p \leq 0.0001 \qquad (5.4)$$

These regression equations clearly indicate that human performance with both devices is predictable by Fitts' law. The mouse has an IP of 4.15 bits/second, and the key joystick has an IP of 1.97 bits/second.

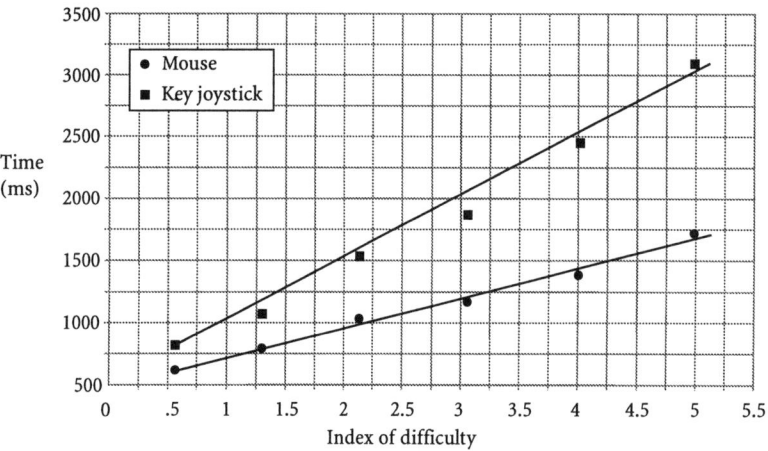

Figure 5.10: Fitts' law *index of difficulty* analysis for pointing tasks.

5.5.4 Error Rate

Although all of the data on performance time analysis reported above represents error-free trials, data was collected during the course of this experiment on the number of trials in which the participants failed to complete the task. In computer-based pointing devices, these error rates usually reflect the ability of the participants to accurately control the pointing device and/or perform the correct action sequences of cursor movement and button pressing for pointing, dragging and context-switching between typing and pointing.

Figures 5.11, 5.12, and 5.13 show the changes in error rate during the experiment for the pointing, mode-switching, and dragging tasks respectively. Table 5.5 shows the overall changes in error rate for the two devices. Although the key joystick had consistently higher error rates for all tasks and for all blocks, only the first block during initial learning is significantly different from the mouse.

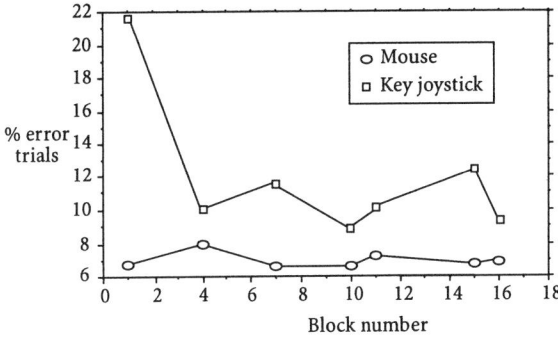

Figure 5.11: Pointing tasks percentage of error trials.

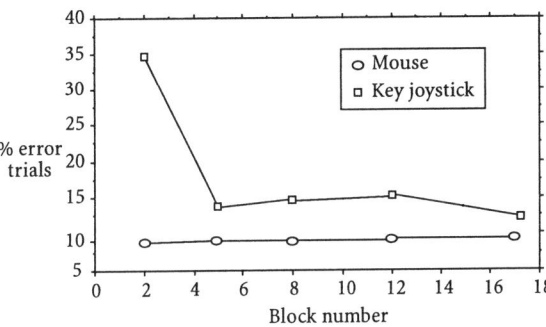

Figure 5.12: Mode-switching percentage of error trials.

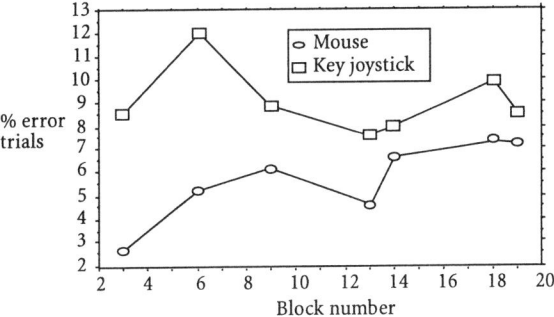

Figure 5.13: Dragging tasks percentage of error trials.

Pointing errors occurred when participants clicked outside the target circle once the trial had begun. (Recall that all mouse events prior to the first click in the home square, which started the trial, were ignored.)

For pointing tasks, a repeated measures analysis of variance shows a main effect by device ($F_{1,17} = 4.278$, $p \leq 0.05$), by trial block ($F_{6,102} = 5.44$, $p \leq 0.0001$) and by device by trial block ($F_{6,102} = 5.14$, $p \leq 0.0001$). However, a contrast analysis with means comparison showed that the only significant difference is in the first block: the mouse mean error rate is 6.8%; the key joystick mean is 21.6% ($F_{1,20} = 11.4$, $p \leq 0.03$).

For the mode-switching tasks a repeated measures analysis of variance shows a main effect by device ($F_{1,20} = 5.89$, $p \leq 0.03$); and by trial block ($F_{4,80} = 16.46$, $p \leq 0.0001$) and by device by trial block ($F_{4,80} = 3.1$, $p \leq 0.05$).

Table 5.5: Change in error rate as a result of practice

Task	Device	Mean error rate by block number			
		1	2	3	Practiced
Point	Mouse	6.8	7.9	6.6	6.9
	Key joystick	21.6	10.0	11.5	10.3
	Key joystick: mouse	+218%	ns	ns	ns
Mode switch	Mouse	18.7	9.1	8.9	8.8
	Key joystick	34.8	13.8	14.5	13.0
	Key joystick: mouse	+86%	ns	ns	ns
Drag	Mouse	2.6	5.2	6.0	3.7
	Key joystick	8.5	11.9	8.9	6.2
	Key joystick: mouse	+227%	+129%	ns	ns

Note: ns = 'not significant'.

Again, however, only the first block shows a significant difference between devices: the mouse mean is 18.7%, and the key joystick mean is 34.8% ($F_{1,20} = 5.1$, $p \leq 0.03$). Mode-switching errors include both pointing errors, typing errors, or a combination of both. For key joystick users, the key joystick's failure to switch correctly to typing mode also caused mode-switching errors.

For the dragging tasks the repeated measures showed no significant differences, although on an individual block level, the first block showed a significant difference: the mouse mean is 2.6%, and the key joystick mean is 8.5%, ($F_{1,20} = 17.4$, $p \leq 0.0005$). The second block also showed a significant difference: the mouse mean is 5.2%, and the key joystick mean is 11.9%, ($F_{1,20} = 15.4$, $p \leq 0.0002$). Most dragging errors are 'dropping' errors when the user fails to sustain the button depression during the movement of the cursor. There are fewer overall errors on dragging tasks because the size of the target did not vary from 32 pixels (0.896cm) which was the largest target and, according to Fitts' law, should be the fastest of the targets to move to.

For the practiced tasks, there is a main effect by device ($F_{1,20} = 6.36$, $p \leq 0.03$) with a mean of 6.6% for the mouse and 9.8% for the key joystick; and by task ($F_{2,40} = 16.17$, $p \leq 0.0001$) with a mean of 10.9% for mode-switching, 8.6% for pointing and 5.0% for dragging. A contrast analysis with means comparison showed that all three tasks were significantly different from each other, $p \leq 0.05$. There was no significant difference in error rate for the interaction of device by task.

5.6 Discussion

5.6.1 Learning to Use the Two Devices

The results of this experiment suggest that the key joystick is more difficult to learn to control and use than the mouse, but that the key joystick can be mastered, with motivated and concentrated practice, to become a usable pointing device. Key joystick users were much slower and had more errors in all three tasks throughout the period of this experimental study. Although key joystick users were learning faster, i.e. they have a 'steeper' slope on their learning curve, they were not able to equalize the difference between the two devices. By the end of six hours of concentrated practice, key joystick users were still approximately 50% slower for pointing and dragging times. The lack of control and difficulty in use that key joystick users experience during early learning is reflected in the much higher error rates (more than three times those for the mouse) for the initial sessions for all tasks. However, key joystick users soon gain better control and have non-significant differences in error rate for the remaining sessions.

We can compare our 2752 task trials as a learning criterion to other published research which shows that the Card, English and Burr (1978) pointing study took participants to 1200 trials, which they found to be a criterion such that performance between consecutive trial blocks ceased to improve by a significant difference of $p \leq 0.05$. MacKenzie, Sellen and Buxton (1991) reported pointing and dragging performance for a total of 800 trials also claiming that performance after the first block of 160 trials did not improve significantly ($p \leq 0.05$). However, on the MacKenzie et al. experiment, participants received a much less complex task environment than ours, so it was much easier to become quickly skilled. Since our experiment gave participants 64% more practice than the Card, English and Burr study and 150% more than the MacKenzie, Sellen and Buxton study, we could expect participants to become skilled users by the end of our study.

We also believe that although our experiments use a classical Fitts task, these tasks were modified to reproduce the environment of the computer user thus establishing greater ecological validity. For example, we extend the tasks to two dimensions and include tasks for dragging and mode switching in addition to pointing. We also use target sizes which conform to common display sizes such as text characters and icons.

5.6.2 Practiced Performance

Previous studies of the mouse have shown human performance to follow Fitts' law (Card et al., 1978; Epps, 1986; MacKenzie et al., 1991). The research on isometric joysticks has been somewhat mixed. Studies by Jagacinski et al. (1980); Jagacinski and Monk, (1985); Epps (1986), and Kantowitz and Elvers (1988) of hand/finger controlled joysticks and Rutledge and Selker (1990) of a single-finger controlled joystick have shown the isometric joystick to follow Fitts' law. However, the study by Card et al. (1978) raised some doubt as to whether the isometric joystick is a Fitts' law device. Our study provides further evidence that human performance using the isometric joystick by finger control is indeed a Fitts' law phenomenon.

The result that the key joystick was approximately 58% slower than the mouse came as a surprise because in the Card et al. study (1978), the joystick was only 22% slower than the mouse (1.57s vs. 1.29s average positioning time). MacKenzie

(1992) provides a framework for understanding this. He suggests that while it is not possible to compare *devices* across experimental conditions, the ratio of *IPs* can be compared. Based on this, we compared our data to data reported by Rutledge and Selker (1990), and MacKenzie (1992) from Epps (1986) and Card *et al.* (1978), which were the studies that compared mice and isometric joysticks. Our results are summarized in Table 5.6, which is a duplication of Table 4.11.

Table 5.6: The IPs and their ratios for mouse and joystick from four studies (in bits/second)

	Card *et al.* (1978)	Epps (1986)	Rutledge and Selker (1990)	Douglas and Mithal (1994, Chapter 4)	Mithal (1995, Chapter 5)
IP (mouse)	10.4	2.6	8.33	4.15	8.13
IP (joystick)	4.5	1.2	4.35	1.97	5.75
Mouse:joystick	2.31	2.16	1.91	2.10	1.41

Note: values for the Epps and Card *et al.* studies are taken from MacKenzie (1992).

Table 5.6 compares mouse and joystick, as suggested by MacKenzie, by the ratios of the index of performance within each study, using the mouse as the base comparison. We have included in this table the results of the Rutledge and Selker (1990) study of the Pointing Stick (later called the Trackpoint™). However, the parameters of the Fitts' law equation in their case are derived from the performance data for one participant with a particular force-to-motion function, not group data as in the other studies.

Table 5.6 demonstrates that the ratio of the index of performance for mouse and key joystick obtained in this study is comparable to those for devices studied by other researchers.

One belief held prior to the study was that because the study by Langolf (1976) indicated that the *IP* for the finger was higher than the *IP* for other body parts, the key joystick would perform considerably better than other isometric joysticks. Our study did not support this. In addition, it should be pointed out that while Langolf studied non-isometric devices, the key joystick is an isometric device, and there is no research to suggest that results for non-isometric devices can be extrapolated to isometric devices. The findings of this study are of relevance to other finger-controlled isometric joysticks such as the PortaPoint touch-sensitive mouse by Interlink Electronics, Toshiba's Accupoint, and IBM's Trackpoint™ II, all of which are similar in design and use to the key joystick.

5.6.3 Device/Mode-switching

5.6.3.1 Device Switching-time and the Keystroke Level Model

The device-switching time for the mouse that the mode-switching task measured was the time it takes to move from the *pointing device to the keyboard*. Our value was 667ms, which is nearly twice the value of 360ms obtained by Card *et al.* (1978). This result is not surprising, as the Card *et al.* study measured device-switching time from the *keyboard to the pointing device*. The target in the first movement is a single key on the keyboard, while in the second movement it is the entire mouse – a larger target. According to Fitts' law, as the movement distances are comparable, the first movement should take longer than the second movement, a result borne out by Rutledge and Selker (1990).

While this statement needs to be studied explicitly, based on our studies and our findings, we hypothesize that there are two separate and unequal device-switching times in the keyboard and mouse combination, and that it takes longer to change from mouse to keyboard than to change from keyboard to mouse, which contradicts the implicit assumption in the *keystroke level model* (Card *et al.*, 1980; Card *et al.*, 1983) that both times are equal.

5.6.3.2 Will a Keyboard Pointing Device Ever be Faster Than a Mouse?

The key joystick achieved its design goal in that it reduces device switching time from keyboard to mouse. However, this savings of 229ms was not enough to compensate for the lower pointing speed of the key joystick – which was 588ms slower.

This finding led us to perform a task analysis of pointing to see what the effect of device-switching time is on the time to complete a task that involves pointing, and to determine whether reducing the device-switching time is an effective technique for increasing the speed of a pointing device.

If the task mix has a lot of switching between typing and pointing, then the key joystick might have an actual advantage in pointing time. It might also be subjectively preferable never to remove the fingers from the keyboard.

In our analysis, a single operation involving pointing starts with the user's hands on the keyboard. The user then switches to the pointing device, performs one or more pointing tasks, then switches back to the pointing device. In general, we can say that there are n switches *to* the pointing device (where $n > 0$), and n switches *from* the pointing device, and m pointing actions (where $m > 0$).

The *keystroke level model* (see Chapter 7, section 7.3) can be applied here, giving us:

$$ActionTime = nT_{to\,point} + mT_{point} + nT_{to\,keyboard} \qquad (5.5)$$

Where *ActionTime* is the total time to complete a pointing task, $T_{to\,point}$ is the device-switching time going from keying to pointing, and $T_{to\,keyboard}$ is the device-switch time going from pointing to keying. In this analysis, pointing time also includes the selection time which involves a key press. Comparing the action times for mouse and key joystick will tell us when the key joystick is faster than the mouse.

A device such as the key joystick cannot eliminate all the device-switching time. This is because it has to wait a finite amount of time after the 'J' key is pressed before going into pointing mode, in order to make sure that the user is not simply typing a 'J'. In an article examining keyboard design, Kinkead (1979) noted that, for highly skilled typists, the average time for a keystroke is 155ms. We can take this to be the lower bound, the absolute minimum time that the key joystick must wait before switching to pointing mode, giving us $T_{to\ point}$ for the key joystick. This will give us the maximum possible savings with the key joystick.

Note that using 155ms for device-switching time assumes that users take no mental preparation time for the device switch. The value we obtained, 438ms to go from typing to pointing, suggests that a mental setup time exists, but our experiment was not designed to determine its value.

The time for a keystroke is also applicable for the $T_{to\ keyboard}$ for the key joystick, because it is the amount of time it would take to release the 'J' key. We can use our result of 1746ms as the pointing time for the key joystick, and therefore get, in ms:

$$ActionTime_{key\ joystick} = n(155 + 155) + m(1746) \qquad (5.6)$$

Taking the mouse-pointing time and the time to switch from the mouse to the keyboard from our study, and the time to switch from the keyboard to the mouse from the Card *et al.* (1978) study, we have, in ms:

$$ActionTime_{mouse} = n(667 + 360) + m(1158) \qquad (5.7)$$

The key joystick will be faster when:

$$ActionTime_{mouse} > ActionTime_{key\ joystick} \qquad (5.8)$$

or

$$n(667 + 360) + m(1158) > n(155 + 155) + m(1746) \qquad (5.9)$$

$$n(667 + 360 - 155 - 155) > m(1746 - 1158) \qquad (5.10)$$

$$717n > 588m \qquad (5.11)$$

where n is the number of device context switches to (and from) the pointing device, and will be 1 for expert actions. Therefore, we have:

$$\frac{717}{558} = 1.28 > m \qquad (5.12)$$

Recall that m is an integer representing the number of pointing actions that make up this operation, and can have values 1, 2, 3 etc. Therefore, with the pointing speeds as measured by our experiment, and the maximal savings in context-switching time that the key joystick can provide, the mouse will be faster for any operation that requires two or more sequential pointing actions. There are many examples of operations in the Macintosh and Windows interfaces that require sequences of pointing or dragging actions, such as selecting an item from the menu or from a drop-down list, and using the mouse to copy or move a file.

The factor that ultimately determines which of the two combinations, mouse and keyboard or key joystick, is faster, is the task mix. Equation 5.12 indicates that in conditions where the task sequence is type–point–type, such as in text editing, a key joystick with the maximum savings in device-switching time would be faster. On the other hand, for activities such as formatting a document, using a drawing program, and manipulating files on the Macintosh, which are sequences of pointing movements with few or no device switches in between, the mouse is faster.

Additionally, the higher the ratio of device switches to pointing actions (the ratio of n to m), the more time the key joystick will save, but this ratio will not be higher than 1 for skilled users, because for skilled users, n will be 1.

5.6.3.3 Bringing the Key Joystick up to Par

The analysis above was for a key joystick with the maximal saving in device-switching time. A task analysis approach can be used to determine how much of an improvement in IP would be required to increase the overall speed of the present key joystick to bring it on par with the mouse and keyboard combination. If we substitute $n = 1$, and the value for homing time of 360ms from Card et al. (1978) for $T_{to\,point}$ for the key joystick in Equation 5.5 and simplify, we get a saving in time when:

$$(667 + 360 - 438 - 155) > m(1746 - 1158) \tag{5.13}$$

$$434 > 588m \tag{5.14}$$

Relation 5.14 is always false, and therefore, the present key joystick is always slower than the mouse. The speeds will be equal when:

$$434 = m(Point\,Time_{key\,joystick} - 1158) \tag{5.15}$$

At a minimum, the key joystick should be as fast as the mouse and keyboard combination when only one pointing action is required. Therefore:

$$Point\,Time_{key\,joystick} = 1592\text{ms} \tag{5.16}$$

Substituting this time into Equations 5.1 and 5.2 and solving for IP gives us a value of 2.77 bits/second as the value at which the key joystick will start approaching the speed of the mouse. This can be compared to 1.97 bits/second, the value of IP obtained for the key joystick, a 40% increase in IP.

5.6.3.4 Fatigue and Device/mode-switching

As we have seen from the above analysis, the key joystick, despite its integration into the typing keyboard to save time, does not save in overall task time due to the slower speed of pointing with this particular type of joystick. Other factors may further increase the task time for tasks combining pointing and typing. For example, we could hypothesize that key joystick users will revert to typing mode after all pointing actions which are followed by a pause longer than about a 5 second duration. This would happen even if the next action was also a pointing action. There are several reasons for this. One is because the user would not find it natural to maintain a contracted muscle position pressing down on the key for a long period without experiencing fatigue. (Several of our key joystick participants complained of fatigue from using the device during our experiments. This was not the case for the mouse participants.) Secondly, many typists have experienced repeating key functions on typing keyboards and have been taught to immediately release the key press. The issue here is not that users don't press down on a key for a long period, e.g. mouse button during a drag, but that the context-switching required of the key joystick is an additional mental effort that can lead to errors if executed incorrectly. Therefore the user opts for safety even though he or she may have to revert again to the same mode of pointing.

These limitations became quite apparent with long-term use despite the initial enthusiasm of users to not remove their hands from the keyboard. Indeed, for some very experienced touch typists it may be subjectively preferable never to remove the fingers from the keyboard, even though overall task time is greater than with a keyboard mouse combination. This would have to be tested in further experimentation.

5.6.3.5 Why Does Mode-switching Have More Errors?

This experiment was designed to collect very rudimentary errors. For pointing and dragging tasks, participants selecting a point outside the target circle were classified as committing an error trial; for device/mode-switching tasks we defined three types of errors categories: the participant selected a point outside the target, the participant typed the word incorrectly, or the participant made both errors (see section 5.4.5.2.)

The large number of key joystick errors demands a further analysis that is useful to the design of the device and to the development of future experimental designs. Figure 5.3 earlier in this chapter is useful for understanding how errors occurred on the key joystick. Mode-switching errors occurred when the participants did not correctly switch the keyboard between pointing and typing modes. For example, if they pressed the 'J' key and released it before the keyboard went into pointing mode, a 'J' would be sent to the computer. This situation is marked in Figure 5.3 as: *Possible error: unintentional 'J'*. On a number of occasions, the participants apparently pressed and released the 'J' key a number of times, causing more than one 'J' to appear. A similar mode-switch error occurred if the participant pressed the 'F' key when the keyboard was not in pointing mode, resulting in an 'F' appearing. We call these *switching errors*.

A second kind of error was caused by the participant placing their hands on the wrong set of keys. As a result, when they tried to press down on the 'J' key, a sequence of 'H's or 'K's would appear. This we call a *hand positioning error*.

Another type of error occurred when, during a click action or during dragging, the participant pressed the 'F' key, and released the 'J' key prior to releasing the 'F' key. This would cause a sequence of 'F's to appear. This is shown in Figure 5.3 by the shaded state box. We call this a *state recognition error*, based on the following rationale. Note that while there is no way of knowing whether the first two kinds of errors are intentional or not, the third kind of error can be prevented within the driver software for the key joystick by preventing the transmission of characters to the computer from the time that the keyboard goes into pointing mode until the time that all keys are released.

5.7 Conclusions

5.7.1 Summary of Findings

This study shows that over a wide range of tasks, the mouse is faster than the key joystick both during learning as well as during practiced performance. However, only during the initial period of learning do key joystick users have a significantly higher error rate. For practiced pointing performance the key joystick is approximately 58% slower than the mouse.

Our studies provide at least one example of a finger-operated, isometric joystick that follows Fitts' law in a situation where the target lies in a two-dimensional plane. While the gross speed of the device was slower than expected, the ratio of the index of performance between the key joystick and the mouse was comparable to that found by other researchers for mouse and isometric joysticks. We note that MacKenzie (1992) suggests that the Fitts index of performance is the most critical value in determining the performance of a pointing device. Our study bears this out.

However, while the finger used in this manner followed Fitts' law performance, we were surprised by the lower index of performances we obtained which was 1.97 bits/second for the finger and 4.15 bits/second for the wrist/hand. In their 1976 study Langolf *et al.* obtained an index of performance of 38 bits/second for the finger and 23 bits/second when the hand flexed and extended about the wrist (Langolf *et al.*, 1976) which is approximately what happens with a mouse.

The earlier Langolf *et al.* study focused on movement in non-isometric conditions. Although there is no motivation to believe that results from the non-isometric situation will carry across to the isometric situation, we did not anticipate the magnitude of the effect. Clearly, there is a complex interaction between limb and device, particularly when comparing a non-isometric device controlling displacement, i.e. the mouse, to an isometric device controlling velocity, i.e. the key joystick. We feel that if the key joystick had not been an isometric device, it might have performed better. Note that this reasoning contradicts that by Kantowitz and Elvers (1988), who felt that:

> ... there are several advantages gained by substituting isometric controllers. Isometric controllers are simpler because limb displacement, and hence muscle strength remains constant.

While the fact that strength remains constant might make it easier to perform the task, constant limb displacement and muscle strength may not be conducive to added control, and we suspect exactly the opposite.

We were interested in whether an on-the-keyboard pointing device does save enough total task time to compensate for slower pointing speed. For the key joystick, the homing time to the keyboard from the pointing device was 438ms, less than the 667ms that it took participants to home from the mouse to the keyboard. This was not enough to compensate for the 58% slower pointing time.

This leads to our theoretical conclusion that continuing to reduce mode-switching time or homing time will have little effect on the overall performance time of this device, and that *IP* is still a better indicator of pointing device performance than mode-switching time. In other words, in order to make this device faster, it is more fruitful to concentrate on improving the pointing speed than on the mode-switching speed.

5.7.2 Future Research

We question the assumption in the *keystroke level model* that the homing times to and from the mouse are the same, and note that Fitts' law itself would suggest that they are different. Card *et al.* (1978) measured time from keying to pointing, and used this 360ms time as device-switching (homing) time in the *keystroke level model*. In this study, we only measured time from pointing to keying for both devices. The reverse study should be conducted.

A number of studies have indicated that velocity control is less effective than position control. It would be interesting to see what would happen if the control algorithm for the key joystick were replaced with one for position control. This question has been investigated in work by Selker and Rutledge (1991). They conclude that selecting a single pixel on a 640×480 screen requires 18.22 bits of information, and a force to position control for the finger-controlled joystick can only provide 7.8 to 12.2 bits. Using velocity control instead allows for arbitrarily precise pointing, provided the transfer function is non-linear to give the user slower speed for high precision pointing and higher speed for fast motion across large screens. (See section 3.1.1.3 for a more detailed discussion.)

The problem that the manufacturers of any isometric device would most like to see answered is the question of how the parameters of the control equations should be set for optimal performance. Isometric velocity-controlled devices often use non-linear functions to compute velocity from force. No method is known to determine that function in advance from knowledge of human psychomotor movement. Current practice is a kind of progressive refinement by changing the parameter and testing it out on users.

Finally, there are several possible things which might be done to improve the key joystick performance for users:

- providing motivated practice environments before attempting work on real problems;
- creating a 'smarter' error-recognition routine;
- (possibly) changing the physical positioning and physical operation of the key-to-joystick interface.

These would be subject to further experimental validation that significant improvement occurs. As our experimental evidence and analysis has shown in this chapter, isometric joysticks are much harder to learn and use than the mouse in the most common GUI computer tasks of pointing and dragging. As our analysis has shown, improving or even totally eliminating device/mode-switching time will not make up for the greater amount of time it takes to point with the isometric joystick. Despite these problems, isometric controllers offer advantages such as very small space requirements, and the lack of moving parts that make them ideally suited for inclusion in laptop and notebook computers. Thus, understanding the causes of the inferior performance of the isometric joystick with an eye to improving pointing time through better design is an important research focus. In the next chapter, we will present experimental findings that explore further the causes for isometric joystick's inferior pointing time performance.

5.8 Endnotes

1   The Trackpoint was tested by Rutledge and Selker (1990) with six participants to determine the optimum acceleration curve.
2   While writing the code for the dragging experiment, an interesting question arose: When has an object been dragged onto another object? For example, of the following instances, when has the light square been dragged onto the darker square?

The answer depends on the implementation of dragging. For example, one object could be considered to be dragged onto another when any part of it obscures any part of the target. The problem with this is that if there are two or more potential targets side by side, the dragged object could obscure parts of both, and it would be unclear which object was the recipient of the drag. Similar objections can be made to schemes which require some specified portion of the dragged object or the target to be covered. For example, we could require that 50% of the target should be covered, and the problem becomes more complicated when the sizes of the dragged object and the target are not the same. There can also be confusion about whether to consider the portion of the drag that is overlapped, or the portion of the target overlapped. Such considerations also have an effect on how the size for Fitts' law analyses is to be measured. For example, if we assume any degree of overlap, the size parameter in the Fitts' law equation becomes the combined size of dragged object and target.

The problem is sidestepped in the implementation of GUIs such as the Macintosh and Microsoft Windows. The notion of a dragged object being on top of the target is determined by the position of the cursor's hot spot. This simplifies both the determination of a target hit, as well as the Fitts' law analysis. A target hit can be determined by checking the position of the target relative to the hot spot when the mouse button is released, and the position of the dragged object can be ignored. For the Fitts' law analysis, we just have to consider the size of the target.

6. *Using the Microstructure of Movement to Understand Device Performance*

6.1 Introduction

Our study of the key joystick described in the previous chapter gave rise to as many questions as answers. We found that both the isometric joystick and the mouse were Fitts' law devices, but mean performance with the joystick[1] was substantially slower and had more errors than the mouse, for practiced pointing and dragging. We also found that users of the joystick found it difficult to learn, and we were struck by the fact that a number of participants complained that the joystick was hard to control. Finally, there was a sharp split in opinion among our participants: some liked the joystick, others did not.

Thus, our experimental data indicated that the joystick was inferior to the mouse for use in basic GUI pointing and dragging tasks – a result supported by previous research comparing the mouse and isometric joystick (Card *et al.*, 1978; Epps, 1986; Rutledge and Selker, 1991). As our next research goal, we wanted to understand why the isometric joystick, in general, performs so poorly when compared to the mouse, and whether we could re-engineer its performance based on better knowledge of human performance. To answer that question, we turn to a different type of experimental study from the experimental Fitts task evaluation of the previous chapter. To understand our motivation for doing this, we first review the limitations of using Fitts' law as our only analytical tool.

Fitts' law studies focus on the relationship between target width, distance and overall movement time. Although Fitts' law can be used to compare devices, tasks, or limbs, it cannot explain why the performance differences exist. Secondly, the data gathered for the traditional Fitts' task does not contain the details of the process of the pointing motion on a microsecond-by-microsecond basis. This can obscure important differences in performance.

An illustration of this is given in Figure 6.1, which shows two pointing task trials that take the same amount of movement time. The graphs plot the velocity on the *y*-axis, and the distance on the *x*-axis. Both trials have the same target distance and target width. The upper trial has a smaller velocity and is made up of three sub-movements, all towards the target, while the lower trial is made up of an overshoot and a return. The lower trial traverses a longer distance, but due to its higher velocity, takes the same amount of time as the trial above. While the two trials are identical from the point of view of Fitts' law, they are very different at the micro-analysis level. As a result, Fitts' law cannot explain differences in performance based on how the movement occurred.

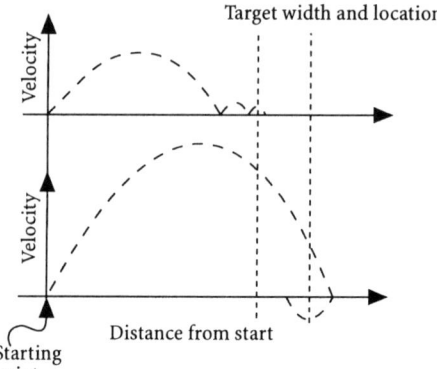

Figure 6.1: Two trials (not to scale) which are identical from the point of view of Fitts' law, but have different microstructures of movement.

On the other hand, the form of the Fitts' law equation does suggest some characteristics of movement. Because of the logarithmic nature of the Fitts' law equation, doubling the target distance does not double the movement time. Instead it goes up a small amount proportional to the value of b (see Equation 2.2). This indicates that as targets get further away the limb reaches a higher peak velocity, leading to curves that look like those shown in Figure 6.2.

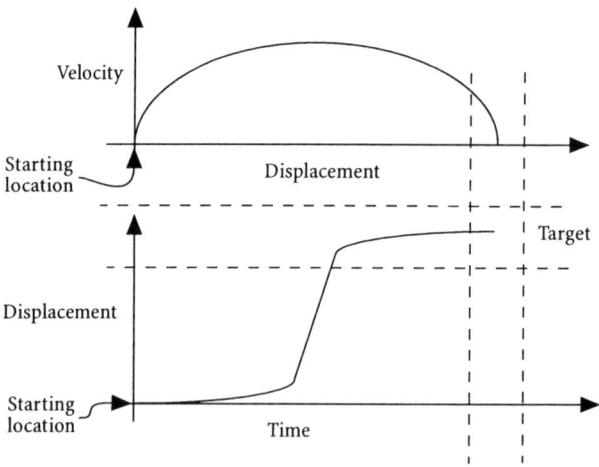

Figure 6.2: Hypothetical velocity and displacement as a limb moves towards a target. Hand-drawn graph, not to scale.

The upper graph shows velocity on the y-axis and displacement on the x-axis, and suggests that the limb accelerates over the first half of the distance to the target, and decelerates over the second half. This in turn leads to the lower graph of displacement as a function of time. In addition, we know from Welford's formulation of Fitts' law that, on the average, the movement takes:

$$MT = a + b log_2 \left(\frac{D}{W} + 0.5 \right)$$ (6.1)

If some function $v = F(t)$ describes velocity as a function of time, then we can say:

$$D = \int_0^\alpha F(t) dt$$ (6.2)

where:

$\alpha = a + b log_2 (D/W + 0.5)$

D is the distance to the target

Knowing $F(t)$ would provide researchers with a concise mathematical model of the pointing task. It turns out, however, that there are two problems that make this task difficult. First, there are many models that predict a movement time that is consistent with Fitts' law, and the number of forms of $F(t)$ is possibly infinite (Kawato, 1992). Second, studies that have gathered displacement vs. time data for pointing trials show that even practiced individuals will perform the same trial differently each time they make the movement. As a result, models describing movement have to be stochastic in nature.

Recent work on hypothesizing and testing competing models of movement is based on studies of the microstructure of movement. Such studies track the position of the limb or cursor from the starting location towards the target. From these data, plots are made of velocity and distance as functions of time for each trial. It is from this data that the *stochastic optimized submovement* (SOS) model (Meyer et al., 1988; Meyer et al., 1982; Meyer et al., 1990) has emerged as the principle theory describing the kinematics of pointing. (See section 2.2 for more background on these concepts.) Although most microanalysis studies have been of pointing unmediated by a computer, Walker et al. (1993) confirmed the SOS model for describing movement with a mouse.

Inspired by the microstructure of movement techniques used in experimental studies of the SOS model, we decided to focus on the kinematics of movement of the isometric joystick.[2] We designed an experiment using both a joystick and the mouse. The mouse functioned as a baseline, in order to repeat the results of the Walker et al. study. We suspected that despite the fact performance with both devices is described by Fitts' law, movement with the joystick might differ substantially in its details from the mouse, since the former uses force as control input and the latter, displacement. We wanted to understand what movements with these pointing devices looked like, how they compared with one another, and whether differences in movement might be linked to differences in the devices and differences in performance.

The remainder of this chapter describes the comparative study that we conducted on a mouse and a finger-controlled isometric joystick called the Trackpoint™ II, manufactured by IBM for its notebook computers. This work constitutes the junior author's Ph.D. dissertation and can be found in Mithal (1995) and Mithal and Douglas (1996).

Our analysis of the microstructure of movement for the isometric joystick reveals that there were random variations in its velocity (which we call jitter or jerkiness). No such jitter is found in mouse movements. We suggest this jitter can be attributed to a combination of human tremor, i.e. variations in muscle force, and artifacts of the hardware and software peculiar to the isometric joystick. We hypothesize that the slower performance of the joystick results from the necessity of the user to adapt to a more complex model of control which is not directly translatable to the psychomotor characteristics of rapid aimed movement.

6.2 Research Questions

Since our study is primarily exploratory, it is useful to describe specific research questions that guide it. The questions fall into three categories: applicability of Fitts' law to the mouse and Trackpoint™ II joystick, the microstructure of movement for the two devices, and modeling movement with the two devices.

- *Applicability of Fitts' law*

1. Do the devices (mouse and isometric joystick) follow Fitts' law? What are the constants in their Fitts' law equations? How do the indices of performance for these devices compare with one another?

   In this first question, we wanted to know whether these are Fitts' law devices. The SOS model makes this assumption. We also wanted confirmation of Fitts' law performance for the Trackpoint™ II. Finally, we wanted to verify the robustness of our experimental study with other studies conducted on these two types of devices.

- *Microstructure of movement*

2. In terms of the duration and accuracy of the first and subsequent submovements, what is the microstructure of movement for the isometric joystick? What is it for the mouse?

   As described in Chapter 2, dichotomous models – such as the SOS model – suggest that the first submovement is larger and faster than the rest of the submovements. This has already been verified for the mouse (Walker *et al.*, 1993) and we wished to extend this to the joystick, leading to question 2.

3. Are there differences in the microstructure of movement of the mouse and isometric joystick, and do these differences explain the difference in performance, particularly the slower speed of the joystick?

We suspected that joystick movement might be quite different from that of the mouse, and could possibly account for the differences in performance.

4. Are there changes over time in the microstructure of movement for individual participant's performance?

   Question 4 looked at the effect of practice on the microstructure of movement while question 5 examined individual differences.

5. Are there differences in the microstructure of movement between individual participants?

- *Modeling movement*

6. Do models of movement that describe isotonic devices describe isometric devices? In particular, does the SOS model describe the movement of both the mouse and the isometric joystick?

   The SOS model has been applied to pointing with the mouse (Walker *et al.*, 1993). Our study was designed to provide additional support for that finding. If we could extend the SOS model to the joystick it would increase our confidence that the model is universally applicable, which leads to question 6. If the SOS model did not hold for the isometric joystick, the microstructure level analysis could be used to develop an alternative model, leading to question 7.

7. If the SOS model does not describe the movement of the isometric joystick, can we modify the model so that it does?

8. Can we use our model for the isometric joystick and the knowledge about its movement microstructure to improve its design?

   Our motivation for modeling pointing devices is to enable designers to make better design decisions, and the eighth question examined whether the knowledge gained through this study could be used to improve the design of the isometric joystick.

6.3 Method

The experiment was designed to be a simple Fitts pointing task that allowed easy comparison of differences between the two pointing devices, differences between participants, and differences over time. It was also designed to give participants enough practice so that data from the end of the study represented practiced performance.

6.3.1 Participants

Six volunteers participated in the experiment. Two participants were women. Four participants were students and two were staff members of the University of Oregon. Of the six participants, four used the mouse on a regular basis and had no experience with the Trackpoint™, and two owned IBM ThinkPads™ which had embedded Trackpoint™ II joysticks. Of the two Trackpoint™ users, one also had extensive experience with a mouse, while the other had only minimal experience with a mouse, but extensive experience with the Trackpoint™. All participants were right-handed. They were promised a home-cooked Indian meal for participating in the experiment.

6.3.2 Experimental Equipment

The hardware used for the experiment was a Gateway 2000 P5-90 XL computer with an Intel Pentium processor running at 90Mhz. Tests showed that the processor did not have the floating-point division error identified with earlier versions of the Pentium. The computer had 16Mb of memory and 1Gb of hard disk. The display adapter was an ATI Mach 64 accelerated video card with 2Mb of video RAM, displaying 65,536 colors at a resolution of 1024 × 768 pixels. This was attached to a 17-inch NEC MultiSync XE17 monitor. The monitor displayed 1024 pixels in 310 mm. The mouse used was a PS/2-compatible mouse from Microsoft, FCC ID C3K5400PS2, part #31660. The isometric joystick was a Trackpoint™ II keyboard from IBM. This keyboard, represented in Figure 6.3, has an isometric joystick embedded between the 'G', 'H' and 'B' keys of a standard keyboard.

Isometric joystick
Mouse buttons

Figure 6.3: The IBM Trackpoint™ II keyboard.

The joystick, being isometric, does not move but senses the magnitude and direction of the force applied to it, and moves the cursor with a velocity proportional to the force in the direction that the force is applied. The mapping of force to velocity is non-linear as described in Rutledge and Selker, 1990. The buttons below the space bar correspond to the buttons on a standard two-button mouse, the left button mapping on to the left button on the mouse, and the right button mapping onto the right button on the mouse.

In the standard touch-typing position, the joystick is equidistant from the index fingers of both hands, and the 'mouse' buttons fall under the thumbs. Some participants chose to click the left 'mouse' button with the thumb of the right hand, while others used the index finger of the left hand (the right button was not used for this experiment). They were instructed to use whatever technique they preferred.

The manner in which the mouse and Trackpoint™ keyboard are connected to a computer is a little unusual, and it is explained below. Understanding these connections is critical for interpreting the results that are presented later in this chapter. A pointing device can be connected to an MS-DOS or Windows computer through either a serial (RS-232c) port, or a PS/2 mouse port (i8042), as shown in Figure 6.4.

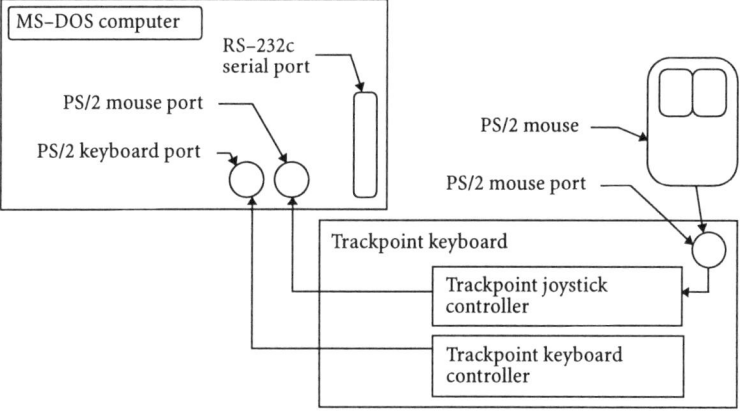

Figure 6.4: Connections for the Trackpoint™ keyboard.

The Trackpoint™ keyboard has two cables that come out of it (Figure 6.4), one going to the PS/2 keyboard port, and the other going to the PS/2 mouse port. In addition, there is a PS/2 mouse port on the keyboard to which a mouse can be attached in addition to the Trackpoint™ joystick. The connection from the mouse goes through the Trackpoint™ joystick controller and feeds signals to the PS/2 mouse port on the CPU through the same set of wires that the Trackpoint™'s own signals are fed to the computer. The same PS/2 software driver running inside the computer responds to these signals, and these are picked up by the program presenting the experimental task. In summary, once the data from either the joystick or the mouse enters the computer through the PS/2 port, there is no way to detect from which device it originated. The operating system will treat all data as if it originated from the mouse.

A PS/2 mouse can, of course, be connected directly to the CPU in conjunction with at PS/2 keyboard, and the PS/2 mouse can be substituted with a serial mouse.

For this study, the configuration shown in Figure 6.4 was used with the PS/2 mouse connected to the PS/2 mouse port *on the keyboard*.

The software used to present the experimental tasks was also used to sample the movement of the pointing devices. It was written in C, and compiled using Microsoft Visual C++ version 2 with speed optimization, and 386-specific CPU instructions to run on Windows 3.11. Data tracking the position of the pointing device was generated whenever the window manager received a mouse movement, mouse button up or mouse button down message. (Since the joystick's input was identical to the mouse's once it entered the PS/2 port, no special processing was required for it.) The message was time-stamped using the Windows 3.11 multimedia function call *TimerCount*. The operating system used for data collection was Microsoft Windows NT version 3.5. Sampling of cursor position occurred every 16ms.[3] The raw data was later processed by use of a specially written data analysis program, a standard statistical analysis package, and MatLab.

6.3.3 Experimental Procedure

During the first session, the goal of the experiment and the operation of the pointing devices were described to participants. The monitor, keyboard and mouse were placed on an ergonomic workstation table with the monitor's center at eye level, and the keyboard and mouse at a position where they could be accessed by participants whilst keeping their arms straight. The monitor was approximately 33 inches (82cm) away from the participant's eyes. Participants were given a height-adjustable chair and a footrest, and were asked to adjust the experimental equipment to maximize their comfort.

Participants were then asked to perform 10 warm-up trials with the experiment. These warm-up trials were repeated at the start of every session and discarded from the analysis. During the warm-up trials, participants were also shown the computer's behavior when an error occurred, and what they had to do to complete the trial.

The program provided a score as motivation. Participants were shown the score bar at the bottom of the screen, and were encouraged to get as high a score as possible. This could be done by hitting the target quickly and keeping errors low. In order to increase motivation the scores were recorded. Participants were told how their scores varied across sessions. At the end of every block of 120 trials, a dialog box appeared telling the participants that a block was completed.

6.3.4 Experimental Task

A one-dimensional Fitts task was used for the experiment, based on the experimental configuration used by Walker *et al.* (1993) in their study of the applicability of the SOS model to mouse movement. It was presented to the users as depicted in Figure 6.5. It had a starting location (the home square) and an ending location (the target ribbon). These elements were presented against a white background. 'A' represents the amplitude or distance from the center of the home square to the center of the target ribbon. 'W' represents the width of the target ribbon.

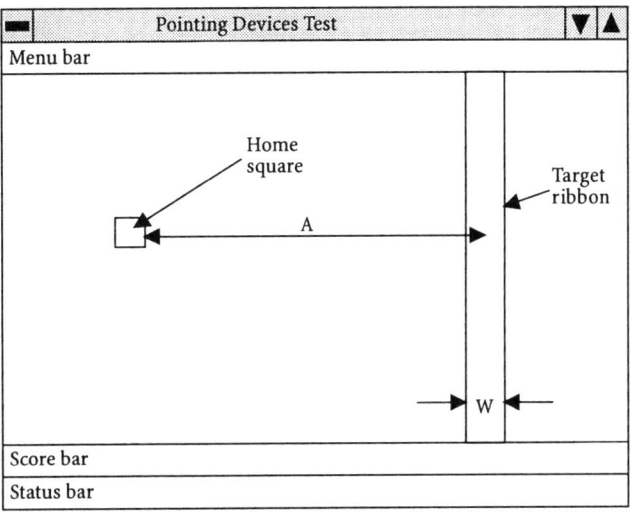

Figure 6.5: The experimental task.

Participants were asked to first click in the home square (which started the trial), and then in the target ribbon (which ended the trial). At the start of the trial, the home square was colored red and the target ribbon white. When they clicked in the home square to start a trial, the home square turned white and the target ribbon turned red, indicating both where they should aim and that the trial was in progress. At the start of every trial, the software repositioned the cursor in the center of the home square.

The time at the start of the trial and the time at the end of the trial were recorded. In addition, the software sampled the position of the mouse cursor between the clicks, keeping track of position and time, generating a sample on the average of every 16ms. After the completion of a trial, the screen was blanked, the data from the trial was written to disk, and the next trial was presented. The home square always appeared in the same location for each trial. The width and location of the target ribbon were varied as indicated in Table 6.1.

Table 6.1: Values for amplitude (distance to target) and width (of target) used in the experiment

Amplitude (A)		Width (W)	
Pixels	mm	Pixels	mm
768	232.5	16	4.84
384	116.3	32	9.69
192	58.1	64	19.38
96	29.1		

These values generated the following six amplitude-to-width ratios (A/W): 48, 24, 12, 6, 3, 1.5. When a participant made an error, i.e., clicked outside the target ribbon, the computer beeped, indicating the error. The participant then had to complete the trial by clicking in the target ribbon. The computer recorded the incorrect clicks and marked the trial as an error trial.

The next trial in the sequence was then presented. The error trial was repeated at the end of the block, so that participants had to complete all trials correctly. Two status bars presented a score and a count of the total number of correct trials, and the number of blocks completed for the session.

6.3.5 Experimental Design

The experiment was a single-factor (two devices), within-subjects design. The software grouped 10 sets of the 12 combinations of width and distance together, randomized the order, and presented the 120 trials in this random order as a single block. The order of presentation was exactly repeated from block to block, except for error trials. A session consisted of 5 blocks of 120 trials, or 600 trials per session. Participants did 3 sessions for a total of 1800 trials per device. Each participant performed 3 sessions with one pointing device, followed by 3 sessions with the other device. To counterbalance order effects, 3 of the 6 participants were randomly assigned to use the mouse first; 3 to the joystick.

For some of our participants, the early sessions represent true learning behavior, since 4 of our participants had no prior experience with isometric joysticks, and one had very little with the mouse. We chose 1800 total trials to allow participants to develop what we hoped would be a skilled performance level for both devices. This would allow us to observe any differences between learning and skilled (practiced) behavior. Prior experimental work of mouse and isometric joystick by Card et al. (1978) and our study described in Chapter 5, have observed practiced performance at about 1200 trials using a two-dimensional Fitts-task paradigm. Practiced performance was defined phenomenologically in those studies when the difference in average movement time compared between two sequential blocks was no longer statistically significant at $p \leq 0.05$. We therefore assumed that the data from the last block of the last session (at around 1800 trials) represents a practiced level performance for all participants, for both devices.

6.4 Results

We present the results in two forms: macro-level analysis and micro-level analysis. The macro-level results, which include the Fitts' law analyses, were unsurprising, while the micro-level results revealed an unexpected jitter in the velocity of the isometric joystick. These results are described below.

6.4.1 Macro-level Analysis

While the primary goal of this study was to perform a microstructure analysis of movement, a macro-level analysis was performed to ensure there was nothing unusual about the data. We looked at trends in the overall trial-completion time over the duration of the experiment by grouping the data into blocks of 120 trials. A Fitts' law analysis was conducted to determine the *indices of performance* (IPs) of the two devices, and to study the effect of movement distance and target width on trial completion time.

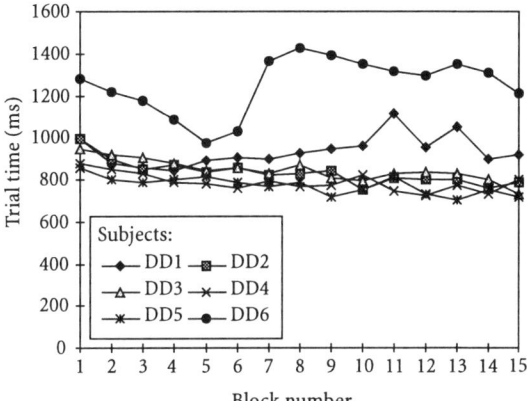

Figure 6.6: Mean block times for the mouse for each participant, n = 6.

Figure 6.6 is a graph of the mean movement time by block for the mouse for each participant. A close examination of the data showed that participant DD6 had very poor mouse trial times which, in fact, *increased* after block 6. We surmised that the participant had tried to minimize errors even if this meant substantially increased trial times.

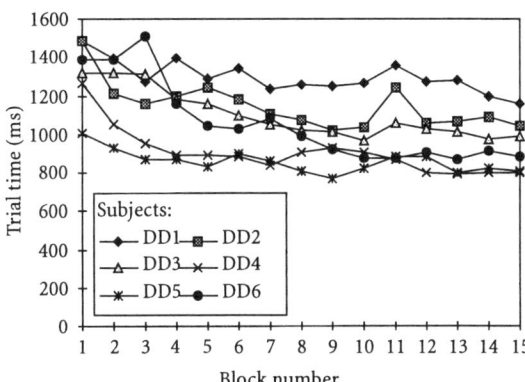

Figure 6.7: Mean block times for the joystick for each participant, n=6.

Figure 6.7 presents the same data for the joystick. As expected, the mean trial times decreased with practice, and the mouse had quicker trial times than the joystick. For the final block, which represents practiced performance for each participant, we computed the means and standard deviations for each device. That data is shown in Table 6.2. We see from this data that DD6 is quite a bit slower using the mouse than the other participants. For the joystick, DD4 and DD5 have the fastest mean times for the joystick, an observation that will become important later in our analysis.

Table 6.2: Final (15th) block times (in ms) for each participant, n=6

	Mouse		Joystick	
Participant	Mean	Standard deviation	Mean	Standard deviation
DD1	921	87	1160	131
DD2	784	72	1040	59
DD3	730	60	992	61
DD4	798	43	797	39
DD5	716	61	805	57
DD6	1211	60	885	51
Total	860		946	

An ANOVA, testing the mean-movement-time differences between subjects for the mouse, confirmed that there were significant differences between subjects, $F_{5,54} = 82.001$, $p < 0.0001$. A Scheffe test for differences between each participant showed that DD6 differed significantly from each of the other participants, $p < 0.0001$. This analysis, and the visual observations of Figure 6.6 made earlier, prompted us to drop DD6's data for both joystick and mouse from the learning and Fitts' law statistical analyses that follow, but not from the micro-level analysis of the next section. We also computed a similar ANOVA for joystick, and confirmed that there were significant differences between subjects, $F_{5,54} = 38.952$, $p < 0.0001$. However, a Scheffe test for differences between each participant showed that no single participant was significantly different from all others. There appeared to be two subgroups: DD4, DD5, and DD6 who differed significantly by individual comparison with DD1, DD2 and DD3. Within these two groups, individuals did not differ significantly.

Table 6.3: Mean and standard deviations of trial blocks without participant DD6, n=5

Joystick

Block	1	2	3	4	5	6	7	8	9	10	11	12	13	14	15
Mean	1312	1181	1112	1106	1084	1081	1017	1013	996	998	1080	1009	991	976	959
Standard deviation	199	191	193	223	209	193	167	170	173	167	218	179	204	172	156

Mouse

Block	1	2	3	4	5	6	7	8	9	10	11	12	13	14	15
Mean	933	869	843	835	832	833	822	835	815	815	861	807	830	788	790
Standard deviation	63.5	45	44	41	41	59	48	66	85	85	145	94	132	67	81

The trial means and standard deviations for each block, without DD6's data, are shown in Table 6.3 and this data is plotted in Figure 6.8.

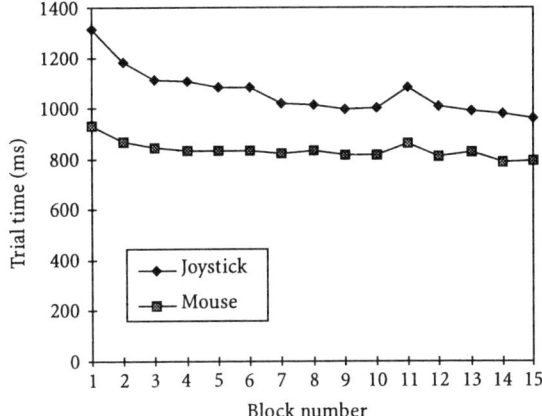

Figure 6.8: Mean trial times by block without participant DD6, n = 5.

In order to determine if there was statistically significant learning from block to block, a pair-wise Bonferroni t-test was performed between successive blocks. The results are listed in Table 6.4.

Table 6.4: P-values for t-test of difference between means of successive blocks, $n=5$

Block	1–2	2–3	3–4	4–5	5–6	6–7	7–8	8–9	9–10	10–11	11–12	12–13	13–14	14–15
Joystick	0.03†	0.01†	0.45	0.21	0.45	0.00†	0.42	0.13	0.45	0.06	0.06	0.17	0.26	0.12
Mouse	0.01†	0.00†	0.28	0.42	0.46	0.22	0.18	0.17	0.50	0.14	0.08	0.19	0.13	0.47

†Significant difference at $p \le 0.05$; s.e. for the mouse is 36.2s, for the joystick, 69.8s.

From the table we can see that for the mouse, the only two blocks which showed significant differences at $p \le .05$ were blocks 1 through 3, after which there was no significant learning. For the joystick, there was no significant learning after block 7. Thus we can assume that by the end of the experiment participants were sufficiently practiced on both devices.

To determine whether practiced performance was significantly different between devices, we computed a t-test for the difference in means for the final (15th) block for the remaining five participants. This test confirmed that when using the joystick, participants had significantly slower mean movement time, $t(98) = 6.416$, $p \le 0.0001$. The mean difference between joystick and mouse times was 169ms, or 21% slower.

Fitts' law indicates that the distance to the target (A) and the target width (W) should have strong effects on trial time. These effects are combined in the *index of difficulty* (ID) term. Figure 6.9 plots mean trial completion time against the Welford formulation of ID (Equation 6.1) for the final (15th) block. We see a good match to a straight line.

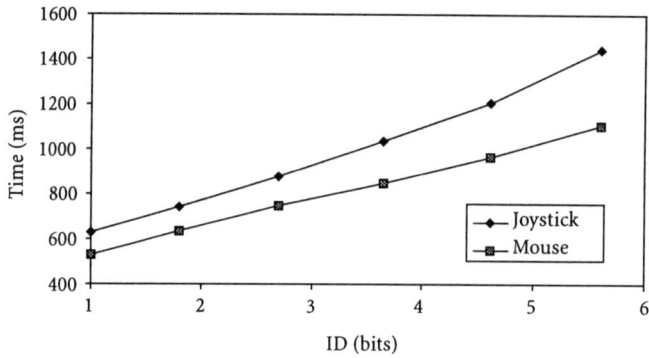

Figure 6.9: Plot of mean trial times with the Welford ID, n = 5.

Performing a regression analysis of mean movement time against *ID* gives the values in Table 6.5. The mouse had an *IP* of 8.13 bits/second ($r^2 = 0.998$), while the isometric joystick had an *IP* of 5.75 bits/second ($r^2 = 0.991$). These results show that the joystick has a Fitts' index of performance (*IP*) below that of the mouse, which was expected from prior research.

Table 6.5: Results of the Fitts' law regression analysis

	r^2	IP
Mouse	0.99	8.13
Joystick	0.99	5.75
Mouse:joystick ratio		1.41

Generally speaking, the macro-level analyses of gross movement did not reveal any surprises. The joystick had a lower *IP* than the mouse. There was no statistically significant learning after block 3 for the mouse, and block 7 for the joystick, and thus we have confidence that the last (15th) block represents practiced performance with a significant difference between devices.

6.4.2 Micro-level Analyses

The analyses of gross movement from the previous sections were conducted to develop confidence in the data, so that we would have confidence in the microstructure level analysis presented in this section.

6.4.2.1 Microstructure of Movement of the Mouse

Because microstructure analysis looks at the kinematics of actual motion for the pointing device, we begin by looking at a graph of motion for a prototypical mouse trial taken from our study. Figure 6.10 represents a single trial, with the time in milliseconds plotted on the x-axis, and distance from the start (displacement) plotted on the first y-axis. Plots of distance moved vs. time are difficult to interpret, and are generally not used for analysis. Consequently, velocity vs. time is plotted on the second y-axis and provides more information. We can see how the velocity varied over the duration of the trial. There was almost no movement for 200ms, which compares well to the reaction time found in other studies (Card *et al.*, 1978; Walker *et al.*, 1993). There was then a large, rapid, submovement followed by two smaller submovements. The first of these overshot the target, and the second was a corrective submovement that moved back to the target.

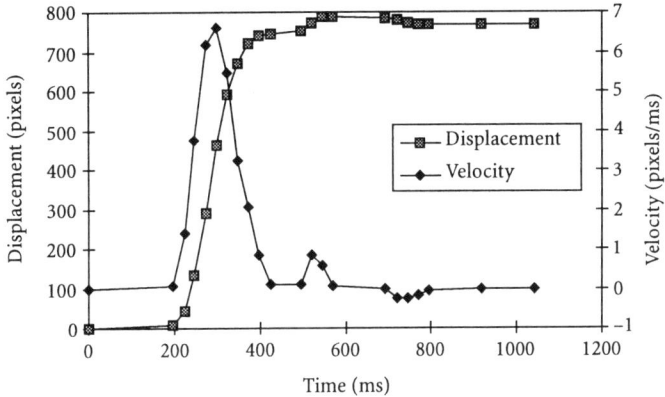

Figure 6.10: Prototypical mouse trial with distance and velocity as a function of time, A = 768 pixels.

A better way of looking at this data is shown in Figure 6.11, with displacement on the x-axis, and velocity on the y-axis. This graph shows the velocity of the cursor along the path to the target. It shows that the movement was a sequence of three submovements. The first submovement covered most of the distance to the target and reached a high peak velocity. The next two submovements were smaller, covering smaller proportions of the distance to the target. The second submovement overshot the target and the third submovement was a correction, bringing the cursor back.

Figure 6.11: Prototypical mouse trial with velocity as a function of distance, A = 768 pixels (same data as Figure 6.10).

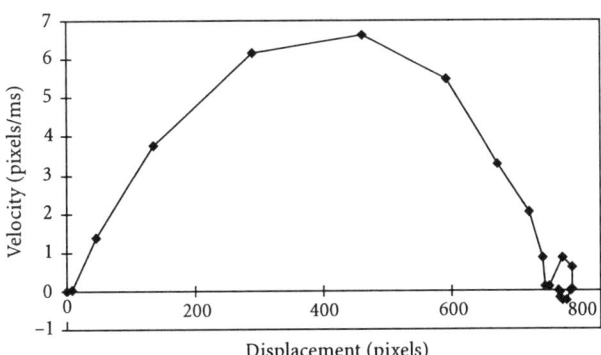

This trial is a good match to the SOS model's prediction that the first submovement is different from the rest of the submovements. The trial is also representative of the majority of mouse trials observed throughout this study.

Figure 6.12 is a trial with multiple overshoots. The participant made a rapid primary submovement towards the target which overshot. Subsequent submovement also overshot, and the participant oscillated around the target until it was reached. This trial is also a prototypical of the SOS model. It has a large primary submovement, followed by smaller secondary submovements.

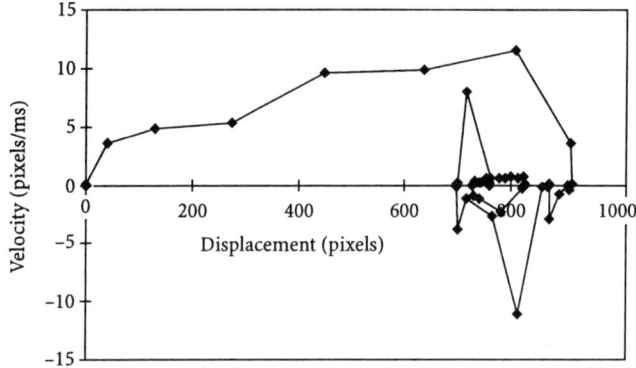

Figure 6.12: First mouse trial participant DD5 – raw data. A = 768 pixels.

These figures show that, in general, mouse movements have a large primary submovement, followed by smaller submovements. While every single trial has not been examined, a large percentage of the trials have, and, generally speaking, for mouse movement we see a large primary submovement followed by smaller secondary submovements.

6.4.2.2 Microstructure of Movement of the Isometric Joystick

Data for the isometric joystick was also obtained. Figure 6.13 and Figure 6.14 show a prototypical joystick trial taken from our study. Note that this trial took a very long time, 3000ms (3s), and there was a significant delay (300ms) before movement occurred.

The distance vs. time subplot in Figure 6.13 does not reveal anything out of the ordinary, but the velocity vs. time subplot shows a rapid variation in velocity which is clearer in the velocity vs. distance plot (Figure 6.14). We called this a 'velocity jitter' or 'jerkiness', and it appeared in the majority of the joystick trials, and persisted over time with almost all participants. Note that again, as in the case of the mouse, this trial is prototypical of trials with the joystick, but that each trial has unique characteristics reflecting the stochastic nature of human movement.

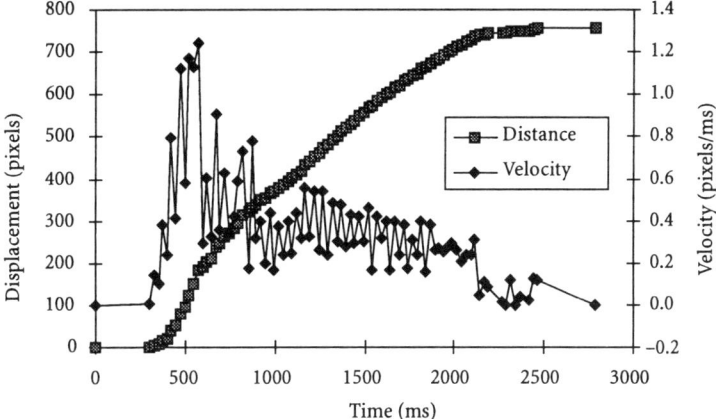

Figure 6.13: Prototypical isometric joystick trial with distance and velocity as a function of time, A = 768 pixels.

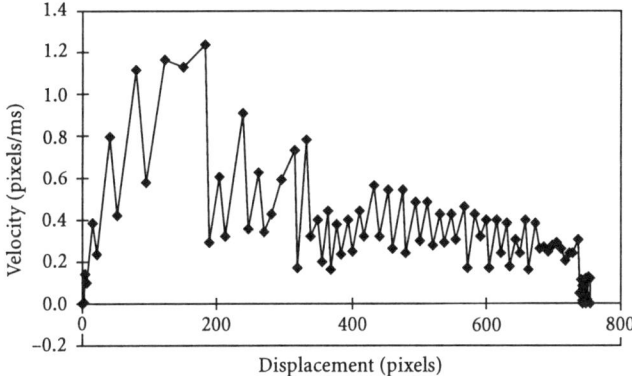

Figure 6.14: Prototypical isometric joystick trial with velocity as a function of distance, A = 768 pixels. (Same trial as Figure 6.13).

The graphs shown in Figures 6.15, 6.16, and 6.17 are representative samples of joystick trials from three other participants, and from three different periods in the experiment. Figure 6.15 shows that the movement towards the target was made up of a sequence of submovements of rapidly-changing velocity.

Figure 6.16 shows a period in the beginning of the movement which might represent a primary submovement with rapid movement towards the target, relatively unaffected by jitter. However, the rest of the movement is quite badly obscured by jitter.

Joystick trials were thus characterized by jerkiness that is visible only when the velocity of the trial is studied either over time or over movement distance. The jerkiness was evident in all trials of the study.

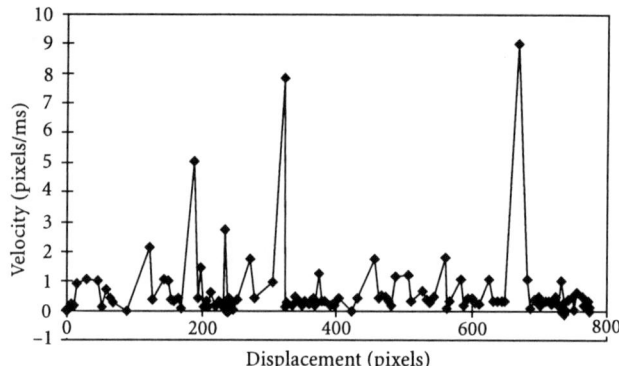

Figure 6.15: First joystick trial participant DD4 – raw data, A=768 pixels.

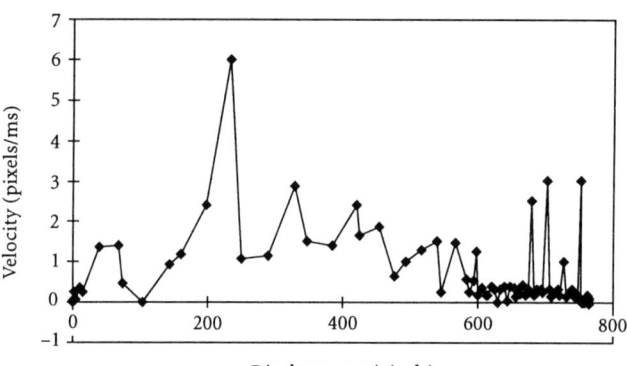

Figure 6.16: Middle joystick trial participant DD2 – raw data, A = 768 pixels.

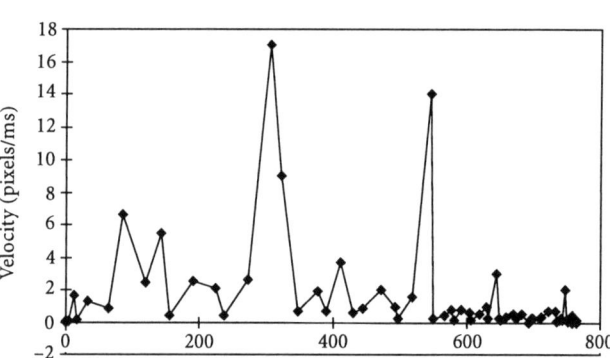

Figure 6.17: Last joystick trial participant DD1 – raw data, A=768 pixels.

6.4.2.3 Applicability of the SOS Model to Joystick Movement

One of the goals of this work was to extend the SOS model to the joystick. It had already been shown to be fairly good at modeling movement with the mouse (Walker *et al.*, 1993). Unfortunately, the jerkiness in joystick movement that was captured in our data caused analytical problems in parsing SOS submovements because the parser used by earlier researchers depends on transitions in velocity and acceleration to determine the start and end of a submovement. Unfortunately, the jitter is exactly such transitions in velocity and acceleration, and the parsing algorithm cannot distinguish between submovements, and variations due to jitter. Because of this, the SOS model analysis could not be performed for the isometric joystick. We did not perform an SOS model analysis for the mouse either because our data, by visual inspection, appeared to confirm the earlier work of Walker *et al.* (1993).[4]

6.5 Discussion

The most problematic aspect of the results was the discovery of jitter for the joystick. After carefully considering all the data we had gathered, we came up with two major plausible explanations for the cause. The first is that jitter is an artifact of the operation of the joystick. This could be peculiar to our particular equipment and experimental test situation, or something inherent in all isometric joysticks, which we call *intrinsic jitter*. The second cause could be that because the isometric joystick is force-sensitive, it picks up physiological tremor in the finger which becomes amplified and causes control problems for the human motor system. Finally, both these causes combined could be responsible for jitter.

6.5.1 Jitter as a Hardware and Software Artifact

When the jerkiness in the velocity was discovered during initial pilot studies[5] an effort was made to determine if there was a defective piece of hardware, something unique to the participants, or a phenomenon that truly affected only joysticks. Since both the joystick and the mouse are connected through a complex interaction of hardware and software (see section 3.1), it is important to review the setup of the experimental equipment. The Trackpoint™ is connected through the PS/2 mouse port. In this configuration, both mouse and isometric joystick feed their signals to the computer over the same set of wires. In other words, the data generated by the joystick emulates mouse data. These signals are then interpreted by the same software driver, and then passed on to the data-gathering program via the operating system. Subsequently, the data gathered for both mouse and joystick receives the same treatment. Any differences in the data between the two devices must be attributable to causes occurring prior to the point of entry through the PS/2 port – either the joystick itself or the person operating the joystick.

The sources of jitter that were eliminated by testing various possibilities during the pilot studies were:

- *Participants:* data from all seven different participants (one pilot, six experimental) showed jitter.
- *The test computer:* other computers showed jitter when sampling using the Trackpoint™ as the pointing device. The computers tested included an Intel 486 processor, Pentium processors, two IBM ThinkPad™s, and a NEC Versa™ notebook.
- *The test Trackpoint™:* a Trackpoint™II and a Trackpoint™III were tested in IBM ThinkPad™s, and a similar keyboard joystick in an NEC Versa™ notebook computer. All showed jitter. In addition, a non-keyboard, isometric joystick manufactured by Interlink and called the PortaPoint was tested. The PortaPoint is mounted in a housing similar in shape to a mouse and uses the same electronics as the key joystick tested in Chapter 5. It attaches to the computer through the PS/2 mouse port.
- *PS/2 connection:* since the entire keyboard used in the experiment was connected through the PS/2 port, we reasoned that the keyboard to port connection might be defective. We then connected the PortaPoint isometric joystick directly to the PS/2 port, and observed jitter. The PortaPoint also had a serial port connection that produced data with jitter.
- *Sampling rates and operating systems:* jitter appeared at a sampling rate of 26ms for Windows 3.11 and 25ms for Windows 95 used in pilot studies, as well as at 16ms for Windows NT 3.5 used to collect the experimental data.

Thus, we found that jitter was observed when, and only when, an isometric joystick was used. We are confident that the cause of jitter is either the joystick itself or the human performance coupled with it. We do not believe that the jitter is introduced as an artifact of our own analysis program. This program takes a file of cursor displacement samples which are time-stamped, differentiates velocity as a function of distance, and then graphs those values. If that were the case, the mouse data would show the same jitter, since data from both devices are handled identically after entering the PS/2 port.

It is possible that the manner in which the joystick generates output is inherently unstable: variations in velocity would appear even under steady-state input. This possible cause was suggested by reviewers of our research, and, consequently, we conducted a follow-up study.

In order to test the steady-state input from the Trackpoint™ without human input,[6] we decided to apply a range of constant forces. Fortunately, Rutledge and Selker (1990) published detailed information on the operation of the joystick, known in their published material as the *Pointing Stick*. They define the operating force input range of the Trackpoint™ from about 2g to 225g and describe the transfer function which computes force to velocity. (See section 3.1.1.3 and Figure 3.2 for a description of the Trackpoint™ transfer function.)

To conduct our test, we applied a lateral force to the joystick by suspending balance weights commonly found in a chemistry lab balance set. This was intended to approximate the force applied by a human finger. The weights used were 150g, 100g, 50g and 20g and were applied for approximately ten-second intervals. Jitter appeared in all cases, and was most marked for the larger weights.

Figure 6.18 shows a plot from this study using a force of 100g over a period of about 9 seconds. This data has been collected and processed with the same programs that were used in the main experiment, although the operating system used was Windows 95 with a sampling rate of 25ms. The data is plotted with velocity in pixels per millisecond on the y-axis, and distance in pixels on the x-axis. A better way of understanding this data is to recompute the velocity in pixels per 25ms which is the sampling rate. Table 6.6 shows this conversion.

Table 6.6: Conversion of pixels/ms to pixels in 25ms interval

Pixels per millisecond (ms)	Pixels per 25 millisecond (ms) interval
0.08	2
0.16	4
0.24	6
0.32	8

Examining Figure 6.18 and using the conversion from Table 6.6, we see a regular pattern of variation in velocity, jumping from 6 pixels per 25ms to 8 pixels to 6 to 2 and repeating in a somewhat random fashion. The application of a constant 100g force should produce a constant velocity. It is important to note that during these tests, we observed that the cursor did not travel at a constant, smooth rate. This observation confirms our sampling results and emphasizes that these variations in velocity are visible to the human user.

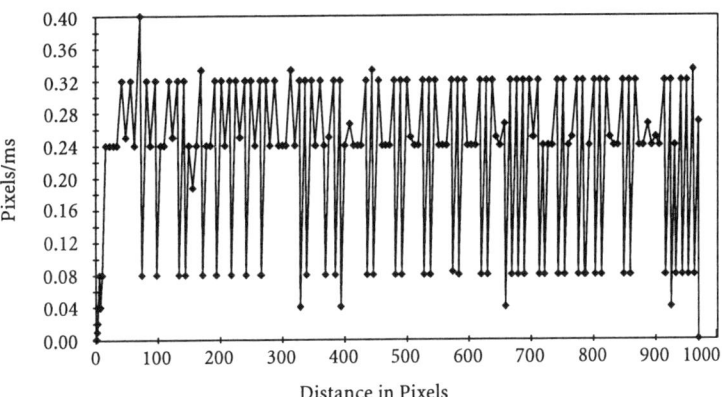

Figure 6.18: Constant force trial, 100g force applied.

This data clearly shows that, in and of itself, the joystick generates a jitter which we will call *intrinsic jitter*. However, from this study we do not know at what stage of the process of converting the input force into the output displacement the jitter appears, and from which sources. Candidates include:

- *The strain gauges* that pick up force do not maintain a constant output introducing noise.

- *The computational processes* which sample the input force, and then use a non-linear function to compute an output velocity, might be susceptible to errors of numerical approximation. These naturally occur when rounding or truncating, or when computing a digital value (velocity) from an analog, continuous, transduced value (force).

- *An artifact* of the process in which the joystick sends its data to the PS/2 mouse driver. After computing the transfer function from force to velocity, the joystick must emulate a mouse. It generates a displacement unit, called a *mickey*, by integrating the velocity value with respect to a time unit, then the displacement data is sent to the computer through the port by an interrupt driven asynchronous protocol. If the unit of time in which velocity is computed differs from the unit of time in which displacement is computed, a higher frequency noise can be introduced into the signal. We estimated the intrinsic jitter at 20Hz or higher frequency and our investigation of this issue is on-going.

6.5.2   A Second Cause of Jitter: Tremor and the Voluntary Application of Force

Although it would seem that the joystick itself introduces rapid variations in velocity, which are the sole cause of jitter, there is evidence of another cause which exists and compounds the complexity of jitter. This cause is that the isometric joystick, which senses force, picks up physiological tremor in the finger. Before we explain this hypothesis in more detail, we discuss a little of what is known about tremor.

All forms of voluntary movement have some time period associated with them. For instance, the early work by Woodworth noted time periods of 300ms for the initial movement (Meyer *et al.*, 1990). It has also been noted that in trying to maintain a steady posture or perform a voluntary movement, involuntary variations in force occur. These variations are called *tremor* (Stein and Lee, 1989).

Tremor is visible in most individuals when holding a limb outstretched. If you hold your arm out with your fingers extended, you are likely to see a twitch in the fingers, and possibly even see that you cannot hold your arm completely steady. The twitch is caused by tremor, which is an inability of the human neuromuscular system to maintain a constant force.

Tremor occurs during the application of steady force in the absence of movement, such as when holding down a button, or pushing an isometric joystick. Tremor also occurs when the applied force causes movement, such as when the arm moves across the body in an arc, or during mouse movement. Tremor even occurs at rest, because of the variations caused by the blood pulsing through the veins and arteries (Stein and Lee, 1989). Finally, tremor tends to increase with increases in applied force.

Stein and Lee (1989) report that the range of frequencies generated by an outstretched limb span the range of frequencies present in voluntary movement. The largest components of tremor occur in the low frequency range, usually below 5Hz, and these movements are quite random. While a large portion of tremor is quite random and generally occurs at low frequencies, some components are more oscillatory and occur at slightly higher frequencies: generally between 8–12Hz. This oscillatory tremor appears to be caused by feedback mechanisms between the skeleton, muscles and the nervous system. In general, tremor occurs with all application of force and is a random noise that occurs throughout the same frequency range as voluntary movement.

Halliday and Redfearn (1956) measured finger tremor in 46 healthy subjects and found tremor frequencies between 5–15Hz. They also found that tremor frequency was virtually unaffected by loading the finger with 50 or 100g weights and concluded that:

> … tremor rates are virtually independent of the mechanical properties of the limb.
>
> *Halliday and Redfearn, 1956:610*

6.5.2.1 Tremor and the Isometric Joystick

Let us now consider how physiological tremor could affect the joystick. Our first piece of evidence is an unpublished IBM technical report by Selker and Rutledge (1991) which documents the difficulty users had applying a constant force to the Trackpoint™. In this experiment, four participants were asked to maintain a constant force for a 2.4-second period. Error (target over- or under-shoots) and dither (standard deviation of the difference between requested and actual force means) were among several measures computed.

Three results were concluded from this study. First, that participants were unable to hold a constant force; second, that there is a large variation in pointing accuracy between individuals; and third, that error and dither increase with increasing force. Selker and Rutledge estimate force precision at about 10% of intentionally applied force. They observed that these variations in force, and, consequently, velocity of the cursor, are fortunately aligned in the direction of the target. They also investigated gripping the Trackpoint™ using two fingers instead of pushing and pulling with one. However, they state:

> Two unsteady fingers are just as unsteady as one unsteady finger.
>
> *Selker and Rutledge, 1991:10*

Although Selker and Rutledge attribute the inability of participants to maintain a constant force under these conditions to human performance, the intrinsic jitter that we observed earlier would also have affected the performance of their experimental participants. However, before entirely dismissing the argument that the jitter is caused by human tremor, we need to consider the evidence of individual differences. Both studies present evidence that large individual differences in performance exist. These cannot be accounted for solely by intrinsic jitter.

Before turning to the examination of that evidence, we first discuss how tremor could be actually amplified by the operation of the joystick. The joystick is a force-sensitive device that translates input force into changes in cursor velocity. When there is tremor present in the finger, the tremor is perceived as changes in applied force.

Tremor is picked up by the joystick and passed on to its hardware controller. The controller employs an 'accelerated' design, i.e. it employs a non-linear translation between input force and output displacement (Rutledge and Selker, 1990). This transfer function accentuates the effect that changes in input have on the output. So tremor is exaggerated in the displacement data that is sent to the software driver. As is also true for the mouse, the software driver is in turn accelerated and accentuates changes in displacement into larger changes in the position of the cursor. The net result is that the velocity of the cursor varies widely as it moves across the screen. Thus the design of the joystick makes it unique in the way that it amplifies tremor.

The isometric joystick is also unique in the manner in which it is affected by tremor. The finger that controls the joystick applies a lateral force on the joystick, and is unsupported. It also does not move. Therefore there is little to damp the tremor. In other types of movement, tremor is damped by two things, inertial mass and friction. Because the finger does not move, inertial mass does not play a role. Again, because nothing moves, friction does not play a role. The only damping factor that we have been able to assume is the friction that exists between adjacent muscle fibers in the finger (Stein and Lee, 1989).

Tremor does not affect displacement control devices in the same way. Tremor also occurs during mouse movement, but it does not have the same effect. When a mouse is moving across a mousepad, any tremor is damped by the friction of the mouse and the hand on the mousepad, as well as by the mass of the hand, wrist and mouse (and perhaps the forearm). The mouse is therefore not directly affected by tremor. So the physical construction of the joystick makes it susceptible to tremor while other devices such as the mouse are not.

To summarize, the isometric joystick is a force-sensitive device, designed to amplify small changes in force. Its physical characteristics make it transduce the tremor signal and the mathematical characteristics of the controller and software driver amplify that signal. In contrast, the mechanical nature of the mouse tends to neutralize any tremor effects.

6.5.2.2   Analysis of Tremor in the Joystick

We now face the issue of attempting to remove the intrinsic jitter from the data we collected in the main experiment in order to directly analyze the contribution of tremor, and observe patterns in movement minus intrinsic jitter. Our general approach was to filter the data from the main experiment to remove the intrinsic jitter, and, then, perform a spectral analysis on the filtered data. This quantitative analysis reveals that there are strong individual differences for participants using the joystick – two of whom appear to have less tremor and achieve a mouse-like SOS movement pattern.

Effect of Filtering Data

Human movement tends to lie in the frequency range below 10Hz, with the upper limit of the range at 20Hz (Stein and Lee, 1989). The intrinsic jitter, as well as sampling error,[7] can therefore be reduced by running the data through a low-pass Butterworth digital filter to remove all the frequency components higher than 20Hz (Kaiser and Reed, 1977).

First, a visual inspection of the smoothed, i.e. filtered, data was done for a large number of trials. These trials were chosen from all participants in early, middle and late sessions of the experiment, for both mouse and joystick. Each trial was passed through a low-pass Butterworth filter using a mathematics package called *MatLab*, published by Mathworks, and available in a Student Edition from Prentice Hall (Student Edition of MatLab for Windows, version 4, ISBN 0-13-184995-6). The data was then graphed in the now familiar plot of velocity vs. displacement.

The resulting plots for both devices were smoother than the plots of their raw data, but the plots for the joystick remained jerky in comparison to the plots for the mouse. Figure 6.19 is a smoothed joystick trial from raw data plotted in Figure 6.15. This trial is the first trial for participant DD4. It shows that some jerkiness persists despite the smoothing effects of the filtering algorithm. Visual inspection of most of the other joystick plots showed a similar pattern. In other words, the jerkiness persisted in the plots despite the low-pass filtering. This is consistent with the literature which says that the frequency range of tremor lies below 20Hz, and the filtering removed frequencies higher than 20Hz.

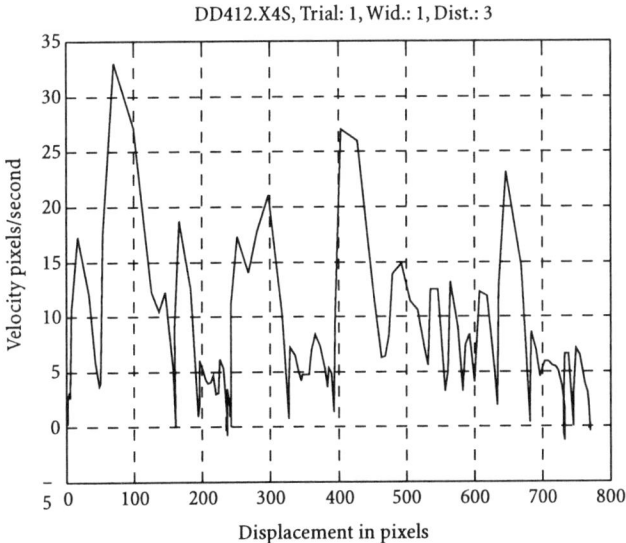

Figure 6.19: First joystick trial for participant DD4 – filtered data. Same trial as Figure 6.15. A = 768 pixels.

There were, however, two participants whose performance with the joystick varies from the other participants. First, DD4 and DD5 had the lowest mean movement times with the isometric joystick (see Table 6.2), and we were interested in seeing whether there were any differences between their movement microstructures and those of the other participants, and whether this developed over time. Could a difference in movement account for improved performance?

Participant DD4 reported having had a lot of experience playing video games that used an isotonic joystick, but had never used an isometric joystick before. Participant DD5 owned an IBM ThinkPad™ and had used a Trackpoint™ for about six months prior to the experiment. Interestingly, participant DD6 had the most experience with the Trackpoint™. He had owned an IBM ThinkPad™ for approximately two years before the experiment and was much more comfortable using it than using a mouse. However, he did not have the highest performance with it relative to the other participants in the experiment, though his final trial times lay in the top half.

Figure 6.20 and Figure 6.21 show two representative velocity vs. distance graphs of trials by participants DD4 and DD5. The data for DD4 is taken from a middle session trial. DD4 appears to have reduced through practice the jerkiness apparent in the initial trial as shown in Figure 6.15 and Figure 6.19. The trial for DD5 is the very last one, and represents a prototype plot for this participant.

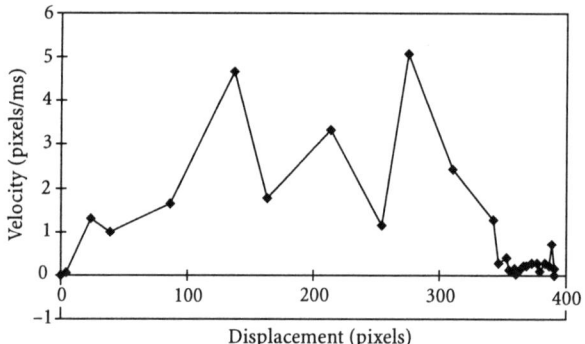

Figure 6.20: Middle joystick trial for participant DD4 – raw data.

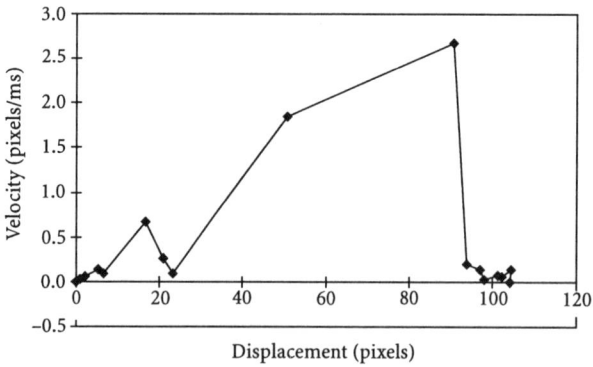

Figure 6.21: Last joystick trial for participant DD5 – raw data.

In general, both DD4 and DD5 appeared to have a mouse-like quality to their joystick movement, i.e. episodes of movement that reach large velocities and are relatively free of jerkiness. If these graphs represent human performance minus the intrinsic jitter of the joystick, then it might be assumed that both these participants are either relatively free of tremor, or have developed movement strategies which reduce its effects. This suggests that individual differences may account for differences in performance.

Spectral Analysis of Jerkiness

Our analysis thus far has been qualitative, depending on visual inspection. We noted that filtered data for the joystick showed less jerkiness, and that some individuals, DD4 and DD5, appeared to have movement patterns which were even less jerky and more mouse-like. This pattern correlated with better performance. While qualitative analysis is useful in early stages of exploratory analysis, it lacks the ability to summarize or quantify effects. This section describes our next step which was to quantify the amount of jitter in individual participants' performance over a period of time to see if there was any noticeable difference.

What we have called jitter or jerkiness is essentially variations over time of a signal we call velocity. What we have observed so far as a difference between the mouse and the joystick data is that the joystick data has higher-frequency components than the mouse. Actually, the data for the joystick is more complex, in that there is a superposition of a higher-frequency signal on a low-frequency signal. The higher-frequency signal is intrinsic jitter from the hardware, an oscillatory tremor component lying in the range from 8–12Hz, a random tremor component at less than 5Hz, and an intentional movement component of below 5Hz. Indeed, visual examination of Figure 6.15, a joystick trial, shows that underneath the jitter appears a series of 4 or 5 submovements. If the average time for that a joystick trial takes 950ms, then the approximate frequency of the submovements would be about 5Hz. Clearly, a mouse movement of the same duration with only two submovements would be less than half the 5Hz.

This sort of data can be analyzed in the frequency domain using Fourier techniques. Based on the analysis above, we would expect that a greater percentage of the signals would exist at higher frequencies for the joystick than the mouse. This is called the *spectral power*. Using this approach, a Fourier analysis was conducted on the last block of data for all participants for both devices. First, each trial from the last block was passed through a low-pass Butterworth filter, and then analyzed in the frequency domain. (The filtering was the same as in the earlier analysis and was intended to filter out intrinsic jitter which was at frequencies higher than 20Hz.) The frequency domain analysis of the smoothed data was performed using MatLab.

As expected, most of the power of each trial was in very low frequencies. The power also varied widely from trial to trial, which is not informative. The spectrograms of individual trials differed greatly from participant to participant and between devices, and no pattern was apparent either between participants or between devices, or even within devices, apart from the very general pattern depicted in Figure 6.24. This pattern tended to have greater power in the low frequencies, and lower power in the high frequencies. The spectrograms for each trial of the last block for each device were aggregated by participant. The power was normalized prior to addition by dividing the power at each frequency by the power of the frequency with the highest power. This generated a power spectrum where the highest power was 1. When summed over all trials for a participant, the maximum power rose to 120. The results are presented in the next few pages.

Figure 6.22 represents the spectrogram for the last block of mouse trials for each participant. Notice a slight bulge at approximately 4Hz for DD6. DD6 had the poorest mouse performance. This suggests that DD6 might have been using a different strategy for controlling the mouse from the rest of the participants, perhaps a series of slow moves to get to the target. Similarly, Figure 6.23 is the spectrogram of the last block of joystick trials for each participant. Here participant DD1 has a slight bulge at approximately 4Hz. DD1 had the poorest joystick performance.

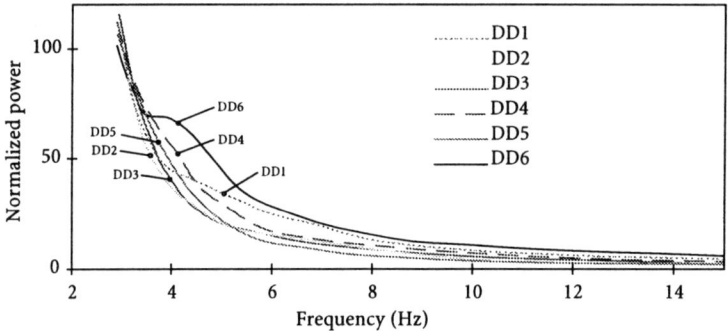

Figure 6.22: Spectrograms for last block of mouse trials.

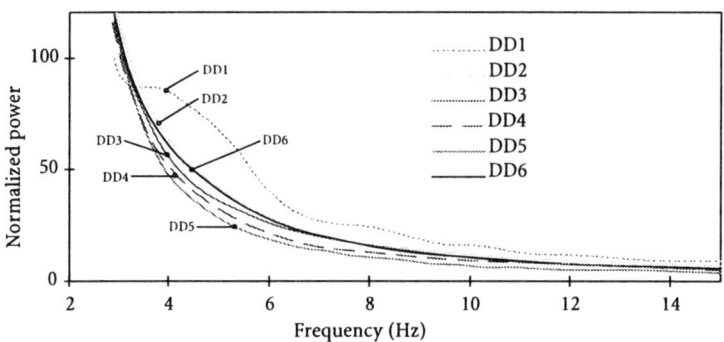

Figure 6.23: Spectrograms for last block of joystick trials.

Figure 6.24 presents the mean frequency data for the mouse for all participants compared to the mean frequency data for the joystick for the participants. It clearly shows a that there is a greater percentage of the power for higher frequencies (between 3Hz and 10Hz) for the joystick than for the mouse, which is what the earlier analysis suggested.

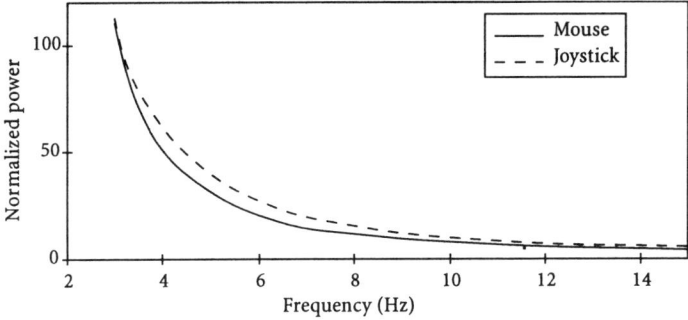

Figure 6.24: Comparison of spectrograms for both devices.

To summarize, the spectral analysis showed that there are more high-frequency components in the joystick movement, which is consistent with more submovements and the presence of a tremor.

These spectral differences can be explored at the level of individual performance. Figure 6.25 through Figure 6.30 plot the spectra of mouse and joystick trials for the last block of each participant. The plots for participants DD1, DD2 and DD3 show a difference between the mouse data and the joystick data. There is more power in the joystick data than the mouse data between 3–15Hz. This indicates that there are higher-frequency components in the joystick data.

In this light, the plots for participants DD4 (Figure 6.28) and DD5 (Figure 6.29), who had better performance with the joystick are very interesting. For them, these figures show a great deal of similarity between the spectra for mouse and joystick movement. Their plots do not show the separation that can be seen in the graphs of the other participants. This suggests a relative lack of the presence of jitter in their trials. This issue is discussed further later in this chapter.

Figure 6.30 is also of interest. It shows the spectra for participant DD6, who did not like the mouse, and in fact had a slower performance with the mouse than the joystick. This participant had more power at higher frequencies for the mouse, and the bulge at around 4Hz suggests some sort of stop-and-go pointing strategy.

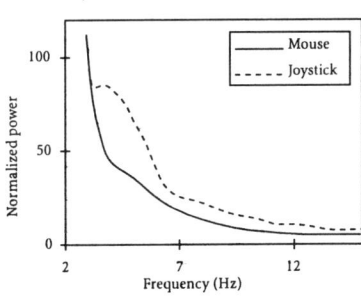

Figure 6.25: DD1's last block.

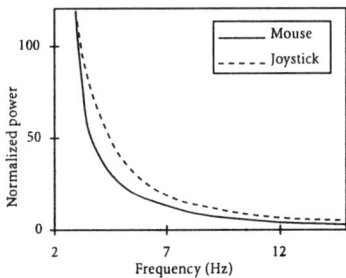

Figure 6.26: DD2's last block.

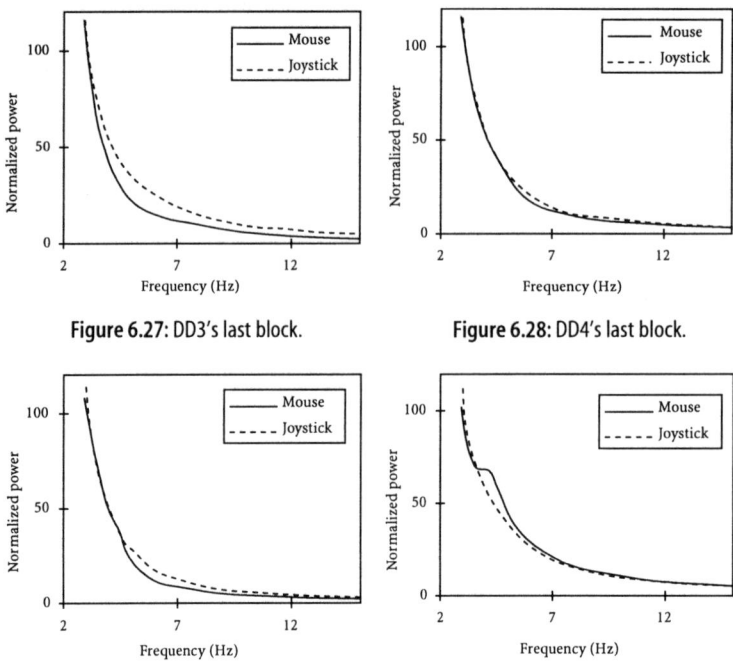

Figure 6.27: DD3's last block.   Figure 6.28: DD4's last block.

Figure 6.29: DD5's last block.   Figure 6.30: DD6's last block.

This analysis showed that there are individual differences between individual participants that appeared in the spectrograms of their movement trials. We believe that both tremor and intrinsic jitter play a role in making joystick movement jerky, and are not mutually exclusive. Both result in jerky motion of the cursor possibly causing problems in motor control using visual feedback. All these factors make control of the isometric joystick more difficult to use and slower than the mouse.

Although we have direct causal evidence through a controlled experiment for intrinsic jitter, our hypothesis of tremor remains based on qualitative and quantitative correlations. To summarize: after filtering out the higher frequency intrinsic jitter, we still observed jerkiness in most joystick data. We note that the spectral analysis showed patterns of individual differences, where subjects with high performance with the joystick appeared to have joystick spectra that were similar to mouse spectra, without the jerkiness. These individuals appear to have either less tremor or to have learned strategies to reduce it. However, a controlled experiment needs to be performed which directly measures tremor, perhaps directly at the strain gauge. Only then will the complex combination of hardware, software, and human performance fully explain the joystick jitter.

6.6 Summary and Conclusions

This study was aimed at developing a systematic understanding of why the isometric joystick is more difficult to use than the mouse. Using a within-subjects longitudinal design and a standard Fitts task, we studied experimentally the kinematics of the two devices by examining the microstructure of movement for six different people. Our initial goal was to test whether the SOS model of movement applied to both devices. We computed movement time for all participants and the standard Fitts' law coefficients and regressions, which confirmed that the data was typical of other studies comparing the two types of devices. Movement times for the isometric joystick were longer on average, and four out of six participants reported that it was harder to control.

By sampling the movement of the cursor, we collected and analyzed data representing changes in velocity of the cursor as a function of distance traveled towards the target. Visual inspection of the mouse microstructure data showed an SOS model of movement, confirming the prior research of Walker *et al.* (1993). However, the discovery of jitter (rapid variations in velocity within a relatively short period of time) in the joystick data prevented us from an analysis of the SOS model, and lead to an additional line of study which was not part of the original research agenda.

We hypothesize that joystick jitter comes from two primary causes. The first, which we call intrinsic jitter, arises from computational and hardware–software peculiarities of converting transduced force to velocity to displacement information transmitted to the computer as an asynchronous interrupt signal. This problem is inherent in several of the isometric joysticks we examined. We confirmed this with an experimental study of the isometric joystick under the application of constant force without human input. That study demonstrated that intrinsic jitter lies at frequencies of 20Hz or greater.

The second cause of jitter which we hypothesize is from human physiological tremor. A prior study by Selker and Rutledge (1991) found that participants were unable to maintain a constant force with the joystick for a period of 2.4 seconds. The variability was about 10%, though they observed large individual differences. Tremor is a natural component of human movement. Most tremor is random and occurs below 5Hz, although some oscillatory components occur in the range between 8–12Hz.

In order to remove the intrinsic jitter from the joystick data, and, hopefully, allow us to continue with our analysis of the underlying movement model, we took the last block of participants' data and filtered out the frequency components equal to or higher than 20Hz. Removing these components smoothed the data. However, it did not remove all the jitter from the joystick data, leaving us with strong, though not direct causal evidence, that there is a contribution of human tremor. Despite this smoothing, the jitter was still significant enough to prevent us from observing and analyzing a clear movement model, either comparable to or different from the SOS model.

An important observation of individual differences was clearly visible in plots of both raw and smoothed data. At the start of the experiment, all participants using the joystick had trials where the velocity of the cursor was jerky. Over time, for participants DD4 and DD5 the shape of the velocity vs. distance plots began to appear more mouse-like, i.e. without jitter and with SOS model shape.

A Fourier analysis and comparison of the spectrograms of mouse movement and of joystick movement for the last block, for each subject, supported this theory. For subjects DD4 and DD5, the mouse and joystick power spectra were very close together. For the rest of the subjects there was a marked difference, with the joystick having a larger percentage of higher frequency components. These higher frequency components we attribute to tremor and more submovements.

While we failed in our original intention to develop a microstructure movement model for the joystick, we were successful in the underlying goal of learning more about how the isometric joystick is used, and as the following discussion will show, there are opportunities to use this knowledge to improve its design.

The study afforded us a number of conclusions. We have a clear explanation about why people find isometric devices difficult to control, and in the process of doing so, we found the study of the microstructure of movement to be a very valuable analytic tool. We also learnt about individual differences, an area that is largely ignored in pointing device research. We now discuss these aspects, ending with a discussion about the research opportunities.

6.6.1 Jitter Makes Isometric Devices Difficult to Control

During the earlier study with the key joystick (see Chapter 5), a surprisingly large number of participants said that they had trouble getting the joystick to stop in small targets. (The smallest target was 8 pixels across.) The reason for this is now easy to understand. Jitter, which is random variations in cursor velocity, makes it difficult for users to stop the cursor at a desired point on the screen and explains why some isometric joysticks are hard to control. A jittery joystick complicates motor control because both intrinsic jitter and amplified tremor prevent fine motor adjustments. The jitter, presented as visual feedback of cursor movement, further complicates fine motor control.

As participants using the joystick try to stop in the target, the random variation in velocity makes this more difficult, resulting in longer trial times for the joystick. Our best evidence of this are participants DD4 and DD5 who had mean trial times much lower than the group means, and practiced joystick trials that look like mouse movement.

6.6.2 An Alternative Model for Isometric Movement

A number of times during the course of the discussion in this chapter, we have hypothesized that the SOS model might hold for isometric joystick movement.

Although we were unable to analyze the data we obtained to confirm or disprove that hypothesis, and while we did see evidence of mouse-like SOS motion for two participants, we also saw some evidence through visual inspection of a second alternative model.

The mouse, as an isotonic device, is able to allow the user to replicate manual rapid aimed motion as described by the SOS model. For mouse movement and for manual movement, a single submovement is made up of two force pulses: one that moves the mouse or limb in the direction of the target, and the second that causes a deceleration. This is depicted in Figure 6.31.

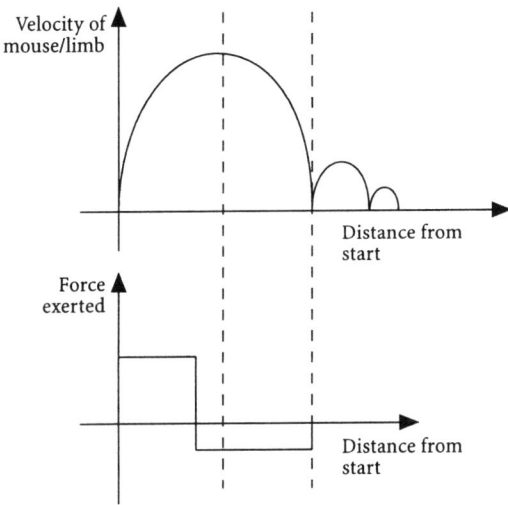

Figure 6.31: Force pulses involved in SOS model submovements.

However, the isometric joystick is an entirely different type of control. The underlying shape of many of the velocity vs. distance plots for the isometric joystick suggests that users of the isometric joystick might use a different movement strategy than that used to control a mouse. Note that the force applied to the isometric joystick is mapped directly onto the velocity of the cursor. In isotonic movement such as with the mouse, the cursor velocity is an integration of the force, and so force only indirectly affects velocity, while it directly affects acceleration.

An alternative model for the isometric joystick is the following: participants push down on the joystick trying to reach a high velocity ramp, hold it at that peak till they come close to the target, then release the joystick, and give a series of small force pulses for fine adjusting motion. This is depicted in Figure 6.32. This model is supported by the finding of our study that targets that were further away took disproportionately longer for the isometric joystick.

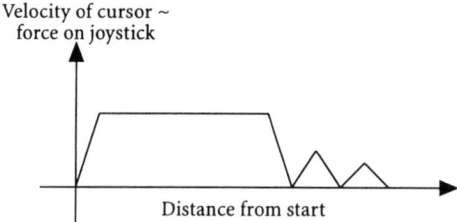

Figure 6.32: Alternative model of isometric movement.

Future research should formalize these two alternative models and determine an experimental test to clarify them. They may be used by different people or even for different pointing situations by the same person. This will be difficult to assess, since the underlying data is stochastic, and, as this study has shown, complicated by complex artifacts that affect human movement.

6.6.3 Individual Differences

Contemporary research on pointing devices has not taken individual differences into consideration. Standard Fitts' law analyses, for example, compare group trial times in order to derive Fitts' law coefficients. This study showed that there might be major qualitative differences between participants who perform well on the isometric joystick, and participants who perform poorly, even though the data presents itself as Fitts' law data.

The split of our participants into poor and good performers with the isometric joystick might help explain a result from our earlier study with the key joystick. In that study, we found that subjects seemed sharply split on whether they liked the isometric joystick or not. The same seems to be true of participants in this study.

This suggests that the isometric joystick might be more intrinsically suitable for some users than for others. Motor control is considered to be made up of components: three important ones being timing, force, and the sequence in which movements are made. A study by Lundy–Ekman, Ivry, Keele, and Woollacott (1991) indicates that clumsy children with soft neurological signs in the basal ganglia have difficulty in controlling the amplitude of isometric force pulses. In the terms of the present study, we could say that there might be strong physiological reasons why some people are better at using the isometric joystick than others. This is a line of research that needs investigation.

By ignoring individual device preferences, and comparing the performance of different pointing devices across the board, HCI has done users a disservice. We need to be able to match pointing devices to users. If, indeed, there are intrinsic qualities such as tremor that affect a person's device performance, pointing device researchers and manufacturers should focus on providing a variety of top quality devices. Individuals could then choose the device that is best for them, rather than 'one size fits all'.

6.6.4 Improving the Finger-Controlled Isometric Joystick

The most visible result of this study was the discovery of jitter in the joystick's trials. Removing this jitter might improve people's performance with the joystick. One possible solution includes supporting the finger to reduce both tremor and fatigue, which a number of participants in this study complained about. Friction and inertia could be re-introduced either by making the device deformable, or through numerical analysis techniques into either the hardware or the software.

It was discussed earlier how some participants in the experiment were able to make the right kind of movements with the joystick a large percentage of the time, and that most users can make them at least some of the time. This raises the possibility of training. Users can be presented with a training program that gives them positive feedback (e.g. a happy sound) when they make a movement with optimal motion. All of these approaches lead to further avenues for research. Each approach needs a microstructure level analysis to understand how the modifications affect the pointing task.

We conclude this chapter with the observation that a number of research opportunities and insights into design arise out of this microstructure of movement study. Earlier research had shown the value of this level of analysis in modeling isotonic devices (Jagacinski *et al.*, 1980a; Walker *et al.*, 1993). While we have not been able to use it to model isometric devices, it was extremely effective in providing information about what happened during joystick trials. The manner in which this study uncovered jitter in the isometric joystick strongly supports this statement. The analysis of movement microstructure has proven valuable in this study, and we highly recommend it for other devices.

6.7 Endnotes

1   Unless otherwise specified, in this chapter the term 'joystick' refers to a finger-operated isometric velocity-control joystick.
2   David Meyer and Charles Wright, developers of the SOS model disagree on whether or not it might be applicable to isometric movement. (Personal communications in e-mail from David Meyer, 10 November 1993 and Charles E. Wright, 16 November 1993.)
3   The smallest period associated with human movement is approximately 60ms, which corresponds to a frequency of 16.7Hz. However, the Nyquist theorem tells us that if a signal is comprised of frequencies up to nHz, it must be sampled at a frequency of $2n$Hz in order for the signal to be accurately represented. Therefore, the sampling rate needed to measure the smallest period of human movement is 33Hz, or approximately once every 30ms. Since the software generated a mouse position update approximately every 16ms, this was almost twice the required period.
4   An analysis of mouse submovement data collected in this study was later performed by Ted Kirkpatrick, a Ph.D. student of Sarah Douglas, using the software developed by Walker *et al.* (1993) and kindly sent to us by them. His analysis confirmed the SOS model for the experimental mouse data, although he found a slightly higher average number of submovements than the Walker study value of 1.51 to 1.94 submovements.

5 Pilot tests were run on a Gateway 2000 with an Intel 486 processor running at 33Mhz, and a Paradise 80c31 video chipset with 1Mb of video RAM. The operating system for the pilot study was Windows for Workgroups version 3.11. Sampling during the pilot study occurred every 26ms.

6 The authors would like to acknowledge the enormous amount of effort that Ted Kirkpatrick, a Ph.D. student at the University of Oregon, put into getting these results.

7 The process of taking a digital sample of a continuous waveform introduces sampling error. In addition, taking the numerical differential of time series data introduces high frequency error.

7. *Performance Models*

Previous chapters have demonstrated the enormous amount of experimental research that has been done on pointing devices and human performance. We have seen the complex interaction between type of device, type of task, type of limb and type of user. We have derived Fitts' law parameters and examined relationships between models of movement such as the SOS model and device type. As valuable as these studies are for a better understanding of device design and for the fundamentals of human psychomotor performance, they may be of little practical value to the ergonomics analyst who, during design of an interactive system, wishes to predict human performance in a situation of real use. For example, given a task in a 3D CAD/CAM design system such as inputting the parameters for the surface of an object, how long will it take to perform with a mouse? With a joystick? Empirically-based approximations called *performance models*, which are the topic of this chapter, attempt to answer these questions.

All performance models which have been developed for human–computer interaction are based on observable and measurable human behavior, primarily in the context of work environments. Because of the universality of GUIs, these models incorporate pointing device performance. They have been most successful at predicting overall performance time for work composed of skilled, repetitive tasks. They have been less successful at predicting performance failure (error behavior), problem solving, or learning. The most important of these models are Card, Moran and Newell's GOMS and the *keystroke level model* or KLM (1980a, 1980b), and their descendants such as John's CPM–GOMS (1988) and Kieras' NGOMSL and EPIC (1988, 1995).

HCI performance models can be used at two different stages in the design and development of user interface software: to help inform the design decisions during the early stages and to evaluate the effectiveness of previously implemented or finished interfaces. The first use is termed *generative*; the second *evaluative*. Most of the researchers who have developed the models we review in this chapter have intended them to be generative. This early design use is advocated because of the difficulty of changing designs the closer one is to full programming implementation. However, an emphasis on a generative model will require a greater emphasis on ease of use. In other words, if the value of the resulting information is not worth the effort to implement the model, it will not be used by developers.

The purpose of this chapter is to present a detailed description and evaluation of the most important performance models, namely GOMS and the KLM, with particular attention paid to how they handle pointing performance. Following these descriptions, we will evaluate the current state of research extending the earlier work of GOMS and the KLM to a more detailed level of psychomotor modeling.

We begin with a discussion of the historical background of performance models in both task analysis and work measurement – concepts fundamental to all human–computer interaction performance models.

7.1 Historical Background

7.1.1 Task Analysis

Task analysis was first developed in the 1950s by human factors engineers working on the design of military systems that required complex allocation of responsibilities between the technology, such as an aircraft, and the human 'operator' – the pilot. The analysis of performance was often couched in the stimulus–response language of the behavioral psychology of the day. For example, Kidd and Van Cott (1972) describe task analysis as follows:

> Such specification covers the psychological aspects of the indication to be observed (stimulus and channel), the action required (response behavior, including decision making), the skills and knowledge required for task performance, and probable characteristic human errors and equipment malfunctions.
>
> *Kidd and Van Cott*, 1972:6

Task analysis reduces the complexity of a task into a hierarchical composition of subtasks. Thus, flying a jet plane has a subtask of controlling the jet engine operation, which itself has a subtask of adjusting engine rpm. Subtask derivation obtains information about the purpose of the task in terms of a system goal or subgoal, as well as information about the performance time.

Table 7.1: Format for task allocation and analysis (from Kidd and Van Cott, 1972:7)

Function: Operate aircraft power plant and system controls								
Task: Control jet engine operation								
Subtask	Action stimulus	Required action	Feedback	Potential errors	Time		Work-station	Skill level
					Allowable	Necessary		
Adjust engine rpm	Engine rpm on tachometer	Depress throttle control downward	Increase in indicated tachometer rpm	a. Misread tachometer b. Fail to adjust throttle to proper rpm	10s	7s	Aircraft commander seat	Low

Furthermore, Kidd and Van Cott suggest that specification of the task and subtasks should be given as an action verb and indicate the purpose in terms of a system goal or subgoal. Table 7.1 represents such task analysis.

In this task analysis most components are *prescriptive* since they are defined as part of what the system's designer envisions in the design. They define what will be expected of the human during performance using a system that has not yet been built. However, some of the elements, for example, the potential errors and skill level are also *predictive* and based on the analyst's experience. Other uses of task analysis include a *descriptive* approach in which an already existing complex system is decomposed into simpler subtasks in order to understand which components can be modified or computerized. Task analysis can be characterized as:

- hierarchical decomposition of performance into tasks and subtasks;
- specification of a task as composed of an action and a purpose (goal);
- prescription/description of task performance in terms of:
  a. perceptual input (stimulus)
  b. physical output (response)
  c. feedback
  d. time
  e. errors
  f. knowledge and skill

7.1.2 Work Measurement

Related to and in fact implicit in the development of task analysis was the technique of *work measurement*. Beginning with the early work of Frederick Taylor in the 1890s and the Gilbreths' in the 1910s, work measurement seeks to predict performance time for repetitive tasks such as those found on an assembly line. The primary purpose of prediction is to minimize overall performance time in order to reduce the cost of labor. When designing a task for an assembly line, during the late 1940s systems known as *predetermined time estimations* were developed. The most popular was *methods time measurement* (MTM) developed by Maynard (latest edition is 1992). MTM takes a task and breaks it down into 23 elementary motions such as reaching for an object or looking at a location. We must note here that these motions are not based on any psychological definitions or taxonomy. 'Reaching' is not a rapid aimed movement like a Fitts pointing task.

The time given to a particular motion was determined by analyzing film records of human motion during typical factory assembly tasks. Each motion has a predetermined time standard which is determined by the nature of the motion and conditions under which it is made. For example, the REACH motion has over 600 possible time values depending on the proper combination of distance, destination and acceleration. The MTM system would predict that a REACH to an object in a fixed location, 10 inches (254mm) away, would take 312ms. These predetermined times have been computed from an empirical database composed of tens of thousands of observations maintained and published by several international MTM associations. The accuracy of the predictions at 95% confidence limits are within ±5% at cycles[1] of 0.27 to 0.558 minutes duration (Eady, 1986).

It is estimated that to analyze a task using MTM will take as much as 150 times as long as the job takes to perform. For that reason in the 1960s, higher-level systems of basic motions were developed. The original MTM system was called MTM-1 and the higher levels, MTM-2, MTM-3, etc. The levels are compositional with lower-level motions combining to create higher level. For example, the MTM-2 motion of GET is composed of a sequence of MTM-1 motions of REACH + GRASP + RELEASE. The 23 elementary motions in the MTM-1 system are reduced to 9 in the MTM-2 system. The average length of an MTM-1 motion was empirically determined to be about 300ms; that of an MTM-2 motion is about three to four times larger.

In the standard MTM system, mental 'work' is basically restricted to the eye motions whose duration incorporates reaction times and very simple decision making. All of these are simple yes–no decisions of the type 'Do I press the foot-pedal or not?'. The introduction of true predetermined mental-process time occurred in the late 1960s with the *Detailed Work-Factor Mento Manual* (Whitmore, 1987). Basic mental processes include REACT, INSPECT, DECIDE, COMPUTE, and IDENTIFY. Unlike observable physical motions, applying mental processes to work measurement has been very problematic and it is not used extensively.

Work measurement can thus be characterized as:

- reduction of work to the notion of skilled, repetitive tasks;
- task described as a sequence of elementary perceptual and motor actions;
- each action has a mean performance time for the worker population;
- adding these times predicts overall task performance time.

Criticisms have been leveled both at predetermined time models, and at work measurement models in general. They make the assumption that each motion is independent of other motions and that a sum of the predetermined times for all motions in a sequence will validly predict the overall task time. Statistical studies do not support this assumption of independence, particularly when durations are short (Abruzzi, 1952). Rather, it is the case that workers organize motions into an integrated whole for the task. For example, when positioning and engaging a nut with a bolt, the engaging movement varies in difficulty according to ease of fit and the ability of the person to adjust to the immediate situation. This inherent variability in movement also was seen in Chapter 6. Many examples in that chapter illustrate the variation in the microstructure of movement for a single person, even though the parameters of the task varied very little – only 12 unique combinations of amplitude and width for the target. Predetermined motion estimation, particularly with constant values, fails to take this variability into account – a concern which will remain with many of the models presented in the rest of this chapter.

7.2 GOMS

A direct link can be made from this early work in task analysis and work measurement by human factors engineers to the most widely used and developed performance model for human–computer interaction, the GOMS model of Card, Moran and Newell (1980a, 1983). However, Card, Moran and Newell's work is far more ambitious since it seeks to integrate these engineering techniques with a very general model of human skill based on an information processing model of human psychology. In their landmark book published in 1983, *The Psychology of Human–Computer Interaction*, they called their approach applied information processing, for they intended not only to explain the behavior that they observed in computer users, but also to predict it with models robust enough to be used for design.

They argued that such an approach must be based on task analysis, calculation and approximation.

> When psychology is applied in the context of a specific task, much of the activity hardly seems like psychology at all, but rather like an analysis of the task itself. The reason for this is clear: humans behave in a goal-oriented way. Within their limited perceptual and information-processing abilities, they attempt to adapt to the task environment to attain their goals. Once the goals are known or can be assumed, the structure of the task environment provides a large amount of the predictive content of psychology.
>
> *Card et al., 1983:10*

Task analysis fits well with the earlier *general problem solver* (GPS) theory of Newell and Simon (1972). This theory has a commitment to the assumption that all forms of problem solving arise out of general cognitive mechanisms which are inherently based on information processing. Problem solving is generalized as a goal-directed, non-deterministic search through a symbolic representation of the problem. Newell and Simon claim the GPS model fits observations of human intelligent behavior in many tasks from architectural design, to chess playing, to proving mathematical theorems. However, in contrast to problem solving, there are other facets of human performance, namely, routine cognitive skill, which do not exhibit the non-determinism of problem-solving behavior but clearly retain the goal-directedness. The challenge for Newell and his students, Card and Moran, was to understand how routine cognitive skill could be integrated into the earlier cognitive architecture for problem solving. The result was the GOMS model.

7.2.1 Description

Fundamental to the GOMS model is a description of tasks. A GOMS description consists of Goals, Operators, Methods and Selection rules. Goals are the purpose of the task and are structured hierarchically with subgoals; operators are elementary perceptual, motor and cognitive acts; methods are sequences of operators that will achieve the goal; and selection rules are heuristics which choose between methods if more than one might apply.

An example taken from Card *et al.* (1983:216) and incorporating pointing illustrates these concepts. In the following example a skilled computer user is editing a computer-based document based on notations given on a physical copy of the manuscript. She scans the manuscript for the next editing change, which she then roughly locates with a few words; then she points (with a mouse) to those same words in the computer document but doesn't select; then she returns to the manuscript to verify the exact target; and, finally, she points and selects. A GOMS representation of this behavior follows:

```
Method for GOAL: SELECT-TARGET
   ZERO-IN-METHOD =
   while VisualSearchTarget isa #APPROXIMATE-TARGET
   do POINT-TO-TARGET (MSPosition, VisualSearchTarget, DON'T-SELECT)
      GET-FROM-MANUSCRIPT ({slot VisualSearchTarget}, PositionType)
   finally POINT-TO-TARGET (MSPosition, VisualSearchTarget, SELECT).
```

This example, called the ZERO-IN-METHOD, is one method for achieving the SELECT-TARGET. Another shorter method might be used when the user already knows the location of the pointing target and doesn't have to refer back to the manuscript. A selection rule would choose between these methods. POINT-TO-TARGET and GET-FROM-MANUSCRIPT are operators. Operators are like functions and have arguments. Visual SearchTarget includes the approximate words extracted from the manuscript and held in the user's memory. PositionType is the type of the target, which varies with the editing task. For example, deleting a segment of text requires a beginning character and an ending character. MSPosition is the user's memory of the manuscript where the editing change is to occur.

At this level of description, the operator for pointing, POINT-TO-TARGET, incorporates selecting the target. If we had a finer grain of description, the physical act of pointing would be one operator and pressing the mouse button down or up, would be another operator. This would allow distinctions between pointing and dragging actions. Likewise, GET-FROM-MANUSCRIPT, could be broken down into TURN-HEAD, SCAN-FOR-TARGET, and FIXATE-ON-TARGET. As the level of description gets finer, the operators approach elementary perceptual, motor and cognitive acts. The hierarchical representation of GOMS allows any level of description depending on the chronometric range of the operators. At the level of description illustrated, the operator POINT-TO-TARGET was estimated empirically at 1.7s, and GET-FROM-MANUSCRIPT at 2.1s.

The operator POINT-TO-TARGET has been represented in the ZERO-IN-METHOD as a direct action from looking at the manuscript to looking at the screen and pointing with the mouse. Typical document editing is more complex and may involve conditional information such as scrolling the window when looking for the target. The GOMS model accommodates this conditionality by the use of selection rule and subgoal control structures.

Selection rules can be used to describe the scrolling behavior mentioned above (Card *et al.*, 1983:217–8):

```
Selection rules for POINT-TO-TARGET:
  TOP-2/3-RULE =
   if ScreenPosition isa #MAIN-PART-OF-WINDOW
     then CHOOSE (POINT-WITHOUT-SCROLLING-METHOD)
  BOTTOM-1/3-RULE =
   if ScreenPosition isa #BOTTOM-PART-OF-WINDOW
     then CHOOSE (SCROLL-AND-POINT-METHOD)
  OFF-WINDOW-RULE =
   if ScreenPosition isa #OFF-WINDOW
     then CHOOSE (JUMP-METHOD)
```

These rules describe the conditions under which the user will select a particular method. If the target is already visible in the top two-thirds of the window, no scrolling is done; if in the bottom one-third, the user will scroll the text up in the window; and if the target is not visible at all, the user will point to the scroll bar and select discrete positions to 'jump' the text in the window.

Subgoals are another form of control structure and GOMS uses a hierarchical decomposition. We can see that the GOAL: SELECT-TARGET is itself a subgoal of a text editing goal such as GOAL: DELETE-TEXT which itself is a subgoal of a higher level GOAL: EDIT-UNIT-TASK. Each of these goals has definite methods for accomplishing them which are sequences of deterministic operators. This can be contrasted with human problem-solving behavior where there is uncertainty about which operator to apply next to achieve a goal. For this reason, skilled behavior can be seen to arise out of problem solving with the sequence of operators becoming deterministic and the methods functioning like packaged solutions.

The previous examples have demonstrated the use of the four representational types used in a GOMS description. A complete GOMS model for text editing would be a description of a particular user's behavior for many goals, subgoals, methods, operators and selection rules. As the level of abstraction becomes more fine-grained, the resulting description becomes more complex and lengthy. There is no set catalog of representational elements for GOMS nor a specific level of detail since it was primarily intended as a scientific study of the fundamentals of human cognitive skill.

Card *et al.* describe models at four major levels of operator detail: the *unit-task*, the *functional*, the *argument* and the *keystroke*. The unit-task level has operators at the level of basic manuscript-editing tasks such as delete sentence or move paragraph; the functional level breaks each unit-task into four subtasks which are get-next task, locate-change, make-change and verify-change; the argument level breaks down each of the functional tasks into operators at the level of our POINT-TO-TARGET operator in the earlier example; and the keystroke level is at basic cognitive, perceptual and motor actions such as press-mouse-button.

Pointing tasks can be represented at any level of detail. The POINT-TO-TARGET operator described in the earlier example is much more abstract than the task descriptions we have concentrated on in this book. We would have to develop much finer grained operators at the perceptual and motor level. These might be operators such as:

```
Method for GOAL: SELECT-OBJECT
  ONE-AT-A-TIME =
    LOOK-AT-TARGET (Target)
    POINT (Target, TargetDistance, TargetSize)
    CLICK-MOUSE-BUTTON (Button)

Method for GOAL: DRAG-AND-DROP
  ONE-AT-A-TIME =
    LOOK-AT-OBJECT-TO-DRAG (Target)
    POINT (Target, TargetDistance, TargetSize)
    DOWN-MOUSE-BUTTON (Button)
    LOOK-AT-DROP-TARGET (Target)
    POINT (Target, TargetDistance, TargetSize)
    UP-MOUSE-BUTTON (Button)
```

As the model represents finer and more detailed aspects of a person's behavior, the model necessarily becomes increasingly complex and much closer to the level of analysis of psychomotor movement we have described in this book. However, Card, Moran and Newell concentrated less on the perceptual motor level in favor of larger-grained behavior. The GOMS research was primarily to substantiate a skill model that was compatible with earlier work whose focus was on cognitive aspects of human behavior in problem solving tasks.

7.2.2 Validation

The GOMS model was validated by three studies (Card *et al.*, 1983, Chapter 5). The first study was of three computer text-editor users. Each participant was given 73 editing tasks on a marked-up manuscript. The first three tasks were discarded as warm-up, leaving 70 tasks for data analysis. A computer-collected log of keystrokes was synchronized with a videotape recording. After the participants completed the tasks, an analysis was made of the computer and video transcripts to derive a GOMS representation. For each participant, a set of selection rules and methods was developed.

The hypothesis first tested was that individual participants would have consistent methods and selection rules usage – that is, they would tend to favor one method over other possible methods for achieving a goal. The results showed that participants tended to have a dominant, most frequently used method, even if that method was inefficient, i.e. took more time. From two to four simple selection rules it was possible to predict a user's method selection an average of 90% of the time.

In a second study, identical in design to the first and also using three participants, Card *et al.* predicted what the sequence and duration of operators would be. They divided the data set of 70 tasks for each participant into two data sets: the derivation dataset and the cross-validation data set. The derivation data set used the odd numbered tasks in the experiment; the cross validation, the even numbered. Each participant's data sets were coded at a fairly high functional level of representation. Then the derivation data set was used to derive the participant's use of methods and selection rules. These were then used to predict the sequences in the cross-validation data set. Operator sequences were accurately predicted for all participants 88% of the time. Again, using the derivation data set to derive operator times, operator times were predicted for each operator in the entire sequence of tasks in the cross-validation data set. The average model error was 33% (root mean square (RMS) error[2]).

In the third study with only one participant, Card *et al.* report on the validity of the model at four major levels of operator detail: the unit-task, the functional, the argument and the keystroke. Again, using the derivation data to predict sequences and duration of operators in the cross-validation data, it was found that as the models became finer and finer-grained, the ability to predict became less reliable, confirming the earlier criticisms of Abruzzi (see section 7.1.2). At the functional level, sequences were predicted with about 94% accuracy; at the lowest level of the keystroke, only 60%. Reliability of predicting operator times ranged from 20–40% RMS error which is comparable to the 33% of the second study which used operators at the functional level only.

These studies were intended to validate the GOMS model in terms of the representation of the model and its ability to accurately predict sequences and durations of actions. However, GOMS was not developed to model all aspects of skilled performance. Performance failures, i.e. errors, were found to be quite frequent even among these skilled, highly practiced participants. Slightly more than 1/3 (36%) of the tasks contained errors and nearly doubled the time to perform the tasks in which they occurred. Repairing these errors consumed 26% of the total time spent on the 70 tasks. Although GOMS cannot predict when a performance failure will occur, or what type of failure it might be, skilled users already have a set of well-developed methods which will repair the problem. These are, by and large, the same GOMS methods they have already developed for routine tasks.

7.2.3 Limitations and Problems with the GOMS Model

It is important to emphasize that GOMS describes and predicts error-free, skilled, i.e. well-learned, procedural behavior, and, at that, only for a single person. It does not purport to describe or predict learning, problem-solving, decision-making or performance failure (error) although it can describe and predict repair behavior once the failure has occurred. Olson and Olson (1990), in an excellent review of GOMS modeling, point out that GOMS fails to capture the user's fatigue, individual differences, or mental workload.

There are difficulties with the Card *et al.* GOMS model validation. They had few participants (although lots of within-subjects data) and a fairly limited task environment – that of very basic text-editing. In the original research that developed the GOMS model (1980a) the task studied was text editing using a non-GUI text editor. In this editor, the user could view the text on a display but commands were typed in an abbreviated command language. Not surprisingly, total performance time was found to be 60% mental and 22% typing.

If the same study were conducted on a modern GUI interface with its numerous pointing actions, would mental time occupy such a large proportion of the observed behavior? Consider the following analysis: assume that pressing a key takes about 200ms and that Card *et al.* (1978) found the average pointing action to take about 1100ms. Then an average pointing action takes approximately five times more time than the average keying action; and if the typical GUI interface menu system requires several pointing actions to select a command, it is highly probable that a GUI editor will take much more physical time than the editor on which the GOMS model is based. This would significantly change the proportion of mental time in the overall activity.

There are also practical problems with the use of GOMS to predict performance. The hierarchical structure creates a complex and time-consuming format in which to describe human behavior. It is written in a formal language, somewhat like LISP, without a formal specification of its representation and interpretation. For that reason, it is difficult to develop a GOMS model and difficult to read one. This limits its practical use by designers in predicting user behavior such as the time to complete a task. Finally, in a complex model, it is difficult to test the model for completeness and 'bugs' in the representation, such as failing to specify a method.

7.2.4 Summary

Welford (1968) describes skilled physical motions as smooth, controlled and having an economy of effort. Card *et al.* describe the skilled computer user's behavior as 'highly organized and under the control of well-learned methods, which are quickly triggered into action by the dynamic features of the task situation.' (1983: 188). The GOMS representation captures this behavior through the analogy to computer programming. The goals and their related methods are similar to procedure calls in a computer program. From a psychological perspective they are well-learned sequences. Using an analogy of computer programming is more than a convenience: GOMS was intended as an implementable computer simulation and thus has a fairly formal representation and control structure. In other words, the GOMS model is the skilled, non-problem-solving counterpart to the earlier GPS model of problem solving.

The compelling thoroughness and ambitious scope of the research program which Card, Moran and Newell pursued in the late 1970s has made the GOMS model the unquestioned foundation for understanding performance in human–computer interaction analysis despite the limitations in its validation. This reputation came from the integration of ideas from GPS problem solving, information processing psychology, and the older heritage of task analysis in human factors engineering. Many researchers have attempted to extend GOMS to error behavior and learning and to revise the original GOMS representations to make it more suitable for designing user interfaces. These extensions are discussed in section 7.5 in this chapter. In the next section, we discuss the *keystroke level model*, Card, Moran and Newell's modification of GOMS to make it a more practical tool for designers.

7.3 Keystroke Level Model

As mentioned previously, the GOMS model is very difficult to apply in practical situations where an ergonomics analyst may wish to predict error-free perform-ance time for a task. The *keystroke level model* (KLM) is a simplification of a GOMS representation at the keystroke level of basic perceptual, motor and cogni-tive operators (Card *et al.*, 1980b; 1983). Unlike GOMS, the representational com-ponents are given and a well-specified technique is described for creating a model of behavior for a specific task. As a derivation of the GOMS model, the KLM was intended to describe and predict only well-practiced, skilled behavior. However, unlike GOMS, the KLM predicts mean performance time for an average user to execute a specified task method; it does not attempt to predict sequences of meth-ods and operators or to predict the cognitive time that it may take to acquire the task. These characteristics of the KLM are similar to the earlier work measurement techniques of the MTM described in section 7.1.2.

7.3.1 Description

A KLM analysis begins with the analyst selecting a task for which predicted task time is desired. Using the GOMS definition of unit-task, the time for the task can be written as the sum of the time to acquire the task and the time to execute it:

$$T_{unit\text{-}task} = T_{acquire} + T_{execute} \tag{7.1}$$

Acquisition times are not predicted by the KLM and depend on the types of task. For example, for manuscript editing from a marked-up page, it is about 2–3s. For a CAD/CAM design task, it is about 5–30s.

The execution time is then computed as a summation of the times of a fixed set of elementary operators. The basic operators are keystroking (**K**), pointing (**P**), homing (**H**), drawing (**D**), a mental operator (**M**), and system response time (**R**).

$$T_{execute} = T_K + T_P + T_H + T_D + T_M + T_R \tag{7.2}$$

Decisions must be made about translating observed behavior into these opera-tors. Keystroking is the basic keying operation, whether typing text characters or pressing a mouse button or function key. Pointing is using a pointing device – a mouse or joystick – to point to a target. Pointing time does not include pressing the mouse button for selection of a target. Homing is device-switching time or moving the hands to or from the pointing device and keyboard. Drawing is using a mouse to define a drawing composed of a number of straight line segments. The mental operator is the time for mentally preparing to execute the previous physi-cal operators. It involves decision-making time as well as recall or retrieval of the operators or method. System-response time is required when the user must wait for the system to respond to a particular physical action. Further definition of these operators and their predicted performance time is given in Table 7.2. As the table demonstrates, the KLM recognizes the importance of pointing devices in GUIs. Of particular note is the fact that the pointing operator is estimated at a mean of 1.1s compared to 0.2s for keying – a factor of five. In a graphical user interface, a great deal of time is spent pointing.

Table 7.2: Operators of the *keystroke level model* (from Card, Moran and Newell, 1983:264)

Operator	Description and remarks.	Time (s)
K	**Press key or button.** Pressing the SHIFT or CONTROL key counts as a separate **K** operation. Time varies with the typing skill of the user. When unknown, use rate given of average skilled typist (55 wpm).	0.20
P	**Point with mouse to target on display.** The time to point varies with distance and target size according to Fitts' law, ranging from 0.8s to 1.5s with 1.1s being an average. This operator does not include the (0.2s) button press that often follows. Mouse pointing time is also a good estimate for other efficient analogue pointing devices, such as joysticks.	1.10
H	**Home hand(s) on keyboard or other device.**	0.40
$D(n_D, l_D)$	**Draw n_D straight-line segments of total length l_D cm.** This is a very restricted operator. It assumes that drawing is done with the mouse on a system that constrains all lines to fall on a square 0.56cm grid. Users vary in their drawing skill; the time given is an average value.	$0.9n_D + 0.16l_D$
M	**Mentally prepare.**	1.35
R(t)	**Response by system.** Different commands require different response times. The response time is counted only if it causes the user to wait.	t

To illustrate the use of the KLM, an example task called, **Make_Labeled_Circle**, will be encoded. Figure 7.1 illustrates the desired drawing. The circle is drawn with a pattern and then labeled 'Target'. The task will be performed using an early version of the Macintosh MacDraw object-based graphics editor whose interface is shown in the figure below.

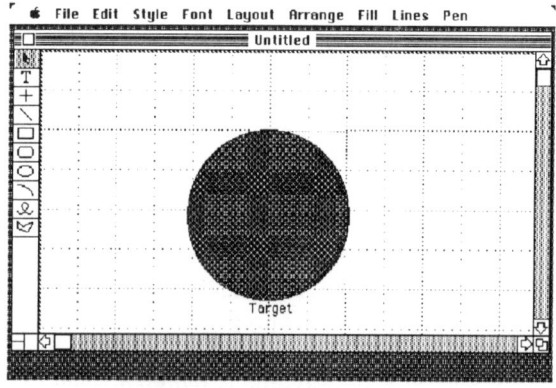

Figure 7.1: Make_Labeled_Circle screen.

The method selected for the **Make_Labeled_Circle** task is roughly described as the following unit-tasks:

Draw_Filled_Circle
Label_Circle

Unlike a GOMS representation, there is no notion of multiple methods for achieving a goal. The KLM lacks the GOMS control structure of goal hierarchy or selection rules for choosing between methods. Unlike GOMS, the KLM will only predict performance for a specific method, not the entire sequence of behavior given multiple tasks and methods. Taking the first unit-task, **Draw_Filled_Circle**, as an example, we write down the actions that the user will perform. Note that the SHIFT key must be held down when drawing a circle to distinguish it from an ellipse.

Draw_Filled_Circle

Reach for mouse from keyboard

Point to command to draw circle (icon looks like an ellipse)

Select icon (click mouse button)

Point to Fill on menu bar

Select menu (press and hold mouse button down)

Drag (Pull Down) menu to Pattern menu item

Select Pattern menu item (release mouse button)

Press and hold down SHIFT key (for a true circle, not ellipse)

Point to position in drawing for perimeter of circle

Press and hold mouse button down

Draw diameter of circle (5cm)

Release mouse button and SHIFT key

Next the task is written out using the elementary operators **K**, **P**, **H**, and **D**. Mental and system response operators are placed later.

Draw_Filled_Circle

Reach for mouse from keyboard	H
Point to command to draw circle	P
Select icon (click mouse button)	K
Point to Fill on menu bar	P
Select menu (press and hold mouse button down)	K
Drag (Pull Down) menu to Pattern menu item	P
Select Pattern menu item (release mouse button)	K
Press and hold down SHIFT key	K
Point to position in drawing for perimeter of circle	P
Press and hold mouse button down	K
Draw diameter of circle (5cm)	D
Release mouse button and SHIFT key	K

This is the sequence of physical actions to achieve **Draw_Filled_Circle**. A minor decision had to be made about how to handle the pull-down menu. The analyst decided that the dragging should be represented by a pointing and two keying operators for the mouse button press, hold, and release. The original KLM does not specify how to handle pull-down menu operations or dragging. We have also introduced a **K̶**, which signifies that there is a keystroke, i.e. a released key, but that its time is counted when the key is originally pressed down. Note also that there is no way in the KLM to handle a 'differently-handed', parallel release of both the mouse button and the SHIFT key on the keyboard, except as a single action. In other words, both the KLM and GOMS can only describe one stream of sequential actions.

There are no waiting periods for system response, but the mental operators need to be added. Table 7.3 is the list of heuristic rules used for placing mental operators. Card *et al.* developed these rules as heuristics since they could not discover theoretically or empirically a deterministic (causal) method for locating where a cognitive 'action' occurs in a pattern of physical and perceptual actions.

Table 7.3: Heuristic rules for placing the M operators (from Card *et al.*, 1983:265)

Begin with a method of encoding that includes all physical operations and response operations. Use Rule 0 to place candidate Ms, and then cycle through Rules 1 to 4 for each M to see whether it should be deleted.	
Rule 0	Insert Ms in front of all Ks that are not part of argument strings proper (e.g., text or numbers). Place Ms in front of all Ps that select commands (not arguments).
Rule 1	If an operator following an M is *fully anticipated* in an operator just previous to M, then delete the M (e.g., PMK⟹PK).
Rule 2	If a string of MKs *belongs to a cognitive unit* (e.g., the name of a command) then delete all Ms but the first.
Rule 3	If a K is a *redundant terminator* (e.g., the terminator of a command immediately following the terminator of its argument), then delete the M in front of it.
Rule 4	If a K *terminates a constant string* (e.g., a command name), then delete the M in front of it; but if the K terminates a variable string (e.g., an argument string), then keep the M in front of it.

Beginning with heuristic Rule 0 given in Table 7.3, the analyst places candidate mental operators in the method where Ks and Ps are located. Rule 0 places mental operators in front of all Ks that do not enter text or numbers. In our example, an M is placed before a mouse button K. (The K̶s are ignored.) Using Rule 0 requires that a decision be made about the structure of the commands since Ms are placed in front of all Ps which select commands (actions). We have decided that there are three separate commands in this method: selecting an icon command, selecting a pattern, and drawing a circle.

Draw_Filled_Circle

Reach for mouse from keyboard	H
Select command icon:	
Point to command to draw circle	MP
Select icon (click mouse button)	MK
Select pattern:	
Point to Fill on menu bar	MP
Select menu (press and hold mouse button down)	MK

Drag (Pull Down) menu to Pattern menu item   P
Select Pattern menu item (release mouse button)   K̶

Draw circle:
Press and hold down SHIFT key   MK
Point to position in drawing for perimeter of circle   P
Press and hold mouse button down   MK
Draw diameter of circle (5cm)   D
Release mouse button and SHIFT key   K̶

An alternative parsing is possible. The entire method could be seen as one action (command): the draw circle command. This single command has two operands: one to select the pattern, and another to specify the parameters of the size of the circle. If that were the case, there would only be one mental operator at the beginning of the pointing operator for selecting the draw circle icon. The KLM was originally developed for simple, typed-command languages, which usually had a simple syntactic structure of action [object, modifiers]. A GUI interface syntax may often specify the object first in the syntax and then the command. Command specification may also be much more complex than typing in two or three characters – such as selecting a command from a pull-down menu.

After placing all candidate Ms in the method, Rules 1 to 4 are applied. In the **Draw_Filled_Circle** method Rule 1 is applied to delete three Ms from the mouse button press after pointing, since the key presses are fully anticipated in the pointing operator. The method now has the following operators:

Draw_Filled_Circle

Reach for mouse from keyboard   H

Select command icon:
Point to command to draw circle   MP
Select icon (click mouse button)   M̶K

Select pattern:
Point to Fill on menu bar   MP
Select menu (press and hold mouse button down)   M̶K
Drag (Pull Down) menu to Pattern menu item   P
Select Pattern menu item (release mouse button)   K̶

Draw circle:
Press and hold down SHIFT key   MK
Point to position in drawing for perimeter of circle   P
Press and hold mouse button down   M̶K
Draw diameter of circle (5cm)   D
Release mouse button and SHIFT key   K̶

Substituting in Equation 7.2, the predicted time to execute this method is:

$$T_{execute} = 4T_K + 4T_P + 1T_H + 1T_D + 3T_M \qquad (7.3)$$

Multiplying by the times given in Table 7.2 is:

$$T_{execute} = (4 \times 0.2) + (4 \times 1.1) + (1 \times 0.4) + (0.9 + (0.16 \times 5cm)) + (3 \times 1.35) \qquad (7.4)$$

giving a predicted total time of:

$$T_{execute} = 11.35s \qquad (7.5)$$

The KLM technique is applied to the second unit-task, **Label_Circle**:

Label_Circle
Select command icon:
Point to command to create text (icon looks like a T)   **MP**
Select icon (click mouse button)   **MK**
Position label:
Point to position in drawing for beginning of text   **MP**
Select position (click mouse button)   **MK**
Reach for keyboard from mouse   **H**
Type word 'Target'   **6K**

Substituting in Equation 7.2, the predicted time to execute this method is:

$$T_{execute} = 8T_K + 2T_P + 1T_H + 2T_M \qquad (7.6)$$

Multiplying by the times given in Table 7.2 is:

$$T_{execute} = (8 \times 0.2) + (2 \times 1.1) + (1 \times 0.4) + (2 \times 1.35) \qquad (7.7)$$

giving a predicted total time for labeling the circle of:

$$T_{execute} = 6.9s \qquad (7.8)$$

The task-execution time for the whole task of drawing and labeling the circle is predicted at 18.25s by summing the two unit-task execution times (Equations 7.5 and 7.3). There is some variability in writing a KLM method as discussed above, so there are really a range of predictions depending on where Ms are placed, etc. Variability from variance in users' behavior is also ignored. (The times for operators in the KLM can be considered means of a normal distribution.) We have also ignored the task-acquisition time, which is not predicted by the KLM, but must be estimated by the analyst. In the next section, we discuss how the KLM was validated and how our prediction for the **Make_Labeled_Circle** task compares to data collected experimentally.

7.3.2 Validating the KLM

A validation study was done by Card *et al.* (1980b, 1983) using 1280 user–system–task interactions. The data came from 28 different participants, 10 different computer systems, and 14 tasks. The systems included three different text editors (four tasks each), three different graphics editors (five tasks each), and five different file-management systems (one task each). For each task–system combination, the most 'natural' method was coded in KLM operations and total task-time computed. This predicted time was compared to the observed time of the participants. The average RMS error for all tasks was 21%, about the same as the prediction error for the GOMS model at the keystroke level. Since the standard (sampling) error[3] was about 9%, the rest of the prediction error, i.e. 12%, is due to a failure of the model to predict accurately. The average coefficient of variation[4] for the tasks is 0.31 which is expected for tasks averaging about 8s in duration and composed of sequences of operators (Abruzzi, 1952; 1956).

The KLM appears to be a fairly robust performance model for predicting well-practiced, skilled, error-free performance time for tasks whose operators, including pointing operators, fit the empirical constraints of the model.

7.3.3 Caveats Concerning Pointing Devices in the KLM

This book has repeatedly raised concerns about context-free prediction that ignores the complex interrelationships between types and characteristics of pointing devices and task environments. The KLM ignores these differences. Thus, concerns are raised about applying the KLM definitions and times for the KLM actions to the operators for pointing, homing and drawing tasks.

7.3.3.1 Pointing

The average pointing operator time is taken from experimental data in a study of pointing device performance by Card, English and Burr (1978). The results of the study found that pointing with a mouse could be described by the Welford version of the Fitts' law equation:

$$MT = 1.03 + 0.096 \, log_2\left(D/S + 0.5\right) \tag{7.9}$$

This equation includes the mouse button press for selecting the target. Card, Moran and Newell (1980b, 1983) use this equation to derive the pointing operator time in the KLM by subtracting a keying time of 0.2s from the intercept of 1.03s. This gives a new equation of:

$$MT = 0.8 + 0.1 \, log_2\left(D/S + 0.5\right) \tag{7.10}$$

However, what is needed is a mean pointing time for the operator without having to compute the Fitts' law equation for every distance/size combination in a task which may be time-consuming, if not impossible. (Note that in a GUI style of interface the 'user is in control' and it may often be impossible to compute the distance since the starting location of the cursor is unpredictable.) Card et al. arrive at the value of 1.1s for the pointing operator by taking the mean time of 1.3s for practiced pointing with a mouse from the 1978 experiment and subtracting 0.2s for the mouse button press. Since this data is experimentally derived from a combination of distance/size targets, it is important to understand that the mean time of the pointing operator is dependent on the range of those combinations. In the 1978 experiment, target distances were set at 10, 20, 40, 80, and 160mm. Target sizes were 1, 2, 4, or 10 characters. This gives sizes of 2, 4, 8 and 20mm. (The actual sizes are not given in the experimental description. We assume for this example that a character is 2mm for 12-point Times Roman, although it depends on the type of font and the pixel resolution.) Thus the most difficult target is 160mm away and 2mm (1 character) in size, for an index of difficulty of:

$$log_2(D/S+0.5) = log_2(160/2+0.5) \approx 6 \qquad (7.11)$$

The easiest target is 10mm away and 20mm (10 characters) in size, for an index of difficulty of:

$$log_2(D/S+0.5) = log_2(10/20+0.5) = 0 \qquad (7.12)$$

In other words, 1.1s mean pointing time is the mean for pointing tasks equally distributed in the range from 0 to 6 in index of difficulty. A specific set of tasks may have a much shorter pointing time because either the range or the distribution of distances or widths varies considerably from this assumption. Similarly, as computer screens become larger and pointing tasks cover larger distances, the pointing operator time of 1.1s in the KLM may under-predict averaged pointing task time.

A second difficulty in applying the pointing operator is the assumption that mouse pointing time is also a good estimate for other efficient analogue pointing devices, such as joysticks. In Chapter 4 we saw that for many different comparison experiments, joysticks are typically less efficient than mice. In Chapter 5 we saw that an isometric finger-controlled joystick was about 60% slower than a mouse for pointing and about 50% slower for dragging. We recommend that different operators for pointing with different types of devices be developed based on experimental studies of pointing device performance.

7.3.3.2 Homing

Homing time, as used in the KLM, is taken from the Card *et al.* (1978) experiment. Homing time is what we have called device-switching time in this book – see Chapter 3, section 3.3.1.4. The homing operator is the mean of the times participants spent reaching from the keyboard to the mouse: 0.36s. In the KLM, homing time is rounded to 0.4s and assumed to be the same for any pointing device. It is easy to conceive of situations where this assumption might not be reasonable. An example is device-switching between different limbs such as a pointing device controlled by the foot and typing done with the hands. Also, as we saw in Chapter 5, some devices such as the key joystick do not have a true device-switching time. They mode-switch between pointing and typing. The KLM fails to distinguish device switching of a device from mode switching. For the key joystick whose performance was assessed in Chapter 5, the mode-switching time was 0.4s – a time which would (somewhat fortuitously) be accurately estimated by the KLM homing operator. However, there may be other devices that would have a lesser or even greater time.

A second problem which must be addressed is that the KLM assumes a homing operator of 0.4s for movement from the keyboard to the pointing device and back. As we saw in the study in Chapter 5, device-switching time for reaching from the mouse back to the keyboard was 0.7s, almost 75% more time than the current homing operator estimates. That this return movement would take longer is predicted by Fitts' law, since a key on the keyboard is a smaller target than the mouse.

7.3.3.3 Drawing

Finally, drawing in the current KLM is quite limited. It assumes the mouse as the drawing device and a specific grid metric. Studies cited in Chapter 4 strongly suggest that the stylus used on a graphic tablet is the most natural and efficient drawing device, with the isometric, velocity-controlled joystick one of the least. For the KLM to be useful, operators for these and other drawing devices need to be estimated empirically.

7.3.3.4 Other Pointing Tasks

Currently, the KLM assumes three GUI tasks for pointing devices: namely pointing, drawing and device switching. To be widely applicable, the KLM needs to be extended to dragging and, possibly, to tracking. In this chapter, we have followed the conventional use of the KLM and modeled the dragging task as a pointing operator with a mouse button keying operator. However, the experimental studies show true dragging tasks to be slower than pointing. While tracking is not a common GUI task and has limited implementation in game environments, the KLM should be extended to include it. Finally, extending the KLM into three-dimensional tasks, such as virtual reality, is an open research topic.

7.3.4 Summary

We have described the KLM as a simplification of GOMS that establishes a technique for calculating total task time for average expert users. The KLM retains only the operators and methods of GOMS and establishes predetermined times of performance for a fixed set of operators.[5] Card *et al.* intended the KLM as a practical design tool to help developers predict overall task time for an average expert user given a particular interface. A typical design use would be to help decide between two possible interfaces, one using an icon panel, the other pull-down menus. Using a common set of core tasks, the designer would write the KLMs for both interfaces and compare the overall predicted performance time. A second type of use would be to analyze an existing method which is known to be too time-consuming to see if faster operators could be substituted.

In many ways the KLM is the HCI version of work measurement tools (such as MTM) used by industrial engineers to estimate time for repetitive factory tasks. Paralleling the usefulness and eventual widespread acceptance of the MTM system, we would expect to see the same with the KLM. However, few applications of use are reported in the literature and few HCI researchers have joined the effort to build a database of empirical data and refine the basic operators. (See section 7.5.3 for a review of those few). Based on the lack of published studies, we can assume that it is not in widespread use. It may be that it is still far too time-consuming to develop a KLM representation of a complete interactive system to justify the results. It may be that constructing a model and use of the operators, particularly the mental operator, are not well understood. It is also the case that designers are not concerned with user task time, and are more directed toward increasing functionality. The lack of applications of the KLM is unfortunate, because the KLM is probably the best-validated, and easiest to understand performance model. In the remaining sections of this chapter we will review these issues as we examine related research on performance models.

7.4 Stochastic Network Models

An alternate representation for the methods of the keystroke level model or GOMS is a state transition network. Arcs of the network can be labeled with the elementary actions of the KLM and given time values. Nodes can represent the mental states of the user such as executing a selected method. A path through the network represents a sequence of methods. It is relatively easy to show the alternate methods, such as in a GOMS model, and method selection probabilities can be assigned to arc transitions. The pictorial nature of the network readily allows an analyst to check the completeness and correctness of the KLM methods.

A more powerful computational device, the *recursive transition network* (RTN), can represent the goal (and therefore method) hierarchies of GOMS. *The augmented transition network* (ATN), which allows state information to be passed from state-to-state, is an even more powerful computational representation. RTNs and ATNs are often used to represent the user interaction level in an interface. One of the first such efforts was that of Jacob (1983, 1985, 1986). Figure 7.2 illustrates an ATN representation of the same **Draw_Filled_Circle** task used in section 7.3. In the figure, the nodes represent the goal structure of the hypothetical user. We see in the figure that there are three major subtasks, Select Circle Icon, Select Pattern, and Draw Circle. In the KLM, each of these states would be preceded by a mental operator. In the figure, two of them, Select Pattern and Draw Circle, are represented by double-circle nodes indicating that they are recursively defined. The lower boxes for these subtasks show the detailed actions.

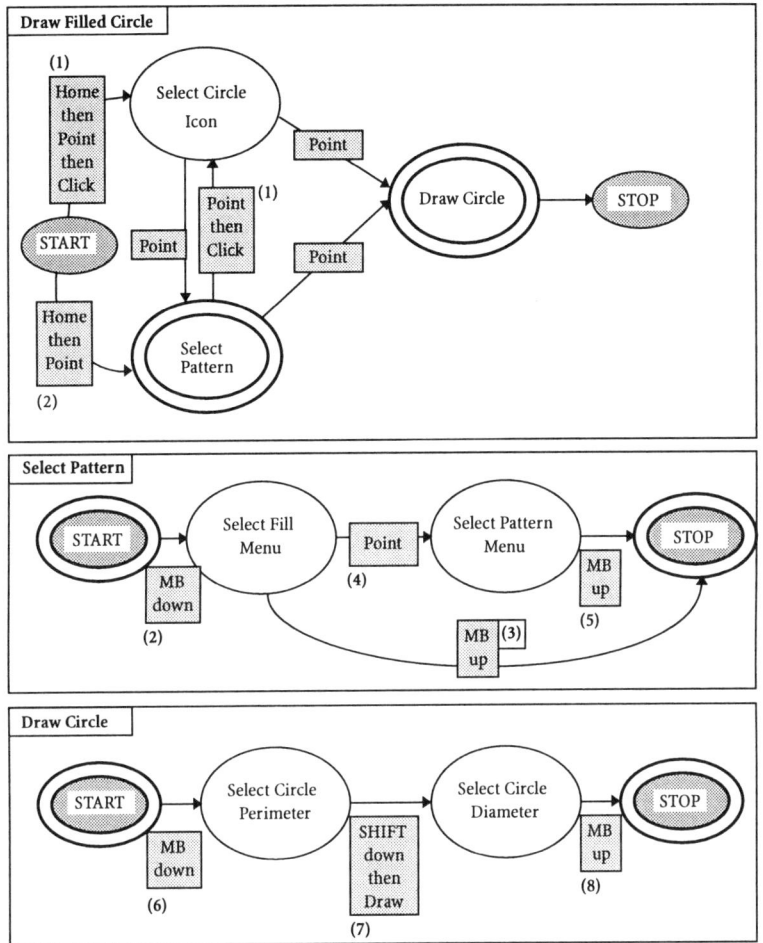

Figure 7.2: Network model for Draw_Filled_Circle task.

The transition net is read by beginning at START and following a path of directed arcs until reaching a STOP node. Figure 7.2 demonstrates the alternate paths a hypothetical user could take in drawing a filled circle: choosing the pattern first, choosing the circle icon, then drawing; or choosing the circle icon, then the pattern, then drawing; or finally, skipping the pattern selection because the desired pattern was already selected. Each arc specifies the KLM physical action primitives. MB down is 'mouse button down' and represents a *key* operator. Dragging is represented by a *point* with the mouse button held down as in the earlier example.

The arcs are annotated with numbers in parentheses which denote condition-action pairs used by Jacob in his state transition diagram language (1985). Similar to the preconditions and post-conditions of a production rule, each condition-action pair describes:

1. *conditions* which are actions by the user;

2. *responses* by the user interface software resulting in a perceptible change to the user interface;

3. possible *actions* that will be executed by the application program.

Table 7.4 defines the condition–action pairs for the **Draw_Filled_Circle** task illustrated in Figure 7.2.

Table 7.4: Condition–action pairs for **Draw_Filled_Circle** network

(1)	Condition	Point to Draw_Circle Icon and MB key click
	Response	Move cursor on screen and highlight icon
	Action	CURRENT_TOOL($Draw_Circle)
(2)	Condition	Point to 'Fill' on menubar and MB key down
	Response	Move cursor on screen, Highlight 'Fill' menu, Display 'Fill' drop-down menu
(3)	Condition	MB key up
	Response	Hide menu and unhighlight 'Fill' menu
(4)	Condition	Point to pattern
	Response	Move cursor on screen; show selected pattern in Current Pattern Rectangle
(5)	Condition	MB key up
	Response	Hide menu, unhighlight 'Fill'
	Action	CURRENT_PATTERN($Selected_Pattern)
(6)	Condition	Point and MB key down
	Response	Move cursor on screen, display XY location when MB down
	Action	DRAWCIRCLE(Point1 ← XY, Point2)
(7)	Condition	SHIFT key down and Draw
	Response	Display rubberbanded circle
	Action	DRAWCIRCLE(Point1 ← XY, Point2 ← dynamic) and
		INVERTCIRCLE(Point1 ← XY, Point2 ← dynamic)
(8)	Condition	MB key up
	Response	Display completed circle
	Action	DRAWCIRCLE(Point1 ← XY, Point2 ← WZ)

A Jacob's type of state transition network can be represented as a directed graph. All types of state transition networks are formally equivalent to different types of grammars. A computer-based interpreter can be written that uses the network specification and the condition–action pairs to simulate the interface. (In fact, Jacob used this specification language to generate implemented code for a target machine.) During this simulation, it is relatively easy to compute times for the KLM operators and to compute task-performance time for a particular path through the network.

7.5 Extensions to the GOMS Model Research

After the publication of the Card *et al.* (1983) work integrating task analysis and work measurement concepts with a psychological model based on cognition as information processing, a number of researchers attempted to substantiate and extend the GOMS model and its cognitive engineering agenda. These research activities can be grouped roughly into four areas: (1) efforts to apply the GOMS model to behavior not covered previously: namely errors and learning; (2) efforts to more accurately model perceptual, cognitive and motor processing; (3) efforts to validate the predictions of GOMS in new domains of interactive software; and (4) efforts to simplify the usability of GOMS as a design tool.

7.5.1 Modeling Performance Errors and Learning in GOMS

Robertson (1983) showed how error and error recovery could be incorporated in a GOMS-like analysis. Polson and Kieras (1985), Kieras and Polson (1985) and Bovair, Kieras and Polson (1990) developed a production system simulation of GOMS principally to predict learning behavior in a transfer of training paradigm for text editing. After representing the GOMS elements as production rules, they tested the theory that the number of productions necessary to perform text-editing tasks is a good predictor of the time it takes to learn a new text-editing system. They also predicted differences in time to learn a second text editor, given similarities and differences in the procedural knowledge captured as production rules. A major difficulty with this approach is that there are many functionally equivalent sets of production rules and no one 'right' representation. This influences the number of productions and consequently the estimation of cognitive complexity.

7.5.2 Modeling Perceptual, Cognitive and Motor Processing

Three major research projects have attempted to build on and refine the performance model research done by Card *et al.* with GOMS and KLM. The trend with all three has been to push the level of modeling to an even finer-grained analysis of perceptual, cognitive and motor processing. Their goal is to more accurately model actual human performance to increase the reliability of predictions. We will review those three projects in this section. The first is John's CPM–GOMS model, the second Jagacinski's two-level model, and the last is Kieras' EPIC model.

7.5.2.1 CPM–GOMS

The most significant research work extending the theory – and application – of GOMS modeling is that of John (1988) with a model called CPM–GOMS. CPM–GOMS directly models the perceptual, cognitive, and motor processors proposed in the information processing theory of Card *et al.* (1983) on which GOMS is based. A significant theoretical contribution of this model is its ability to handle parallel operators. In order to easily introduce this parallelism into the GOMS model, John represents the activities of each processor as a scheduling network used in engineering project management. CPM stands for two concepts. The first is Cognitive Perceptual and Motor processors; the second, Critical Path Method, which is a method of analyzing the schedule of a network of activities for the dependencies due to time constraints. The critical path is the sequence of activities that gives the minimal total time for the task.

Modeling of the perceptual, cognitive and motor processors is done in the following ways. The perceptual processors have visual and auditory operators (activities). The motor processors have right-hand, left-hand, verbal and eye-movement operators, which are *saccade* and *fixate*. The cognitive processor has only one basic cognitive operator. In general, the processors work in parallel with each other, but individual types of activities of each are sequentially ordered. The individual operator activities are the familiar elements of the low-level (keystroke) GOMS operators. For example, the motor processor can have concurrently ordered activities of pressing the SHIFT key with the left hand while pressing a sequence of letter keys with the right hand while the auditory perceptual processor listens to the name given by a caller. The operator durations in CPM–GOMS tend to be very low-level and range from about 50–300ms.

CPM–GOMS is the result of an ambitious research program to validate the GOMS theory of human procedural skill. By refining the operators of the various perceptual, cognitive and motor processors, and by modeling their activities in a direct stochastic manner, John has argued that CPM–GOMS is sufficient to describe interactive tasks in many domains from routine telephone operator tasks (Gray *et al.*, 1993) to real-time, dynamic video games (John and Vera, 1992).

Although the CPM–GOMS model theoretically accommodates motor processing for pointing tasks, none of the published research by John and colleagues specifically analyzes pointing; focusing instead on keying operations as the main motor activity. That research must be done and must be based on detailed psychomotor studies at a level of description on the order of 50–300ms. Since the CPM–GOMS model incorporates eye movements, the complex interrelationships between visual feedback and pointing will have to be modeled directly.

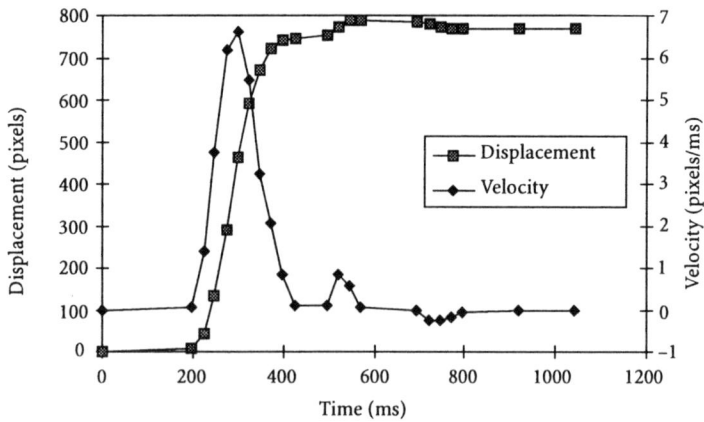

Figure 7.3: Microstructure of pointing movement (1100ms).

We now present a first attempt at a CPM–GOMS model of pointing based on microstructure of movement research from Chapter 6. In that chapter, we presented a typical mouse pointing movement of 1100ms which consisted of three submovements and is well described by the SOS model of movement. Figure 7.3 illustrates the temporal course of motor activity for that pointing movement. We can see that for the first 200ms there is almost no movement. Then, there is a large, rapid submovement, followed by two smaller submovements each preceded by a pause of 100ms.

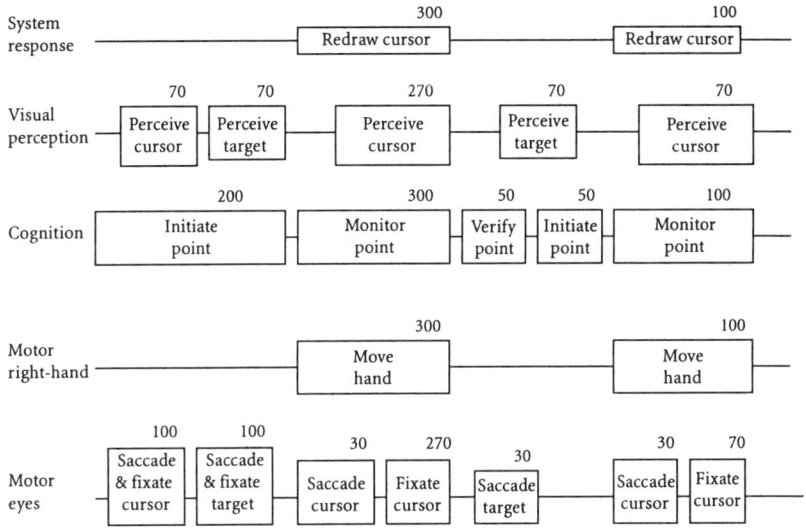

Figure 7.4: CPM–GOMS for Point (first 700ms).

Figure 7.4 is a CPM–GOMS representation of the previous figure for the first 700ms of the pointing movement. Following the SOS model, this movement consists of three submovements and a mouse button click; the figure shows the first two pointing submovements. We have added hypothetical information about various perceptual, and cognitive processing based on the current understanding of psychomotor research. Time is read from left to right. The top horizontal line is system-response time and the next horizontal lines in Figure 7.4 each represent activities in the multiple processors: *Visual-perception, Cognitive, Motor-right hand,* and *Motor-eye movement.* The duration of each activity is the number placed at the upper-right corner of the activity's box.

As the figure shows, the cognitive processor initiates pointing for 200ms during which the motor control for the eyes is directed to look at the cursor, which is then perceived visually, then motor control for the eyes is directed to look at the target, which is then perceived visually, then a motor movement of the right hand initiates the first ballistic submovement lasting 300ms during which the eyes track the cursor. After this first submovement, there is a cognitive activity of 50ms during which the person verifies that the target has not been achieved and a·50ms cognitive initiation of the second submovement, followed by a motor movement of the right hand of 100ms which is continuously monitored and tracked by the cognitive and visual processes.

The processors overlap in activity (parallelism) as well as synchronize sequentially. The critical path would be determined by the initial cognitive process, then the visual perception, then the first submovement of motor activity, then the cognitive verification, then the second cognitive initiation, and finally the second submovement of motor activity. Summing those activity durations gives a critical path of 700ms. (*Note*: a second, parallel critical path is the activities of the cognitive processor which is also 700ms.)

7.5.2.2   Jagacinski's Two-level Model

Jagacinski *et al.* (1987) have proposed a model of movement control that integrates a (rule-based) GOMS-type of representation with (skilled) motor functioning. In their model, movement is represented as activity states with start–stop rules and associated motion generators. The start–stop rules determine when a particular motion-generating process is activated and when it is interrupted or terminated. The motion generators determine the spatio–temporal patterning of the movement.

Based on empirical data gathered during a tracking task experiment, they describe the participants' behavior as consisting of four activity states: *reaction time, close following, fast acquisition*, and *predictive response*. The following is an example of an activity state for close following taken from Jagacinski *et al.* (1987):

Start–stop rules
Goal: Follow closely
Activation: When tracking error < 0.65 cm
Termination: When tracking error < 0.1cm for 0.4 seconds

Motion generator
Input: Target position and target velocity 150ms and 300ms into the past and error and error velocity
Output: Cursor position
Control law: Position cursor at the damped-sinusoid-plus-offset estimation of current target position, and closed-loop error nulling by a high-gain crossover model with lead and slight velocity limiting

From these definitions and the participants' empirical data, Jagacinski *et al.* constructed Markov state transition networks of these activities, their durations, their transitions and transition probabilities. To test their theory of two-level control, they implemented each activity state as set of start–stop rules and motion generators in a computer simulation that presented the tasks of the human experiment. The simulation then generated a state transition network which they compared to that of the human participants. The simulation network was qualitatively evaluated for similarities and differences with the human participants' performance.

Generally, it accurately represented the overall episodic quality of the participants' trajectories. However, it was only as good as the worst participant on the most difficult target. They suggest that the model needs more heuristic knowledge about capturing targets whose trajectories exhibit non-linearity.

The Jagacinski *et al.* model for tracking tasks is an important step in integrating motor control into cognitive activity. But general performance models of pointing for human computer interaction tasks will require much more complex representation and control in cognition. Such a model should include modeling relationships between the mental operations of intention, categorization, and planning, and the motor control of pointing.

7.5.2.3 EPIC

Building on the CPM–GOMS work and that of the earlier work of Kieras and Polson with production system models, Kieras has recently begun to develop a new engineering model for human performance called EPIC (Kieras *et al.*, 1995). EPIC incorporates many recent theoretical and empirical results about human performance in the form of a computer simulation framework. Given external stimuli, the model will execute procedures as a simulation of a human performing the task; the simulation purports to predict the time course of action.

In a similar structure to CPM–GOMS, the EPIC architecture represents perceptual, motor and cognitive processors. There are separate perceptual processors for visual and auditory information and separate motor processors for vocal, manual and oculomotor (eye) movements. There are feedback pathways from the motor processors as well as tactile feedback from the effectors, which are important in coordinating multiple tasks. The cognitive processor has a working memory, production memory and long-term memory as well as a production rule interpreter. The distinct time-processing characteristics of these processors are directly modeled and parallel.

EPIC represents the hands as a single manual processor which are normally operated either one at a time, or synchronized with each other. Input to the motor processors is symbolic and represented as a symbolic name for the desired movement or movement feature. EPIC thus models the open-loop system of programmed motor control (see section 2.3) which most psychologists believe represents a general model for the motor system (Rosenbaum, 1991). The effectors can be directly initiated to perform the movement, or preprogrammed if the movement can be anticipated. The latter allows movements to be made as early as is logically possible. This advance preparation can save 100–250ms and allows modeling of preprocessing in motor movement.

EPIC models pointing movement directly in the following manner (Kieras, 1995). To simulate a motor movement of a specific limb, the cognitive processor commands the motor processor to make an aimed movement of a specified limb to a specified object. The motor processor computes the required movements in terms of features and carries it out. The features involved are movement style (point), hand, finger, direction and extent (distance) to object. Direction and extent are essentially polar coordinates from the current position as origin to the target. Subsequent movements can reuse features that don't change. The total time to complete the movement involves the time to generate the features, to initiate the movement, and to execute the actual physical movement itself. Physical movement duration is computed using Welford's version of Fitts' law, using a set of coefficients and a physiological minimum duration of 100ms. Concurrent with the motor processing of aimed movement is the coordination of cognitive processing and the use of the eyes. In the EPIC model, the eye is moved to the target of the movement no later than when the movement is initiated by the motor processor for the limb.

EPIC was tested for its ability to predict execution times with multiple versions of motor activity from a straight GOMS model of sequential motor operators to a fully parallel model that had movements made as far in advance as possible. A fully parallel model anticipates keystrokes by moving the hand to the location of the key in advance and then actuating the keystroke at the appropriate place in the sequence of keystrokes. The results of the test show that highly optimized models – such as the fully-parallel advance-movement model – did not fit the data as well as a simpler parallel model. Kieras *et al.* conclude that while users take advantage of the parallel preparation and execution capabilities of their motor processors to speed up their performance, they make little use of pre-positioning the eyes and hands in advance. The simpler parallel model was able to predict total task execution times to within 7% average absolute error. Using the same tasks, Kieras *et al.* also tested a KLM prediction of task time and found that it predicted to within 28%, the usually reported range for that model.

7.5.3   GOMS Validation and Extension to Non-text-editing Domains

In addition to research done by John, Jagacinski, and Kieras extending GOMS and the KLM into a finer-grained modeling of perceptual, cognitive and motor performance, there has been some research effort to further validate GOMS (and its derivative the KLM) and the whole approach of performance modeling. Most of this latter effort has been directed at extension into task domains other than text editing in which the bulk of the GOMS work was validated. In this section we will review studies by Olson and Nilsen applying the KLM to spreadsheet tasks; Gray, John and Atwood applying CPM–GOMS to telephone operator tasks; Gong and Kieras to CAD tasks; and Haunold and Kuhn applying the KLM to map digitizing tasks. Both the Olson and Nilsen, and the Haunold and Kuhn studies propose adding new operators to the KLM. The Gong and Kieras study found the KLM pointing operator consistently overestimated pointing time. The Haunold and Kuhn study proposed adding another pointing operator to the existing KLM model.

7.5.3.1   Spreadsheet Software Tasks

The first major study extending and validating the GOMS and the KLM model to
another task domain appears to be that of Olson and Nilsen (1988). The domain
was spreadsheet software, a cognitively-intense task. The experiment used two
groups of seven participants each. One group was composed of Lotus 1-2-3 expert
users; the other Multiplan expert users. They performed four tasks over a period of
from one to two hours. The KLM methods were matched to the actual performance and a new operator called scanning, S, was created to better account for
mental time. This operator with a mean duration of 2.29s was added whenever a
spreadsheet coordinate had to be typed. The absolute difference was computed
between the original KLM predicted total task time for both spreadsheet programs, the modified KLM predicted time, and the mean actual time. The original
KLM model prediction differed by 3.4s or 32% of the actual time. The modified
KLM model (with S operators) differed by 2.7s or 26%. In matching the predicted
times for a method to each individual participant's task time, the original KLM
predicted 70% of the variance, and the operator times taken from actual times in
this study predicted 83%.

7.5.3.2   Telephone Operator Tasks

A study published by Gray *et al.* (1993) did an extensive evaluation of CPM–GOMS
models for predicting toll and assistance telephone operator (TAO) task times for
the NYNEX corporation. The purpose of the study was to aid in a decision of
whether or not to install a new workstation for these operators. The TAO tasks are
very routinized and without multiple methods for tasks, i.e. there are no GOMS
selection rules.

The current TAO tasks were studied by videotaping experts, creating CPM–
GOMS methods for the tasks, and then comparing the predicted GOMS times to
the actual times. The difference, 3%, was minimal as was expected since the methods were predicting data from which they were derived. The time to perform the
same tasks on the new workstation was predicted by creating CPM–GOMS methods and using the times prescribed by the model. The new workstation was predicted to be slower by 0.63s than the current one, at an increased cost of $2million
a year. (NYNEX computed costs at $3million per second for humans performing
TAO tasks.) A field study was then conducted with 24 TAOs using each workstation as part of their normal work. The study lasted four months and collected
on-line data on 78,240 calls.

The results of the field study showed that for the average call on the average
month, the proposed workstation required 1.05s more time than the current one.
Comparing the CPM–GOMS prediction of total time to the actual field study data
showed a 11.3% difference for the current workstation and 11.87% for the proposed workstation. For each task, CPM–GOMS was able to predict about 70% of
the variance. Furthermore, the analysis demonstrated why the new workstation
was slower, which was in replacing keying operations by pointing.

7.5.3.3 CAD Tasks

Recent work by Gong and Kieras (1994) applies the practiced execution time and learning predictions of both the original GOMS and the Kieras and Polson production rule model to a new, more realistic domain – that of a specialized CAD program. After a GOMS analysis, the original system was redesigned to reduce predicted execution time by 39%. Both the original and revised systems were tested experimentally, with 21 participants assigned randomly to one of the two conditions.

Comparisons were made between the predicted and actual execution times for a task and the learning times. In relative execution time, the predicted mean of 39% improvement was upheld by an actual mean improvement of 40%. However, the model failed to predict actual absolute task execution times, in most cases overpredicting time by a factor of two.

Gong and Kieras suggest two issues that may account for the failure to accurately predict absolute task time. The first is that the time for the pointing operator (1.1s) assumed by GOMS and the KLM was consistently inaccurate. They used Fitts' law to estimate the mouse-move times for their task, and found values ranging from 0.1s to 0.5s. (Not enough details are given in the published paper to determine how they computed the Fitts' law coefficients.) The second problem is that the sequential assumptions of the GOMS model may be incorrect. If, as John has hypothesized in CPM–GOMS, operators occur in parallel, the total execution time would be significantly reduced.

7.5.3.4 Map Digitizing Tasks

Work by Haunold and Kuhn (1994) extends the keystroke level GOMS model (KLM) to model and optimize manual digitizing of maps at a national mapping agency. Differences between predicted and actual performance time were measured for unit tasks under experimental conditions involving seven users for two to four hours each. The purpose of the empirical study was to validate the KLM operators and their times for use in this particular task domain.

The KLM pointing operator time of 1.1s was found to be an accurate estimate of the actual mean time of 1.16s with a standard deviation of 0.26s, although there were only 50 occurrences of the pointing operator in the data. Likewise, the KLM homing time operator of 0.4s was corroborated with the actual data mean of 0.38s and standard deviation of 0.16s, again for 50 occurrences.

However, two new operators were defined for manual digitizing. The first was a pointing operator, which is shorter than the usual KLM pointing operator; the second was a keying operator for selecting a button from a 16-button cursor. The shorter pointing operator, P_s, occurred in two cases. The first was after an initial, normal, pointing action to search for a vertex target, detecting it where the line breaks and then pointing directly to the vertex. This second pointing time is shorter because of the shorter pointing distance. The second case for P_s occurred when using a snap function to point at an already digitized vertex. Using the snap function increases the target size. In both of these cases, pointing time is reduced because of the Fitts' law relationship between movement time, distance and target. The new P_s operator has a mean of 0.85s with a standard deviation of 0.19s based on 100 observations.

After introducing these two new operators in the methods, Haunold and Kuhn matched the predicted times for methods versus the measured actual performance. There was an average difference between predicted and actual of 5%, and a maximum difference of 11%. This is within the expected variability of the KLM prediction. Haunold and Kuhn noted special placement of mental operators before certain digitizing methods because of user-decision time regarding the digitizing operation itself. This is a task-sensitive heuristic not covered in the original KLM proposal. The value of this study is that it is one of the few empirical studies attempting to validate the KLM, and not GOMS. Secondly, Haunold and Kuhn use the KLM predictions to optimize procedures. They estimate that the cost of digitizing the entire cadastral map of Austria will be about $12million, with about three-quarters of the total digitizing time spent on routine tasks. Thus, there is great economic motivation to optimize the methods using the KLM.

7.5.4 Simplifying GOMS as a Design Tool

A fourth difficulty with the GOMS and KLM performance models is that they are very difficult to teach to software developers, who would most benefit from their application in user interface design decisions. Related is the difficulty that building a GOMS or KLM model of user interface tasks for a particular user interface is time consuming with the original models as proposed by Card *et al.* Software developers are reluctant to invest that amount of time in such effort if it has to be taken away from other design and programming implementation activities. Two research projects, one by Kieras on NGOMSL and the other by Foley on UIDE, address these difficulties and are described in this section.

Kieras proposes a model called the natural GOMS language (NGOMSL) which introduces more precision into the description of GOMS models using a predefined language. Although Kieras calls this a 'formal' language, he has attempted to keep it 'natural' in its usability. In contrast, the Foley research project integrates the KLM model into an interactive system design specification environment. This allows automatic generation of a KLM or NGOMSL analysis.

7.5.4.1 NGOMSL: 'Natural' GOMS Language

In the Kieras (1988) study the four components of the GOMS model are assigned a structured language description in NGOMSL. Goals are action–object pairs in the form <**verb noun**>. Operators are actions that the user executes reduced to a set of primitives, similar to the KLM operators. The pointing operator is **Move-cursor to** <**target coordinates**>. Unlike the KLM, the mental operator is classified by type of cognitive activity: *decide, set-up goal, store or retrieve from working memory*, and *store or retrieve from long-term memory*. Methods are sequences of steps that accomplish a goal. A method may call a submethod. Selection rules in NGOMSL, as in GOMS, are used to choose between methods. To illustrate the NGOMSL language, the following is a method written in NGOMSL and taken from Kieras (1988:151):

Method to accomplish goal of issuing a command

Step 1. Recall that command name is X, **retrieve from LTM** that Y is the menu name for X, and **retain** that menu name as Y.

Step 2. Recall that menu name is Y and **move cursor** to Y on Menu Bar.

Step 3. Press mouse button down.

Step 4. Recall that command name is X, and **move cursor** to X.

Step 5. Recall that command name is X, and **verify** that X is selected.

Step 6. Release mouse button.

Step 7. Forget menu name, **forget** command name, and **report** goal accomplished.

Kieras conceives of each step in a method as a single production rule in an underlying production system model of behavior. Using the notion of a production system and the primitive operators from the KLM, Kieras proposes that the human performance:

... time to execute a method depends on the time to execute the operators and on the number of cognitive steps, or production rules involved.

Kieras, 1988:154

Thus, each of the seven NGOMSL statements above will require an execution time. NGOMSL statement-execution time was estimated at 0.1s based on prior empirical work by Kieras. Kieras takes primitive operator times from Card *et al.* (1983) with 0.28s for a keystroke, 0.1s for a mouse-button press or release, 1.1s for a mouse move, 0.4s to home the hand to a keyboard or mouse, and 1.35s for any mental operator that lacks a better specified execution time. In the method above, step 2 will take one NGOMSL statement execution, plus one mental operator 'recall' execution, plus one pointing operator execution, giving:

$$ExecTime_{step2} = StatementTime_{step2} + MentalTime_{step2} + PointTime_{step2} \quad (7.13)$$

$$ExecTime_{step2} = 0.1 + 1.35 + 1.1 = 2.55s \quad (7.14)$$

In addition to predicting performance time by an expert user, Kieras argues that the production system model of NGOMSL can allow estimation of learning times. The assumption is made by Kieras that operators are already well-learned and that it is the composition of the methods associated with goals that are learned. The learning predictions are based on work by Bovair *et al.* (1990), but will not be considered further in this discussion since they do not address learning a psychomotor skill. For example, the NGOMSL model cannot predict the time it would take for a user to learn a novel input device such as the key joystick (Chapter 5).

The NGOMSL approach is an important attempt to reformulate the GOMS model in informal natural language that would help software developers reduce the time to analyze and predict performance time for a proposed interactive system. It also extends the GOMS work by formulating an underlying production system which can simulate human cognition and action during both learning and skilled performance.

7.5.4.2   UIDE: Generating the KLM and NGOMSL from Software Specifications

A system called the *user interface design environment* (UIDE) has integrated both the KLM and the NGOMSL models into its software with the purpose of allowing the software developer to analyze the impact on human performance of particular choices in the design of a particular user interface.

In UIDE an application is created by specifying a model of the interface. According to Foley *et al.* (1988, 1989) this model is a knowledge-base representation of the conceptual design of a user interface consisting of:

- the class hierarchy of objects that exist in the system;
- properties of the objects;
- actions which can be performed on the objects;
- units of information required by the actions;
- pre- and post-conditions for the actions.

Once the knowledge base has been developed, transformations can be applied which allow the designer to evaluate alternative, functionally equivalent conceptual designs. In Foley *et al.* (1989) user tasks are represented as scripts which are then translated into sequences of the KLM operators using the KLM model rules. The predicted task time can then be used to aid in the choice of user interface design elements.

In later UIDE work described by Byrne *et al.* (1994), a UIDE model specification consists of application actions, interface actions, and interaction techniques. This description is less object-oriented, and more in keeping with GOMS-like descriptions. Application actions are user actions at the user-task level, such as 'create a gate' in a digital circuit design application. These actions operate upon the objects specified in the design. Application actions are performed by executing one or more interface actions, such as 'select a command from a pull-down menu'. Interface actions are composed of interaction techniques which specify the actual physical actions such as 'click-left-mouse-button'.

The following, taken from Byrne *et al.* (1994), is an example of the proposed user actions for the task to create an AND gate in a circuit design system:

```
Application Action: CreateANDGate {location} {gate}
  1. SelectCommandIcon {CreateAND}
    1) ClickObject_LeftButton
  2. SelectPosition-DM {canvas} {pos:location}
    1) ClickPosition_LeftButton
  3. InvokeAction
```

In this example, the application action is specified as `CreateANDGate`, which is accomplished by three interface actions, one of which is `SelectCommandIcon`. In turn, `SelectCommandIcon` is achieved by the action of `ClickObject_LeftButton`. Note that this description of the interface is still fairly high-level. The physical action of `ClickObject_LeftButton` assumes, but does not specify, pointing actions.

To create an NGOMSL analysis, UIDE hierarchical action sequences generated from the UIDE model are translated into NGOMSL statements. Then, an NGOMSL interpreter takes the NGOMSL methods and a description of the tasks to be performed in that interface, and produces an estimate of the time it will take a user to perform the tasks. Byrne *et al.* (1994) describe such a translator and interpreter and show how it can be used to evaluate the user performance times of alternative interfaces for the same task.

7.6 Summary

This chapter has reviewed the extensive research on performance models for predicting the behavior of users interacting with graphical user interface software. Early models such as Card, Moran and Newell's (1983) GOMS and the KLM were developed from earlier human factors engineering work in task analysis and work measurement. Research by John, Kieras, Polson, and Foley in the last decade has primarily focused on empirically validating and extending the GOMS model, particularly as it is used for predicting practiced task time as part of user interface design and development. Prediction to within 30% accuracy is possible with the GOMS–KLM model; better accuracy to within 10% has been achieved with the more recent CPM–GOMS and EPIC models.

Generally, these models have been shown to be less useful in predicting performance failure and learning time, and they appear to be rarely used in engineering practice. Whether this is due to a lack of information about their application, the time-consuming nature of building the representation, or their total focus on prediction of practiced performance time, is not known. Concerning the first case, almost every standard text teaching HCI techniques discusses GOMS, but does not usually present the more practical KLM. In the second case, other predetermined time systems, such as MTM, take approximately 150 times longer to create the analysis than the actual time duration of the task. We estimate a KLM analysis would be within that range. Finally, the efficiency of saving time (on the order of seconds) for a computer-based task, unlike a factory assembly task, has little importance in most task domains.

The basic computer pointing task, i.e. target acquisition, is handled well by the GOMS–KLM approach, but there has been less interest in modeling the full range of pointing device tasks such as dragging or drawing. The GOMS–KLM model simplifies dragging to pointing. This makes sense in that dragging has been shown to be a Fitts' law task similar to pointing; however, dragging is slower than pointing (MacKenzie *et al.*, 1991). The drawing operator, which is not a Fitts' law task, is roughly defined in the KLM, but lacks true empirical validation and extension to computer-based drawing domains. Given the caveats expressed in this book concerning the complex interrelationships between task, device characteristics and performance, caution must always be used in applying the operators. In other words, the appropriate use of performance models must always be considered in light of the specific task context.

The GOMS–KLM model assumes a constant time for all pointing devices and tasks based on experimentally derived times for mouse pointing. Research has not developed along the lines of gathering empirical data for pointing with different devices to establish an extensive data base similar to that of MTM. (The US, UK and Swedish MTM association in the 1970s collected 22,000 observations for the basic MTM actions.) The GOMS–KLM model could certainly accommodate this information. It is important to note that empirically-fitted coefficients used in Fitts' law for a particular device – such as a mouse – may vary from experiment to experiment and do not readily translate from one experimental condition to the next (see section 4.2).

Operator values, intended as population means, are assumed to be normally distributed and should always be used as say, a 95% confidence interval, which takes the variance in human motion into account. Those studies that report a good fit between predictions of the models and the data (Gray *et al.*, 1993; Gong and Kieras, 1994; Haunold and Kuhn, 1994) use operators and times derived directly from the task. This, of course, reduces the variance of the predictions. Systems that use the predetermined time approach of the KLM and NGOMSL, such as UIDE (Foley *et al.*, 1989), will consequently have much more variance, and less reliability. What each analyst must decide is whether a greater investment in creating a model is worth its greater predictive power. Finally, little work, except for that of EPIC, has been done to scientifically model low-level behavior of pointing – particularly the coordination between cognition, motor movement and visual and kinaesthetic feedback. This is a rich area for future research, since the combination of computer simulation and cognitive modeling could contribute to a basic understanding of how the human psychomotor system functions.

7.7 Endnotes

1   A cycle is a repetition of the sequence of motions.
2   Root mean square (RMS) is defined by:

$$\mathrm{RMS}(e) = \sqrt{e_i^2/n}$$

where e_i is the prediction error on the ith unit task.

3   Standard error (SE) of estimation of the population mean for samples of size N is defined as:

$$\mathrm{SE} = \mathrm{SD}/\sqrt{\mathrm{N}}$$

4   Coefficient of variation (CV) = SD/mean. Coefficient of variation partially normalizes the standard deviation to make it more comparable for operators of different durations.
5   Despite the fact that there are major differences between a KLM and GOMS model, current research literature often conflates the two, referring to a KLM model as a keystroke level GOMS model.

8. *Challenges of the Present and Future*

It is difficult to imagine ergonomics research on pointing devices becoming more challenging, or essential, than it is at the present time. The graphical user interface with integrated pointing is now widely available for home, play and work environments – almost 30 years after the invention of the mouse. Furthermore, advances in hardware and software technology are moving interactive systems into 3D and virtual reality, and distributed real-time interaction such as computer-mediated conferencing and tele-operation. These demands and innovations will provide the incentive for the invention of novel pointing devices and the improvement of existing ones.

How do we ensure that ergonomic values and empirical findings based on human performance and evaluation are reflected in the design and development of pointing device software and hardware? Firstly, we need to directly address the problem of how to integrate findings from research into current and future design. We feel that key methods for success are building on past research findings, testing and standards, usability engineering, and guidelines. Second, we need to be aware of directions of future innovation in pointing device technology and user interfaces. This will allow us to assert the importance of an ergonomic perspective. Thirdly, we need to actively direct future research based on prior knowledge by setting our own research agenda.

This chapter begins with a brief review of the major research findings that have been developed in this book and goes on to present three major sections: integrating ergonomic research into design, opportunities for innovation in pointing device technology and interfaces, and recommendations for future research. We see these as the challenges of the present and future.

8.1 Review of Pointing Device Research Findings

In the course of this book we have advocated and described the use of experimental performance analysis to improve the design and use of pointing devices in modern interactive computer systems. We now briefly review the findings of this research.

8.1.1 Ergonomic Study of Pointing Device Findings

- **Finding #1:** Experimental ergonomic studies of individual pointing devices or comparisons between devices have focused primarily on these factors: overall pointing time, errors, and time to reach skilled pointing. Less attention has been given to fatigue and injury, user satisfaction with and (preference for) a device or its features, and the microstructure of movement during pointing.
- **Finding #2:** The best way to test the performance of a new pointing device is to conduct an experimental study comparing its performance to that of a baseline device such as a mouse. The study should take into account learning, practiced performance time, errors and qualitative observations of the participants.

8.1.2 General Psychomotor Findings

- **Finding #3:** Pointing is a common type of human motor movement known as *rapid aimed movement*. Computer-mediated pointing shares many characteristics of rapid aimed movement.
- **Finding #4:** Practice greatly reduces movement time as a power function. Variability of movement time is also reduced. On most usable pointing devices tested, practiced performance occurs within 1000 trials.

8.1.3 Fitts' Law Findings

- **Finding #5:** Fitts' law is an extremely robust description which predicts overall movement time for pointing. Fitts' law describes movement time as a log inverse relationship between distance to the target and width of the target known as the *index of difficulty* (*ID*). Smaller targets and longer distances take more time. Fitts' law describes movement times for many different limbs and many different tasks. Fitts' law can be tested in an experimental environment where distance and width of the target are varied according to *ID*.
- **Finding #6:** Fitts' law for computer-based pointing has been confirmed experimentally for the following pointing devices: mouse, touch tablet, isotonic and isometric velocity-controlled joysticks, trackball and head and eye tracker. Given the target distance and width and the correct coefficients, which are determined experimentally, movement time for a pointing task can be accurately predicted. Fitts' law has been experimentally confirmed for pointing and dragging with computer pointing devices, but not tracking or drawing. Fitts' law has been experimentally confirmed for one- and two-dimensional computer-based pointing tasks, but not in 3D or virtual reality environments.
- **Finding #7:** Different limbs have different levels of strength, degrees of freedom and efficiency. A limb's pointing efficiency can be measured as Fitts'

index of performance, but this must always be considered in the context of a particular device, its operation and the task. There is no way to predict this limb–device performance *a priori*. It must always be experimentally tested and evaluated.

- **Finding #8**: Comparisons of pointing speed between pointing devices across Fitts studies can be made by calculating the ratios of the index of performance within each study and then using those to compare across studies. Computing this ratio from the existing published studies indicates that the mouse is faster than the isometric joystick.

- **Finding #9**: Caution must be exercised when comparing Fitts' law results *across* experimental studies. Fitts' law is not an absolute measure of device performance independent of particular experiments. Experimental results can vary due to differences in experimental task, limb used, device features, practice levels of participants, etc. See section 4.2.

8.1.4 Movement Microstructure Findings

- **Finding #10**: The stochastic optimized submovement (SOS) model is commonly held to be the best microanalytic description of rapid aimed movement. According to this model, such movement consists of an initial, fast ballistic motion of high velocity followed by zero to several corrective movements. The motor system programs the initial ballistic motion using parameters such as the distance the hand must move. Visual and haptic feedback after this motion are critical for programming the secondary submovements. The SOS model can explain the relationships observed in Fitts' law.

- **Finding #11**: The SOS model has been supported by experimental studies of the microanalysis of pointing movement for the mouse. A similar study of pointing with a single finger, isometric, velocity-control joystick has not confirmed the SOS model. In that study it appears that amplified tremor from human muscles and computational problems associated with computing and transmitting the results of the transfer function (from force to velocity to displacement) introduces irregular, visible motions of the cursor. It has been suggested that this might account for the observation from the research literature that isometric joysticks are more difficult to learn and slower than the mouse.

8.1.5 Pointing Device Design Findings

- **Finding #12**: Display/control gain has a range within which the device is usable, and within that range, the gain does not appear to have much effect on pointing time. Accelerated (non-linear) transfer functions for mice and studies of hand motion conclude that the non-linear transfer functions do not improve pointing speed, but are popular because they reduce the mouse footprint area required for moving across large screens.

- **Finding #13:** Non-linear transfer functions in general present numerous design problems. There is no known method for picking the form of the function and the constants of the equation. A sigmoid parabolic has been proposed and tested in a limited empirical way as the best transfer function from force to velocity for isometric joysticks.
- **Finding #14:** Perceptual feedback from a pointing device is an under-appreciated aspect of design. Feedback is not usually designed into the device but occurs inadvertently through use. Haptic feedback is often characterized as a device's 'feel' as well as spatial information during movement. Designers should consider using shape and texture information to help users position their limbs in the correct posture for use. The weight and friction associated with the device during movement may provide important information about displacement of the pointing device. The haptic feedback during selection, such as pressing and releasing a mouse button, informs the user that selection has been activated and accomplished. The lack of such feedback in isometric devices may account for some of their difficulty in use. Visual observation of the movement of the pointing device itself during movement also provides feedback, albeit somewhat indirect, that helps control the device.
- **Finding #15:** Visual and auditory feedback during pointing can be integrated into the design of the graphical user interface. Motion of the cursor is important visual feedback and the software system must be fast enough to display its motion without lag. Small lags in display response have been found to degrade human performance on Fitts' law tasks. Auditory feedback can provide activation information for selection when a key or button is pressed. Some pointing devices are now directly incorporating force feedback about objects located in the graphical user interface into their operation.

8.1.6 Performance Model Findings

- **Finding #16:** Performance data on pointing and device-switching time with the mouse has been integrated into a task analysis model called the keystroke level model (KLM). Using this model, the designer of interactive software can predict practiced human performance within 80% accuracy.

In this section we have briefly summarized what we think are the most important research findings. This is, by necessity, a very incomplete list and one which reflects our personal interests and biases.

8.2 Integrating Ergonomics Research into Design

Although ergonomics research can be used to evaluate and compare devices in a particular situation of use, or to discover scientifically interesting and important phenomena about the human psychomotor system, the challenge of how to use those findings in the design of devices and interfaces is ever present. We address this issue from three perspectives: hardware design, device driver and UIMS-level software, and application-level interactive software design.

8.2.1 Hardware Design

Designing a new pointing device, or even improving an older one, is not a straightforward process. We have advocated throughout this book that developers base hardware design on a knowledge of research findings about the human performance of similar devices, and on a process of experimental testing with typical users (not friends of the developer!).

We now briefly describe the process of a typical development study using a real study conducted by the senior author, Sarah Douglas, on an innovative product which we will call the 'XYZ Mouse'. The initial testing with prototypes can be conducted as pilot studies using from three to five participants. The purpose of the pilot is to assess the general usability of the device with particular emphasis on approximate quantitative and qualitative aspects of the performance and subjective evaluation. In particular, the following issues are of major importance:

- Learning and practiced performance:
  - time
  - errors and problems
- Gross speed and fine positioning motor control on tasks:
  - pointing
  - selection, including single- and double-clicking, and multiple buttons
  - dragging
  - device switching (pointing and typing)
- Repositioning on a relative device
- Transfer function usability ranges for varying function types and parameters
- Accommodation to individual differences
- Physical comfort during use:
  - 'feel' of the device
  - fatigue or other physical problems
- Device reliability
- Participant's subjective evaluation and comments.

All participants should be given and sign an informed consent document. (See Figure 8.1.)

Informed Consent – XYZ Mouse Pilot Study

For purposes of this pilot study, I understand that I will be asked to do the following:

(1) Learn how to use the XYZ Mouse (10–15 minutes);

(2) Practice pointing with it until I reach a reasonable level of skill (30 minutes);

(3) Use the XYZ Mouse in some simple editing and spreadsheet tasks (30 minutes);

(4) Answer a questionnaire about using the XYZ Mouse (10 minutes).

There will be a break between each task. The total task time will be approximately 1 hour and 30 minutes.

I understand that I will be videotaped throughout the study. One video camera will be focused on my hand, while the other will be focused on the screen. This will help ensure my anonymity. (We need to do this in order to be able to see how well you can learn and use this device. Please remember that it is not you who are under test, but the pointing device.) I understand that I will be interviewed after the study to find out what I felt about the device.

I understand that any information that is obtained in connection with this study that can be identified with me will remain confidential and will be disclosed only with my permission. The Screening Questionnaire that I have filled out will be destroyed at the end of the study. The videotapes, computer data and Post Questionnaire will be kept, but will be identified only by a code number. There will be no means of linking my name to the number.

During the course of the study, I understand that if I find the task too fatiguing or if I feel eyestrain, I can pause for a break. My participation is entirely voluntary. I understand that I can discontinue participation at any time without penalty or loss of benefits to which I am otherwise entitled. However, I understand that I may be discontinued without compensation if I have not accurately represented my skills and information about myself on the Screening Questionnaire.

There are some benefits for me. I will help evaluate an innovative pointing device and I will be paid $10 per hour for my time, paid when I complete the study.

If I have any questions about the research at any time, I understand that I can call the director of the research study, Sarah Douglas, at 346-3974.

I agree to accept all risk of any personal injury that may arise in connection with these activities and release PNW Usability Consulting, its subsidiaries, affiliates and employees from any liability in connection with this study.

I agree that I will not disclose any information about the study (including the nature of the study, the nature of my participation, its results, or information about any products involved) in any form, oral or written, to anyone outside of PNW Usability Consulting.

My signature below indicates that I have read and understood the information provided above, that I willingly agree to participate, that I consent to the use of data gathered during the course of this study and through the screening questionnaire, that I may withdraw my consent at any time and discontinue participation at any time without penalty or loss of benefits to which I am otherwise entitled, and that I will receive a copy of this form.

Signature _____   Date _____

Figure 8.1: Informed consent form for the XYZ Mouse.

The informed consent document describes the purpose of the study, what the procedure is, what the responsibilities of the participant are, and any payment or confidentiality. It is particularly important to ensure and guarantee the anonymity of the individual, and their right to end the experiment if they do not feel able to continue. The participant should be assigned a code which is used to identify the individual for the rest of the experimental procedure and analysis. The entire session should be videotaped, with multiple cameras if necessary, to show cursor motion on the screen as well as movement of the pointing device.

A typical pilot session will consist of three types of activities: learning, Fitts' task testing, and realistic task testing. The total session length for the session should not exceed 1 to 2 hours including suitable breaks for resting. A brief introduction and teaching/practice session should be conducted. In our experience, the Solitaire game is an excellent environment for this activity, since it provides large targets, both pointing and dragging tasks, and no penalties for dropping during dragging or selecting the wrong target. Then, pointing, dragging and combined tasks of pointing and typing should be tested using a two-dimensional (full screen) Fitts task environment. (See Soukoreff and MacKenzie, 1995 for free software, or the designs of Chapter 5 in this volume.)

The target sizes should range from a character-size level (2mm) to larger targets of icon size (9mm). Distances should cover ranges for a typical monitor. An early feel for the device can be obtained with about 200 trials for each task. After the Fitts tasks, the participants should spend time performing pointing in a realistic, typical task environment appropriate to the eventual use of the device, such as word processing with Microsoft Word®. Figure 8.2 shows tasks chosen for the XYZ Mouse study. These tasks were chosen to give the participant a range of pointing, dragging and pointing/typing word processing tasks, the major work environment for the typical XYZ Mouse user.

Word Processing Tasks – XYZ Mouse Pilot Study

1. Create a new document.
2. Type the following paragraph:
He sighed. And that was the end of the discussion. Over the years that we've been married, we've learned to sidestep the subject of my family, my duty. It was once the biggest source of our arguments. When we were first married, Phil used to say that I was driven by blind devotion to fear and guilt.
3. Insert a comma after "Over the years".
4. Replace the comma after "my family" with "and". Use dragging to select the comma.
5. Change the word "biggest" to "only". Use dragging or double-clicking to select.
6. Delete " that we've been married,". Use dragging to select the text.
7. Insert a title at the beginning of the paragraph "Excerpt from Amy Tan's The Kitchen God's Wife". Center this title and make it bold with a larger font point size.
8. Scroll the window down.
9. Save the document with the name "temp".

Figure 8.2: Word processing tasks for the XYZ Mouse.

A pre-questionnaire should be given which assesses the participant's prior experience with similar devices, and possibly used to screen out certain types of participants. Figure 8.3 illustrates this for the XYZ Mouse evaluation pilot.

Screening Questionnaire – Code: _____ XYZ Mouse Pilot Study

Name: _____

Work phone: _____ Hours at this phone: _____

Home phone: _____ Hours at this phone: _____

Address: _____

Computer System Familiarity

1. Which computer systems do you use: (please check appropriate box)

	Never used	Use once a week	Use daily
IBM PC or clone	☐	☐	☐
Macintosh	☐	☐	☐
UNIX	☐	☐	☐

2. How many years have you used a computer?
3. What are your principle uses for a computer?
4. How familiar are you with the following: (please check appropriate box)

	Never used	Use once a week	Use daily
Computer Mouse	☐	☐	☐
Trackball	☐	☐	☐
Joystick	☐	☐	☐
Trackpad	☐	☐	☐
Microsoft Windows	☐	☐	☐
Microsoft Word	☐	☐	☐
Microsoft Excel	☐	☐	☐

Physical Performance

5. Are you right- or left-handed?
6. Have you ever had repetitive strain injury (RSI) or carpel tunnel syndrome with any limb? Please describe.
7. Do you have any problems using your hand? This includes soreness or disability. If so, please describe.

General Information

8. What is your age?
9. What is your gender?
10. What is your occupation?
11. When are you available for two consecutive hours?

Figure 8.3: Pre-questionnaire for the XYZ Mouse.

The purpose of this questionnaire was to: obtain general background and experience level for participants that might correlate with performance, screen for participants with physical problems, and schedule a session.

A post-questionnaire and interview should be performed immediately after the performance testing. The purpose of this questionnaire and interview is to assess the immediate responses of the participant, including observed problems. Figure 8.4 illustrates such a questionnaire. The person supervising the study should immediately follow-up on any issues noted in the responses to the questionnaire.

Post Questionnaire – XYZ Mouse Pilot Study

Learning

1. Did you find this device easy to learn? Explain.
2. How would you compare learning the XYZ Mouse to learning the regular hand mouse?
3. What did you find hardest to learn about the XYZ Mouse?

Practiced Skill

4. At the end of the study did you feel like you could control the XYZ Mouse in all situations? If not, where did you have problems?
5. Did you find the XYZ Mouse comfortable to use? If not, why not?
6. Do you have any fatigue from using the XYZ Mouse? Where?

Overall

7. If you had the opportunity to use an XYZ Mouse with your computer, would you? Explain.
8. Would you prefer to use it for certain tasks? Examples: word processing, spreadsheets, video games.
9. Would you like to be able to switch between the hand mouse and the XYZ Mouse?
10. Can you imagine any circumstances in which you or someone else might prefer the XYZ Mouse over other pointing devices?

Figure 8.4: Post-questionnaire for the XYZ Mouse.

Data from the pilot study should be analyzed statistically to give average movement times and error rates both for each participant and for the group. Fitts' law parameters can also be computed. The videotape and questionnaires should be thoroughly evaluated to provide insight into design weaknesses and improvements.

When design has converged towards a usable device, a full experimental study using at least 10 participants should be conducted. The study will necessarily take a number of hours for each participant since practiced performance usually emerges after 1500 trials of Fitts-task pointing, and practiced performance is usually the primary focus in usability.

Additionally, the results from this full experimental study will allow comparison with another device as a baseline. For example, we used the mouse as a baseline of comparison in our experimental study of the key joystick in Chapter 5.

8.2.1.1 Guidelines

In addition to empirical studies, heuristic guidelines do exist to aid the design of pointing devices. They can be used throughout the design and development process as checkpoints for usability. Because of the complexity of human performance when determined by the interaction of types of device, person, limb, and task, it is very difficult to create a set of guidelines which are comprehensive without being too vague. One such attempt was done by Chapanis and Kinkade (1972). They claim that these principles apply to the design of all types of controls, whatever their purpose or mode of operation (Chapanis and Kinkade, 1972:354). Their guidelines appear useful to us as overall questions which the designer of a task incorporating pointing or a new pointing device should review several times during development.

The following are the guidelines suggested by Chapanis and Kinkade:

1. The maximum force, speed, accuracy, or range of body movement required to operate a control should not exceed the limits of the least capable operator, and normal requirements for control operation should be considerably less than the maximum capabilities of most operators.

2. The number of controls should be kept to a minimum, and the control movements should be as simple, and as easy to perform as possible.

3. Control movements that seem 'natural' for the operator are more efficient and less fatiguing than those that seem awkward or difficult.

4. Control movements should be as short as possible, consistent with the requirements of accuracy and 'feel'.

5. Controls should have sufficient resistance so as to reduce the possibility of inadvertent activation by the weight of a hand or foot. For controls requiring single applications of force, or short periods of continuous force, a reasonable maximum resistance is half of the operator's greatest strength. For controls operated continuously, or for long periods, resistance should be much lower.

6. When an operator cannot apply enough unaided force to operate the controls and power-boosted or fully-powered control systems are necessary, artificial resistance cues should be provided.

7. Controls should be designed to stand abuse; for example, emergency or panic responses frequently impose large forces on controls.

8. Controls should provide a positive indication of activation so that malfunction will be obvious to the operator.

9. Control actions should result in a positive indication to the operator that there has been a system response.

10. Control surfaces should be designed to prevent the activating hand, finger, or foot, from slipping.

8.2.1.2 Standards

Finally, no discussion of hardware design would be complete without addressing the issue of standards. In this section we briefly review and critique the existing and anticipated standards work for computer pointing devices of the International Standards Organization (ISO) and the American National Standards Institute (ANSI). The purpose of the standards produced by these organizations is to establish uniform guidelines and testing procedures for evaluating interactive computer products. Standards on pointing devices are included as one of the principal sections. The primary motivation of the standards effort is to influence the design of these devices so that they accommodate the user's biomechanical capabilities and limitations, allow adequate safety and comfort, and prevent injury. In addition, the standards provide users of such devices with a reliable method of evaluation. The standards are written by committees whose members are drawn from the research and applied research communities.

The International Standards Organization has proposed a standard entitled ISO 9241: *Ergonomic Requirements for Office Work with Visual Display Terminals*. In this section we review the details from Part 9, *Non-keyboard Input Device Requirements*, still in draft form. Certification of conformance to this standard will be legally required for devices sold in the European Community. The general description of the standard and the particulars of Part 9 are described in Smith (1996). Part 9 applies to the following hand-operated devices:

- mice
- light-pen and styli
- touch-sensitive screens
- thumb-wheels
- pucks
- remote-control mice

- trackballs
- joysticks
- tablet-overlays
- hand-held scanners
- hand-held bar code readers

Part 9 does not cover the following pointing devices:

- eye-trackers
- head-mounted controllers
- devices for disabled users

- speech activators
- datagloves
- foot-controlled devices

Part 9 specifies general guidelines for physical characteristics of the design including the force required to operate them as well as their feedback, shape, and labeling. General requirements for all covered devices are shown in Table 8.1.

These requirements and recommendations cover performance, as well as physical aspects of the design. As can be seen from the table, most are recommended, not required. The requirement expected to cause the most impact on design is that a user must be able to operate the device with his or her hands in a neutral position. This is to avoid long-term biomechanical stress leading to permanent injury, such as repetitive strain injury (RSI). In addition to these general guidelines, there are requirements for each covered device. Interested readers should consult the standard itself for more specific information by device.

Table 8.1: ISO 9241, Part 9: General Requirements

Requirement	Required	Recommended
Fine positioning anchor		X
Appropriate resolution provided	X	
Resolution appropriate for task		X
Easy target acquisition and manipulation		X
Repositioning possible without tools	X	
Resistance to unintended input	X	
Force displacement		X
Displacement	X	
System adjustable gain		X
Expected cursor movements		X
Visual feedback on input	X	
Non-obstruction of screen targets		X
Lack of parallax between target and device		X
Ambidexterity		X
Neutral hand operating posture	X	
Accommodation of hand sizes	X	
Provision of hand rest surface		X
Grasp stability		X
Stability		X
Surface temperature		X
Weight		X
Edge characteristics		X
Access from work position	X	
Cable non-interference		X
Button design		X
Feedback (button) provided	X	
Buttons resistant to inadvertent activation		X
Buttons shaped to assist positioning		X
Button lock		X
Button lock provision		X

In addition to these guidelines, ISO 9241 defines ergonomic standards through evaluation procedures for measuring the ergonomic quality of a product. Compliance can be demonstrated through testing of user *performance*, *comfort* and *effort* to show that a particular device meets ergonomic standards or that it meets a *de facto* standard currently on the market. As we have noted many times in this book, usability testing is required because design specifications are not sufficient for an evaluation of a device. The ISO 9241 standard also argues that evaluating user performance is not enough for a complete evaluation of a device, since most studies are very short-term. Excessive effort and discomfort may only occur with longer usage. In addition, good performance may not be correlated with comfort, and users are often not aware of negative physiological effects such as nerve compression, reduction in blood circulation and oxygen deprivation which come though effort. Consequently, the ISO 9241, Part 9 requires biomechanical measurement during performance testing. Comfort is assessed by requiring participants to rate the devices using a questionnaire form.

In the proposed standards, the ISO experimental protocol for testing devices defines subject samples, stimuli, experimental design, environmental conditions, furniture adjustments, data collection procedures, and data analysis recommendations. Each task is intended to collect data on performance, i.e. time and error rate. It requires a subject population size that is representative of the intended user population, and recommends at least 25 participants.

The ISO includes six tasks: horizontal tapping (1D pointing), multidirectional tapping (2D pointing), dragging, freehand tracing (drawing), freehand input (hand-written characters or pictures) and grasp and park (homing/device switching). The tasks selected for testing should be determined by the intended use of the device with a particular user population. The standard does not appear to cover as a separate issue learning or reaching a criterion level of practice before administering performance tests. This is a serious flaw, since transfer of training effects have a significant effect on performance and subjective assessment.

The horizontal tapping-task is modeled on the original 1D Fitts tapping-task and has the participants move a cursor along a horizontal axis from one rectangle to another. The rectangles' sizes, and the distances, are varied. The standard requires 25 trials in each test session. Feedback is provided for 'hits' and 'misses' and if a miss occurs the participant should repeat the task to obtain a correct hit before continuing. There are limitations to the experimental design. The standard does not specify a range of target sizes and distances that are sufficient to ensure comprehensive coverage of a range of Fitts' index of difficulty. Also, it does not randomize sizes and distances, only requiring that they be varied between test trials.

Multidirectional tapping does not appear to be designed as a Fitts task. The task presents participants with a circle of squares which are equally spaced around the circumference. The participant moves a cursor across the circle to a highlighted target square. The size of the circle is varied between trials, but not the sizes of the squares. Again, as in horizontal tapping, no specification is made for the sizes of the squares or the distances.

The dragging task is not designed as a Fitts-type of task, nor does it resemble normal computer dragging. Instead, it requires dragging a circle between two horizontal parallel lines until the end of the lines is reached. We find this more like drawing or tracing. Determining the end of the task appears ambiguous: must the entire circle leave the lines? The size of the circle and the distance between the lines are varied. If the circle touches a line, the trial is recorded as an error and repeated. Time to drag is recorded.

The tracing task is intended to assess freehand drawing. The participant must move a circle around a circular track composed of two concentric circles without touching the lines. The size of the circle, the width of the track and the circumference of the track should be varied. If the circle touches a boundary line, it is recorded as an error and repeated. Time to complete the circuit is recorded.

The freehand input test is intended to compare drawn characters or symbols created with an input device with those drawn with traditional writing instruments such as pen or pencil on paper. It requires the participant to write or draw a legible symbol in each of a horizontal string of boxes as rapidly as possible. The size of the boxes and the distance between them should be varied. The time taken to complete the task should be recorded.

The last task, the grasp-and-park test, is intended to test hand movement between keyboard and pointing device. It requires the participant to move the cursor to a specified location on the screen and then use a key on the keyboard to select the position. This task must be done by a single hand. The time difference between this and the equivalent pointing task is the 'grasp and park' or homing time.

During the tasks, biomechanical effort must be measured. The measurement method must not interfere with the performance of the test tasks or cause discomfort to the participant. Three methods of biomechanical assessment are recommended: posture deviations from neutral, muscle effort, and muscle strength. All three should be used because of their complementary effect and differing indications. These measurements require special equipment and trained personnel to administer them. They are intended as an assessment of effort to use the device.

Comfort is determined by having the participant fill out a questionnaire after completing the tasks. If more than one device is used, an overall comparison should be assessed. The questionnaire consists of rating scales on either a five-point or seven-point scale. Non-parametric statistics are used for analysis. A sample questionnaire is shown in Table 8.2.

Table 8.2: ISO 9241 Subjective rating of device

	Least positive				Most positive
	1	2	3	4	5
Force required to use device					
Smoothness of operation					
General effort to use the device					
Soreness or fatigue in wrists					
Soreness or fatigue in fingers					
Soreness or fatigue in arms					
Soreness or fatigue in shoulders					
Posture during input device use					
Impression of accuracy					
Overall device operation					

The ISO 9241, Part 9, standards are primarily an ambitious attempt to promote the design and marketing of devices which are empirically demonstrated to encourage and protect the user's health. Secondly, they are an attempt to focus attention on usability values as an integral part of the design process. Since the certification of a device may be required in the European community, these standards need to be taken seriously.

However, as this book has pointed out, there are many complex issues which must be taken into account when measuring human performance with a device or when comparing performance between devices. The most serious problem with the standard is in the area of the task definitions. They often appear unclear about specifics of experimental design. For example, the standards do not adequately deal with:

• training participants to use the device;
• selection of subjects to screen out or control for prior experience with a device;

- transfer of training effects between devices; and,
- criteria to measure true practiced performance.

If these are not defined or are ambiguous, it is impossible to ensure replication of an evaluation environment. Without such assurance, comparisons across devices or other tests cannot be made. Since this is a draft document as of late 1996, further clarification and specification is possible.

The ANSI efforts at standardization for pointing devices are based on the ISO standards. The ANSI/HFES 100 standard covers the same content as the 'hardware' parts of ISO 9241 including Part 9, but includes substantial new material (Billingsley, 1995). As of late 1996, the committee of the Human Factors and Ergonomics Society was still working on the ANSI standard – which is strictly voluntary for vendors. ANSI cannot, and does not, require vendors to comply, although sometimes ANSI standards are adopted by legislative bodies for inclusion in laws and regulations. If that is the case, compliance becomes a legal requirement within a particular jurisdiction. Without legal requirements for compliance, vendors may voluntarily adopt ANSI standards if they are perceived to provide a competitive advantage without prohibitive cost.

8.2.2 Device Drivers and UIMS Software Design

In this next section we will discuss the possibilities of integrating ergonomics research findings into the design of device drivers and user interface management systems (UIMS) design.

8.2.2.1 Adaptive Software Control

In some sense, every computer pointing device has a transfer function partly implemented in software. We discussed the design issues of transfer functions earlier under hardware design and will now restrict ourselves to driver-level software that is expressly designed to adapt to individual human motion. Non-linear transfer functions for displacement devices attempt to indirectly vary device performance, but they do not anticipate or dynamically alter the transfer function itself based on information sampled during device movement.

As far as we know, no device as ever been built based on this type of direct modeling of human motor movement. We suggest that the potential exists since computing systems are capable of collecting and analysing human motor movement information in real-time (50–200ms). Pointing device design in general might benefit from empirical studies such as Meyer's stochastic optimized submovements (SOS) model for mouse movement (Walker *et al.*, 1993) and Mithal's study of the SOS model for the isometric joystick (Mithal, 1995; Mithal and Douglas, 1996; Chapter 6).

8.2.2.2 UIMS

The operating system of the modern GUI computer is either kernel-based, such as the Macintosh toolbox, or a network-based client–server model. In the client–server model, the software is usually called the user interface management system (UIMS). Both the kernel-based and UIMS software incorporate a *window manager*, which collects the input events from the pointing device, sends them to either the operating system (or application), and then responds to either the event directly, or another event generated by the application by creating a visual or auditory display. Window management software must insure that the speed of redrawing the screen provides adequate feedback to the user. The cursor must smoothly move around the screen in a 'natural' real-time response to movements of the pointing device. Small lags in display response have been found to degrade human performance on Fitts' law tasks. (Hoffman, 1992; MacKenzie and Ware, 1993)

Most GUIs recognize the basic tasks of pointing devices, which include selecting, dragging, and drawing. However, due to differences in hardware and operating system software, not all systems interpret these tasks in the same way. Design of software and hardware for pointing devices must be sensitive to the complexities and differences of these relationships. *What* functionality the device needs depends on *how* the system expects to interpret the actions of the device.

Many of these differences can be understood from the fact that all contemporary user interface systems are built on the event model of user interaction. In the event model, all user actions are considered asynchronous events. When an event, such as a mouse-button click, occurs, information about the event is recorded. This information may include the time of occurrence, the (x, y) position of the cursor, etc. The event is given a predetermined priority and placed in a priority queue. The system takes events in priority and interprets suitable action. If the (x, y) position of the mouse is in a window-close box, the system will close the window; if the (x, y) position of the mouse is in a menu item, the system will pass the information on to the application program to interpret. Note that these problems are common to all pointing devices, although in the following examples, the mouse is used as the prototypical pointing device.

Event-based systems, such as the Macintosh, Microsoft Windows, and X Window all differ in their interpretations of mouse-button events. The Macintosh was designed for a single-button mouse and has an event for button-down and one for button-up. Microsoft Windows supports a two- or three-button mouse. Microsoft Windows has separate events for the left, middle and right buttons. X Window must work for many different platforms using one-, two- or three-button mice. Events for mouse-button up and down are labeled with the number of the button that was pressed. This can cause a problem since a one-button mouse on a Macintosh workstation might use software designed for use with a three-button UNIX workstation.

The original Macintosh one-button mouse had limited functionality compared to multi-button mice. Consequently, the developers created the double-click and triple-click. Although the triple-click is rarely used, the double-click and its semantics are a fully integrated part of the Macintosh user interface, signifying, for example, the launching of applications from the desktop. Double-clicking is interpreted when two mouse-down events are separated by less than a *time-constant*. Systems allow this time-constant to be set by the user for slower or faster mouse double-clicking. In X Window, double-clicking is a problem, since X was designed as a client–server networked system. The second mouse-down event may be delayed in transmission over the network. Because of this problem, the X server does not recognize a double-click event. Client-side software, such as the Motif toolkit, can simulate it by checking the system clock.

In Chapter 3 we defined *selection* as an inherent part of pointing in a GUI. There are, however, situations in existing systems that do not require a separate selection action to terminate a pointing task. These are situations where moving the cursor into a particular area of the screen will cause user interface state changes as if that area were selected by a separate selection action, e.g. mouse-button press. Examples are the activation and highlighting of a window in X Windows when the cursor moves into it; and the activation of 'Balloon' help in the Macintosh or 'Tool Tips' for Microsoft Windows when the cursor moves into various icons. These are enter and exit events.

The perception, or notion, of an event is as an 'instantaneous' moment in time while, in fact, many actions for pointing devices are processes that represent a *duration* of time. Unlike pointing, where the endpoint of cursor motion is captured as input, both dragging and drawing require that the path of mouse movement be available to the UIMS. Early graphic systems used a sampling algorithm which would continuously read the mouse position at a predetermined sampling rate. On a single-user system without multitasking this approach is not a problem. However, on a multitasking system such as UNIX, this is too expensive in system resources. These systems have a special mouse-motion event which is generated only when the mouse moves. If the application receives this event while in a dragging or drawing mode (usually mouse button held down), the graphics are redrawn to reflect actual motion of the object during a drag, or path during a draw.

One of the most important ergonomic issues during dragging or drawing is that of providing the user with adequate visual feedback. Redrawing the screen must occur so that changes fuse into a perception of smooth motion. This occurs at about 60–70 redraws per second. The rate can be as low as 5 times per second to preserve the 'feel' of movement despite the visual perception of jerkiness. Interpreting mouse events based on continuous movement, where path is important, presents special problems over networked systems such as X Window, where the client and server are on different machines. This is due to the transmission time of the communications network. If timing, in addition to path, is required in applications using pointing devices, X Window has a motion history buffer which allows the server to accumulate motion events and send them as a block when requested by the client.

Not only do user problems with feedback occur in dragging and drawing if the screen is not redrawn quickly enough, but a similar problem may occur on simple tasks such as menu selection. If the redraw does not occur quickly enough, the user may have already moved the mouse and his or her attention to another task. Delayed feedback such as highlighting a menu item may be misinterpreted and present a confusing interaction.

Finally, event-based systems such as the Macintosh Toolbox, Microsoft Windows, and X Window are currently not capable of dealing with input from multiple, simultaneous pointing devices, such as two devices controlled by a hand and a foot, or in each hand. The most extreme demand for this type of control is in virtual reality interfaces. These are special purpose computing systems at this time. This suggests that future directions in UIMS research should accommodate pointing devices as truly continuous, multiple synchronized input devices.

8.2.3 Application Software Design

Having just reviewed approaches and issues for integrating ergonomic findings and concerns into hardware and operating system level design, we now turn to application-level software design. We will cover three areas: usability engineering, task analysis, and user interface design.

8.2.3.1 Usability Engineering

Usability engineering (Nielsen, 1992; Whiteside, Bennett, and Holtzblatt, 1988) not only defines a philosophy of design, but also methodology that is *user-centered*. Usability engineering requires the developer to focus on measurable human performance goals which are determined to be important for the particular design problem. These goals direct the design process. Usability engineering assumes that a particular design situation will select from a set of goals. The selected goals may also be prioritized. For example, the following list would define some potential usability goals for the design of software that incorporates pointing:

- by task, i.e. pointing, dragging, drawing, *speed of performance* for practiced use;
- by task, *incidence of error* for practiced use;
- ability to *recover from errors*;
- by task, *effort in learning*;
- *retention of learned skills*;
- *device-switching speed*;
- *physical comfort* in using device, i.e. shape;
- ability to *customize to individual differences* (e.g. handedness, children);
- *freedom from fatigue or injury*, e.g. repetitive strain injury;
- *physical robustness* of device in the context of use;
- *user's satisfaction.*

Although the usability goals can be described as part of the design specification, usability engineering defines a methodology of software engineering that can best be described as an iterative design process with the development of multiple prototypes throughout the design cycle. After each prototype is developed, human performance evaluation becomes the primary source of feedback for evaluating the success of the design and for selecting design alternatives.

8.2.3.2 Task Analysis

Historically, task analysis has been the primary tool of user-centered design and is frequently recommended as a tool of usability engineering. In Chapter 7, *Performance Models*, we examined the most detailed approaches, the earlier keystroke level model developed by Card, Moran and Newell (1983), as well as more recent models such as CPM–GOMS (John, 1988) and EPIC (Kieras *et al.*, 1995). The goal of these models is to predict the overall time of the task, including pointing time, for a skilled user. In addition, to this detailed level of task analysis, two other very high level approaches have been suggested to match the appropriate pointing device with the task: *stimulus–response compatibility* and *perceptual matching*.

One of the oldest theories in the human factors literature is that of stimulus–response compatibility. This theory argues that human performance improves when the nature of the stimulus is most similar to the nature of required response. This effect was first noted with choice reaction time and error rates in the spatial arrangement of controls (Fitts and Seeger, 1953). Jagacinski's studies (1980b; 1989) on target acquisition with moving targets suggest that there is an issue of stimulus–response compatibility for pointing devices, so that position-control devices would be better for stationary targets, and velocity-control devices for targets moving at a constant speed (which makes the target-acquisition problem a tracking problem). By extrapolation, it may be reasonable to suggest that acceleration-control devices might be best for capturing accelerating targets.

Although perceptual matching and stimulus–response compatibility can possibly predict differences in initial performance between devices, caution must be used in drawing conclusions about practiced performance. It is known that effects due to choice reaction time, which is a common measure of stimulus–response compatibility, can be diminished through large amounts of practice (Welford, 1976). Thus we recommend that stimulus–response compatibility results only be used for prediction of performance with novice users.

Jacob, Sibert, McFarlane, and Mullen (1994) have argued that performance can be greatly affected by perceptual qualities of the task and how compatible that is with the control properties of the pointing device. (See section 4.1.6 for a description of their experiment.) Jacob *et al.* apply Garner's theory of perceptual processing to interactive manipulation tasks. In this theory attributes of objects in multidimensional spaces can have different dominant perceptual structures, *integral* or *separable*. Attributes that combine perceptually are said to be integral; those that remain distinct are separable. For example, value (lightness) and chroma (value) of a color are perceived integrally, while size and lightness of an object are perceived separably.

Jacob *et al.* use two different 3D tasks, one defined as integral and the other separable, to test differences in performance using a 3D Polhemus tracker and a mouse whose movements are mapped to 3D movement.

The Polhemus tracker was defined as an integral device and the mouse as separable. Both speed and accuracy were significantly improved when the type of the task was matched to the type of device. This result seems contrary to accepted knowledge about the performance of pointing devices – that the integral device would always be superior. Jacob *et al.* explain their result by arguing that the attributes of a separable object cannot be ignored and are manipulated along each attribute in turn. If the input device supports the type of motion required by the task, then the task can be performed in an efficient manner. Although Jacob *et al.* do not relate their work to stimulus–response compatibility research, their notion of perceptual matching might be construed as such.

In summary, task analysis has been effective in predicting overall task time of experienced users using the detailed descriptions of performance models. Despite limitations to these models (see section 7.6), they are still an effective and robust method of integrating the empirical findings of human performance into interactive system design. On the other hand, stimulus–response compatibility and perceptual matching are appropriate at a much higher level of analysis: matching the pointing device to the task. Both these approaches, due to their more abstract nature, appear unable to make robust predictions about human performance such as learning time, practiced task time, and errors.

8.2.3.3 User Interface Design

Usability engineering and task analysis provide an overall framework during design that can effectively incorporate human performance values into software engineering of interactive systems. In addition, we suggest the following ideas for software written at the level of the detailed user interface.

Application software can benefit from the incorporation of Fitts' law relationships between target size and distance – a simple demonstration is the layout of icon palettes and menus or other selectable GUI objects. The most frequently used paths between selection targets of the same size should be minimized if other goals of the design are not violated. In any GUI interface the pointing time, especially on large displays, can be quite significant and the designer should consciously attempt to organize the display to reduce pointing time.

Several designs illustrate this idea. In a pull-down or pop-up menu, the most frequently selected items can appear first. Another suggested design is a 'Fittsized' menu developed by Walker, Smelcer and Nilsen (described in Olson and Olson, 1990) whose items grow in size according to distance from the beginning of the menu. While such a design improved pointing time over the standard fixed size menu items, the difference was only 80ms – a small effect. In a second experiment Walker *et al.* placed a virtual border on the top, right and bottom edges of a pop-up menu. The cursor could not move beyond this border even though the mouse moved. This greatly increased the effective target size. This second type of menu significantly reduced the average selection time by 450ms – nearly 25%.

In an application of Fitts' law principles to cursor design, Kabbash and Buxton (1995) conducted a 1D Fitts task with two types of cursors: one, the traditional

arrowhead, and the other a larger square cursor. Their hypothesis was that pointing with the tip of the arrowhead cursor to small targets presented a more difficult
task than pointing to the same targets with a larger-area cursor. A secondary
implication of this experiment is that the area of the cursor has an effect on
movement time, in addition to target size and distance. Their hypothesis was confirmed and pointing with both cursors was shown to follow Fitts' law. They estimate that with a pointing device such as a mouse, the savings in using a large area
cursor, 96 pixels, to point to a small target, 6 pixels, could save roughly 0.75s per
mouse selection. On a device which has a lower index of performance than the
mouse, such as a trackball during a dragging task, the savings could be well over
2.0s per selection. Kabbash and Buxton propose switching back and forth between
the two cursor representations as well as two-handed control: the traditional
'point' cursor by the dominant hand and the larger area cursor by the non-
dominant hand. These ideas must be tested further to include mode-switching
time to see if the savings in pointing time is lost by switching time. (See Chapter 5
for a similar study relating pointing speed to mode- and device-switching time.)

8.3 Innovations in Pointing Device Technology and Interfaces

In this section we will review a number of trends and innovations which we see
becoming significant over the next five years: 3D pointing devices, virtual reality,
pointing devices with force feedback, pointing using body states and brain waves,
multi-modal interfaces, and pointing in distributed environments.

8.3.1 3D Devices

Many graphical environments such as computer-aided design (CAD) and computer-aided manufacturing (CAM) present a three-dimensional graphical environment on the display. All traditional pointing devices have been designed for use in
two-dimensional displays. Thus, developers who wish to retain the advantage of
using widely-available 2D pointing devices have been faced with the problem of
mapping movement in a three-dimensional space[1] with a device designed for des-
ignating two-dimensional space. Most mouse-based 3D environments introduce a
mode for changing the interpretation of mouse motion from 2D (x, y) motion to
using 1D forward and backward motion of the mouse as an additional up or down
z-dimension. Mode-state change is often created by pressing a mouse button (for a
two- or three-button mouse) or key on the keyboard. Such a device was used in the
experimental work of Jacob *et al.* (1994) discussed in section 4.1.6. There has been
very little experimental research on the ergonomics of such moded-mice.

Another approach to using a traditional mouse in 3D environments has been device modification of the mouse hardware. A roller mouse has been invented (Venolia, 1993) which adds two wheels on either side of the front of the mouse to control the z-dimension. The user can move the mouse around in a 2D plane while simultaneously moving the roller with the index finger. The mouse button is retained in the traditional position on the top of the mouse. Auditory feedback is used extensively for initiation, duration and termination of interface state including touching, dragging, and aligning objects, and mode changes to 3D. Unfortunately, this device has no description of any studies of human performance.

Three-dimensional motion can become much more complex. Motion in three dimensions must always be specified from either the point of view of an object of interest (which may be guided by the user), *or* from the user's point of view. This latter is termed egocentric motion. Furthermore, interfaces may not only require motion in space but change of egocentric viewpoint or gaze of the user. We previously introduced this topic in section 4.2.1 with the taxonomy of Mackinlay, Card and Robertson (1990) and their invention of a mouse-based egocentric (movement of the viewpoint) motion controller. Egocentric motion in three dimensions not only requires motion in the (x, y, z) direction (from the object's or user's point of view), but also viewpoint, or gaze, motion. Their 3D virtual device depends on mapping three-dimensional movement and gaze to moded motion of the mouse (using the middle mouse-button) coupled to on-screen displays of a type of 'virtual position joystick'. They have respected the results of stimulus–response compatibility research in this design so that movement or gaze right and left correspond to right and left motion of the mouse.

8.3.2 Virtual Reality

Virtual reality (VR) is a 3D environment which integrates dynamic visual display with the user's body posture and motion, eye gaze and hand movement. Orienting the body or looking in a particular direction controls the scene presented to the user's visual system. Standard virtual reality systems usually present the display through two small displays, one for each eye, contained in an enclosed head-mount. The user also wears a dataglove which is used as the input, i.e. pointing, device. The head-mount and dataglove may have Polhemus trackers attached to give positional information in 3D space. The combination of these devices allows the creation of environments in which the user can move about, view, select and move objects. Virtual reality is thus an egocentric environment.

Very little experimental research has been done on virtual reality and most of the literature consists of descriptions of the technology and anecdotal work. An exception to this is an experiment by Ware, Arthur and Booth (1993). They compared a head-coupled stereo display to a stereo image of a 3D scene viewed on a monitor using a perspective projection coupled to the head position of the observer. This second condition, called 'fish tank' VR has a number of advantages over the first (which is a traditional 'immersion' approach):

- better resolution – close to the limits of the human eye;
- creation of a simulated depth-of-field effect with a background that approximates an out-of-focus image;
- stability in the presence of eye movements;
- it allows VR to be used in an everyday workspace with support for peripheral vision of that workspace.

The results of the experiment suggest that head-coupling may be more important than stereo in yielding a strong impression of three-dimensionality. Furthermore, in a path-tracing task, error rates for the 'fish tank' interface were four times higher that of the head-coupled interface.

VR immersion 3D technology has a major benefit to offer the user: a better understanding of the space he or she inhabits. Tasks which are usually performed in a 3D space can be 'intuitively' performed without the complexity of translating a 2D interface into a 3D space. On the other hand, there is also anecdotal evidence that the technology has a number of problems. The virtual world can be confusing. Computational limitations in displaying images in real-time often prevent objects from having enough detail to be recognized and remembered. This in turn causes problems in finding your way around. People get 'lost' in VR environments (Boyd, 1995). While virtual objects are visible, there is often no tactile feedback when they are touched or grasped. (Some feedback can be incorporated into the dataglove in the form of resistance in the finger joints.) Clearly, much more research needs to be done in understanding the ergonomics of VR environments.

8.3.3 Pointing Devices with Force Feedback

Existing pointing devices are not designed to provide any tactile feedback from the GUI objects which are displayed on the computer screen. The relationships between the cursor (which is really a virtual pointer substituting for the finger) and objects pointed to are all visual. Recently, a number of new devices have been invented which attempt to provide force feedback from GUI objects. The user then has the direct sensation of touching those objects thereby gaining shape or texture or elasticity information. Applications for these force-feedback devices include surgical training and visualization of molecular structure.

One such device is the PHANToM developed at MIT by Massie and Salisbury (Massie, 1993; Salisbury, 1995). Users insert their fingers into a moveable thimble suspended from a lightweight rod, which is driven by motors with encoders mounted on a desktop. The coordinates of the user's finger tip are tracked with the encoders and the motors control the x, y and z forces exerted back through the rod. The PHANToM is only one of several inventions for force feedback. Two other devices are Immersion Corp.'s 2D force-feedback joystick and 3D stylus which have integrated force feedback.[2] No experimental ergonomic studies have been done on any of these devices, but they represent an intriguing innovation in user interfaces for pointing.

8.3.4 Body States and Brain Waves

A number of innovative devices have attempted to control cursor movement through body states or brain waves. A product called MindDrive uses a device wrapped around the finger to sense pulse, temperature and electrical activity (Associated Press, 1995). Using a technology akin to polygraph and galvanic skin-response tests, the user learns to control body states of tenseness and relaxation through mental imagery. As body state changes, so too does the direction of a moving cursor. The product is seen as most usable in video games.

Other researchers have proposed using direct EEG (Wolpaw, McFarland, Neat and Forneris, 1991), alpha waves which correlate with 'relaxed' states, or *event related potentials* (ERP) sampling. In a manner similar to other brain-state record-ing, the latter are measured by electrodes attached to the scalp. Differences in ERP electrical activity in specific areas of the brain can signal whether words are understood or not, whether the word fits a mood state, and the participant's alert-ness (Tucker, 1995). These techniques are still laboratory curiosities.

8.3.5 Multi-modal Interfaces

A multi-modal interface is one which uses multiple sense modalities of the user for both control and display. Combining speech (sound mode) with pointing (haptic mode) is one such multi-modal system. A general theory of modalities in inter-action is found in an article by Bernsen (1994). His approach is to generate a tax-onomy of modality types in terms of their information representations showing the advantage in combining modalities.

There has been one major research effort for the past decade by Richard Bolt and the Advanced Human Interface Group at MIT to fully integrate pointing gesture and speech into a graphical interface. Pointing gesture in this context is *deixis*, or resolving reference by pointing to objects in the environment. In the interface described by Thorisson, Koons and Bolt (1992), the user controls objects in the graphical user interface by saying 'Delete *that* object' while simultaneously giving a pointing gesture to the object and looking at the object displayed on a large wall-projected display. The interface incorporates speech recognition and synthesis, an eye tracker, and dataglove with a 3D Polhemus spatial tracker.

Recent research by Cohen and Oviatt has focused on combining speech recogni-tion with natural language processing, and pointing with traditional GUI pointing devices. Cohen (1992) has argued that the strengths of natural language (and weaknesses of GUIs) are in identifying objects not on the screen, for specifying temporal relations, for identifying and operating on large sets and subsets of enti-ties, and for using the context of interaction. On the other hand, the strengths of pointing in GUI interfaces (and the weaknesses of natural language) involve the establishment and use of context and pronominal reference. A multi-modal inter-face, then, is a much more usable interface.

Oviatt (1996) conducted a within-subjects factorial study of an interactive map-ping system with three types of input: spoken, pen-based, and multi-modal spoken and pen. The spoken interface had numerous performance difficulties including increased errors and lengthier task-completion time, in large part due to difficulties in computer-based recognition of spoken descriptions of spatial locations. Ninety-five percent of the users preferred the multi-modal system. Both the Cohen and Oviatt studies demonstrate the advantages of using pointing, as deixis, integrated into natural language processing. While this particular interface research is unique, the integration of speech recognition with natural language processing and pointing information will become more common in the future. One clear usage is in the integration of pointing information from traditional pointing devices, such as a stylus or touch screen, to resolve reference ambiguity in a natural language interface.

8.3.6 Pointing in Distributed Environments

Research in *computer supported cooperative work* (CSCW) has developed remote face-to-face interaction with shared virtual workspaces. In these shared virtual workspaces pointing can be done with individual or shared cursors. In individual cursor environments each user's cursor is displayed as an individualized icon. Difficulties occur if several users are active at once. It is difficult to follow what is happening and is very costly in network traffic. With a shared cursor, multiple users manipulate their own individual pointing device, usually a mouse, to control a shared cursor. Several issues related to pointing tasks become problems with shared cursors: floor control, lags in pointing, and use of the cursor for other than object selection.

Floor control is a term borrowed from conversation analysis for conversational turn-taking. It is used to denote which user has control over the cursor and in these systems is often a source of confusion. Two users may simultaneously try to move the cursor causing confusion over who 'controls the floor'. Doerry (1995) found that these confusions were a significant source of communication breakdown and are related to a lack of visual access to the hand actions of the other users. A technical solution to this problem is a floor-control policy in which a user who wishes to use the pointing device presses a key or an on-screen button. This then locks out other users until the current user relinquishes control by pressing another key or button. A second problem also common to multiple cursor environments is difficulty in maintaining smooth movement of the cursor without significant lag between hand motion of the mouse and movement of the cursor on the screen. When cursor movement depends on network communication, as in these remote systems, the user may not get adequate visual feedback.

Finally, researchers in CSCW have often noticed that remote users will use the cursor for gestural (deictic reference) pointing while they talk. This is a new, communicative function for the traditional pointing device. An example of such use is when a user will point to a graphical object or text segment in the shared workspace and say, 'I think *that* should go *there*'. Observations of remote CSCW environments with shared workspaces indicate that deictic pointing is quite prevalent, e.g. Doerry, 1995.

CSCW is an exciting new area of human–computer interaction that offers many challenges to pointing device technology and GUIs as they are now conceived. It is an area where there will be increasing innovation and, thus, an increasing need for experimental study.

8.4 Future Research Directions

We conclude this book by briefly summarizing the future research challenges and directions for ergonomics research on pointing devices.

8.4.1 Overall Research Approach

1. More basic science research on psychomotor models of pointing including the time course of action, individual differences, differences in limb control, the role of attention, and time–accuracy tradeoffs. Psychomotor research on human movement could be guided to some extent by challenges in pointing device design.

2. More basic science research on empirical studies of the role of haptic and visual feedback in human movement. The challenges of virtual reality technology requires a better understanding of the integration of perception into movement and spatial perception. More traditional pointing devices also fail to incorporate haptic feedback into design which often accounts for their poor performance.

3. Better understanding of muscle movement and its interaction with device control. Chapter 6 suggested that tremor accounts for difficulties in controlling an isometric joystick. Other aspects of muscular control include fine vs. gross movement, and differences due to various limbs.

8.4.2 The Relationship Between Research and Design

1. Base the design and development of pointing device technology on psychomotor theories and empirical studies of the human motor system. This is a recommendation for a change away from the control systems theories of human performance. We have shown in Chapter 6 that surprising results can come from empirical studies at the microstructure of movement level. More studies of device performance at this level are needed.

2. Integrate experimental research results into design and development. Engineers and inventors need to be persuaded that the philosophy and methods of usability studies can promote improved products. Methods must be invented which give the developer timely and cost-effective information about human performance in a form which can influence design. Information about the results of experimental studies of human performance needs to be disseminated to the engineering community.

3. Development of standards. The move to standardization and certification of devices needs cautious review. The current ISO 9241, Part 9, standard is correctly motivated but needs improvement in recommendations for experimental design.

4. Further development and evaluation of performance modeling to include a wider range of pointing device performance measures, device differences, task differences and device switching.

8.4.3 Specific Research Topics for Device Design

1. *Better understanding of how to set the parameters for non-linear transfer functions.* Developers of devices such as an isometric joystick have no guidelines for determining parameters based on human performance. It is currently done by somewhat arbitrary settings and gradual refinement. Experimental testing of a variety of functions, for a variety of devices, needs to be done. Solving this problem will require a combination of experimental studies of human performance and a sophisticated mathematical understanding.

2. *Better understanding of isometric device design and its relationship to human performance.* Isometric devices with velocity control are poorly understood from a human performance perspective. Yet there are situations where they are perhaps the only possible pointing device.

3. *Development of adaptive software control.* Many pointing devices have not taken advantage of the potential for optimizing pointing control through dynamic, adaptive software. Pointing devices are still treated as though they were simpler mechanical/electrical devices. Such adaptive software could optimize pointing time as well as errors.

4. *Development of innovative pointing devices with haptic feedback.* This area is an exciting area of research demanding both engineering innovation as well as a total rethinking of GUI objects and the user interface.

5. *Development and experimental studies of 3D pointing environments.* Virtual reality presents a novel interface. Very little is known about human performance with these systems, even such basic issues as whether Fitts' law applies.

6. *Experimental studies of health issues related to long-term device usage.* The increasing prevalence and need for prediction of potential repetitive strain injury has created a liability for manufacturers of pointing devices.

7. *Development of pointing devices which are controlled by limbs other than the hand.* Individuals with physical limitation or injury of the hand require a reliable alternative limb device. There is a potential for innovative devices which are controlled by the foot or head.

8.4.4 Specific Research Topics for User Interface Design

1. *Experimental studies of human performance with 2D pointing devices used in 3D environments*, including tasks of pointing, dragging, and drawing, and mode switching. While there are innovative 3D interfaces under development, 2D devices will probably be used for many years because of their widespread availability and reasonable cost.

2. *Experimental studies of human performance and visual, auditory, and haptic feedback presented as part of the user interface software.* Very little is known about what kind of feedback should be given in response to user actions.

3. *Experimental and conversation analytic studies of pointing as gesture (reference resolution) in multi-modal and CSCW environments.* Use of pointing devices for other than traditional GUI object selection demands a better understanding of pointing as deixis.

4. *Experimental studies of human performance with gestural interfaces.* Gestural interfaces extend limb movement into tasks such as grasping, pushing, pulling, tapping. Very little is known about the human performance characteristics of these tasks.

5. *Development of UIMS which support simultaneous use of multiple continuous pointing devices, such as two-handed controls.* Existing user interface operating system technology supports an event-based model with a stream of events coming from various input devices. This technology needs to be redesigned to accommodate concurrency.

8.5 Conclusions

We began this book with an appeal to recognizing and incorporating empirical research about human performance into the design and development of pointing devices and interactive systems using pointing devices. We have stressed the importance of correctly designed and executed experimental research. We know that designers have often neglected these types of studies, only to discover later that their device was quite unusable by ordinary people.

We suggest that performance studies can be combined quite successfully with other measures such as user preference for a device, and recordings of muscle fatigue which predict repetitive strain injury.

The early chapters presented background material on pointing, first from the perspective of the human psychomotor system and, later, from that of computer-based pointing. We included a comprehensive review of Fitts' law research and microanalysis models such as the SOS model, and details of applying these concepts to pointing devices with a consideration for device operation, limbs and computer-specific tasks.

We next surveyed the research on specific pointing devices: the digitizing tablet, the touch screen, the mouse, the trackball, the joystick, the head and eye tracker, the dataglove, and foot-operated controls. We have urged caution in predicting human performance of a particular device without due regard to the type of user, the type of device (including its detailed features and limb control), and the type of task. We have also argued that comparison based on absolute measures across devices is risky, despite the initial promise of measures such as Fitts' law.

To illustrate the experimental methods we advocated in earlier chapters, we presented two experimental studies: the first compared a single-finger, isometric, velocity-controlled joystick to the mouse in order to test the proposition that the joystick was the faster device, since device switching between typing and pointing was not required. The second examined differences in the microstructure of movement comparing another finger-controlled isometric joystick with the mouse. The latter study had the goal of trying to understand the results of the first study – why pointing time with isometric joysticks is generally slower than with the mouse – with an eye to improving device design. After both these detailed studies, we turned to a survey, use and critique of performance models, such as GOMS and CPM–GOMS, to predict pointing embedded in complex tasks.

Finally, in this chapter, we surveyed the research findings on pointing devices, described how to integrate these findings into hardware and software design for pointing devices and interactive systems, described areas for innovation in pointing devices, and sketched out future research directions. We hope that we have convinced the reader that, in many ways, the 'golden age' of pointing device technology is just around the corner. We will be able to meet its challenges by grounding our design in empirical studies of human motor system performance.

8.6 Endnotes

1   While we term this three-dimensional movement, it is not technically so. What the user sees on the display is a two-dimensional visual representation of three-dimensional space. Movement in this space is a complex relationship between what is seen and the operation of the particular device. Virtual reality, on the other hand, is a true three-dimensional environment, both for what is seen and for operation of the pointing devices.

2   These are commercial products available from Immersion Corp., 2158 Paragon Drive, San Jose, CA 95131, USA. E-mail is immersion@starconn.com

9. Bibliography

Abrams, R. A., Meyer, D. E. and Kornblum, S. (1990). 'Eye–Hand Coordination: Oculomotor Control in Rapid Aimed Limb Movements.' *Journal of Experimental Psychology: Human Perception and Performance*, 16(2), pp. 248–267.

Abruzzi, A. (1956). *Work, Workers and Work Measurement.* New York: Columbia University Press.

Akamatsu, M., MacKenzie, I. S. and Hasbroucq, T. (1995). 'A Comparison of Tactile, Auditory, and Visual Feedback in a Pointing Task Using a Mouse-Type Device.' *Ergonomics*, 38(4), pp. 816–827.

Albert, A. E. (1982). 'The Effect of Graphic Input Devices on Performance in a Cursor Positioning Task', in *Proceedings of the Human Factors Society 26th Annual Meeting*, pp. 54–58. Santa Monica, CA: Human Factors Society.

Anderson, N. S., Sobiloff, B., White, P. and Pearson, G. (1993). 'A Foot Operated PC Pointer Positioning Device', in *Proceedings of the Human Factors and Ergonomics Society 37th Annual Meeting.* Seattle, WA: Human Factors Society.

Andres, R. O. and Hartung, K. J. (1989). 'Prediction of Head Movement Time Using Fitts' Law.' *Human Factors*, 31(6), pp. 703–713.

Arnaut, L. Y. and Greenstein, J. S. (1986). 'Optimizing the Touch Tablet: The Effects of Control–Display Gain and Method of Cursor Control.' *Human Factors*, 28(6), pp. 717–726.

Associated Press (1995). 'Sensor on Finger Replaces Joy Stick in New Video Games.' Appeared in *The Plain Dealer*, September 10, 1995.

Avons, S. E., Beveridge, M. C., Hickman, A. T. and Hitch, G. J. (1983). 'Considerations on Using a Lightpen-Interactive System with Young Children.' *Behavior Research Methods & Instrumentation*, 15(1), pp. 75–78.

Baggen, E. A. (1987). *A Human Factors Evaluation of Current Touch Entry Technologies.* Unpublished doctoral dissertation. Virginia Polytechnic Institute and State University, Blacksburg, VA.

Barrett, R. C., Selker, E. J., Rutledge, J. D. and Olyha, R. S. (1995). 'Negative Inertia: A Dynamic Pointing Function', in *Human Factors in Computing Systems CHI '95 Conference Companion*, pp. 316–317. New York: ACM.

Becker, J. A. and Greenstein, J. S. (1986). 'A Lead–Lag Compensation Approach to Display/Control Gain for Touch Tablets', in *Proceedings of the Human Factors Society 30th Annual Meeting*. Santa Monica, CA: Human Factors Society.

Bentley, T. L., Custer, G. M. and Meyer, G. M. (1975). *An Alternative Editing Console for the Palo Alto Research Center, Xerox Corporation.* (Unpublished project report). The Design Division, Stanford University. Abstract also available as T. L. Bentley, and G.W. Meyer, 'Design and Evaluation of a Text Editing Console'. *SID International Symposium Digest of Technical Papers*, VII, pp. 66–67, 1976.

Beringer, D. B. and Peterson, J. G. (1985). 'Underlying Behavioral Parameters of the Operation of Touch-Input Devices: Biases, Models and Feedback.' *Human Factors*, 27(4), pp. 445–458.

Beringer, D. B. and Scott, J. (1985). 'The Long-Range Light Pen as a Head-Based User-Computer Interface: Head-Mounted "Sights" versus Head Positioning for Computer Access by the Disabled', in *Proceedings of the Human Factors Society 29th Annual Meeting*, pp. 114–118. Santa Monica, CA: Human Factors Society.

Bernsen, N.O. (1994). 'Foundations of Multimodal Representations: A Taxonomy of Representational Modalities.' *Interacting with Computers*, 6(4), pp. 347–371.

Billingsley, P. (1995). 'ANSI/HFES 200 Standard Well Underway.' *SIGCHI Bulletin*, 27(3), July 1995, pp. 8–9.

Blouin, J., Teasdale, N., Bard, C. and Fleury, M. (1993). 'Directional Control of Rapid Arm Movements: The Role of the Kinetic Visual Feedback System.' *Canadian Journal of Experimental Psychology*, 47(4), pp. 678–696.

Boritz, J., Booth, K. S. and Cowan, W. B. (1991). 'Fitts' Law Studies of Directional Mouse Movement', in *Graphics Interface '91*, pp. 216–233. Toronto, Ontario, Canada: Canadian Man–Computer Communications Society.

Bovair, S., Kieras, D. E. and Polson (1990). 'The Acquisition and Performance of Text Editing Skill: A Cognitive Complexity Analysis.' *Human Computer Interaction*, 5(1), pp. 1–48.

Boyd, C. (1995). 'Human and Machine Dimensions of 3D Interfaces for Virtual Environments', in *Human Factors in Computing Systems CHI '95 Conference Companion*, pp. 41–42. New York: ACM.

Buxton, W. (1983). 'Lexical and Pragmatic Considerations of Input Structures.' *Computer Graphics*, 17(1), pp. 31–37.

Buxton, W. (1990). 'A Three-State Model of Graphical Input', in D. Diaper (Ed.), *Human–Computer Interaction – Interact '90*, pp. 449–456. Amsterdam: Elsevier.

Buxton, W. and Myers, B. A. (1986). 'A Study in Two-Handed Input', in *Human Factors in Computing Systems: CHI '86*, pp. 321–326. New York: ACM.

Buxton, W., Hill, R. and Rowley, P. (1985). 'Issues and Techniques in Touch-Sensitive Tablet Input', in *Computer Graphics, Proceedings of SIGGRAPH '85*, 19(3), pp. 215–224.

Byrne, M. D., Wood, S. D., Sukaviriya, P. N., Foley, J. D. and Kieras, D. E. (1994). 'Automating Interface Evaluation', in *Human Factors in Computing Systems CHI '94 Conference Proceedings*, pp. 232–237. New York: ACM.

Cakir, A. E., Cakir, G., Muller, T. and Unema, P. (1995). 'The TrackPad – A Study on User Comfort and Performance', in *Human Factors in Computing Systems CHI '95 Conference Companion*, pp. 97–98. New York: ACM.

Calhoun, G. L., Janson, W. P. and Arbak, C. J. (1986). 'Use of Eye Control to Select Switches', in *Proceedings of the Human Factors Society 30th Annual Meeting*, pp. 154–158. Santa Monica, CA: Human Factors Society.

Card, S. K., English, W. K. and Burr, B. J. (1978). 'Evaluation of Mouse, Rate-Controlled Isometric Joystick, Step Keys, and Text Keys for Text Selection on a CRT.' *Ergonomics*, 21(8), pp. 601–613.

Card, S. K., Mackinlay, J. D. and Robertson, G. G. (1990). 'The Design Space of Input Devices', in *Human Factors in Computing Systems CHI '90*, pp. 117–124. New York: ACM.

Card, S. K., Mackinlay, J. D. and Robertson, G. G. (1991). 'A Morphological Analysis of the Design Space of Input Devices.' *ACM Transactions on Information Systems*, 9(2), pp. 99–122.

Card, S. K., Moran, T. P. and Newell, A. (1980a). 'Computer Text Editing: An Information Processing Analysis of a Routine Cognitive Skill.' *Cognitive Psychology*, 12, pp. 32–74.

Card, S. K., Moran, T. P. and Newell, A. (1980b). 'The Keystroke Level Model for User Performance Time with Interactive Systems.' *Communications of the ACM*, 23(7), pp. 396–410.

Card, S. K., Moran, T. P. and Newell, A. (1983). *The Psychology of Human-Computer Interaction*. Hillsdale, New Jersey: Lawrence Erlbaum Associates.

Chapanis, A. and Kinkade, R. G. (1972). 'Design of controls', in H. P. Van Cott and R. G. Kinkade (Eds.), *Human Engineering Guide to Equipment Design* (rev. ed., pp. 345–379). Washington, D. C.: U.S. Government Printing Office.

Cohen, P. R. (1992). 'The Role of Natural Language in a Multimodal Interface', in *Proceedings of UIST '92*, pp. 143–149. New York: ACM.

Crossman, E. R. F. W. and Goodeve, P. J. (1983). 'Feedback Control of Hand-Movement and Fitts' Law.' *Quarterly Journal of Experimental Psychology*, 35A(2), pp. 251–278.

Dix, A., Finlay, J., Abowd, G. and Beale, R. (1993). *Human–Computer Interaction*. New York: Prentice Hall.

Doerry, E. (1995). *An Empirical Comparison of Copresent and Technologically-Mediated Interaction Based on Communicative Breakdown*. Unpublished doctoral dissertation, Computer and Information Science Department., University of Oregon, Eugene, Oregon, USA.

Douglas, S. A. and Mithal, A. K. (1994). 'The Effect of Reducing Homing Time on the Speed of a Finger-Controlled Isometric Pointing Device.' in *Human Factors in Computing Systems, CHI '94 Conference Proceedings*, pp. 411–416. New York: ACM Press.

Douglas, S. A. and Mithal, A. K. (1993). *Human Performance Evaluation of a Finger-Controlled Pointing Device*. CIS TR 92–11. Department of Computer Science, University of Oregon, Eugene, 97403–1202.

Drury, C. G. (1975). 'Application of Fitts' Law to Foot-Pedal Design.' *Human Factors*, 17, pp. 368–373.

Eady, K. (1986). 'Today's International MTM Systems: Decision Criteria for their Use', in R. L. Shell (Ed.), *Work Measurement: Principles and Practices*. Norcross, GA: Industrial Engineering and Management Press.

Eccles, J. (1977). 'Cerebellar Function in the Control of Movement.', in F. Rose (Ed.), *Physiological aspects of clinical neurology*, pp. 157–178. Oxford: Blackwell.

Ellingstad, V. S., Parng, A., Gehlen, G. R., Swierenga, S. J. and Auflick, J. (1985). *An Evaluation of the Touch Tablet as a Command and Control Input Device* (Tech. Report). Vermillion, SD: University of South Dakota, Department. of Psychology.

Elliott, D. (1985). The Utilization of Visual Feedback Information during Rapid Pointing Movements. *Quarterly Journal of Experimental Psychology: Human Experimental Psychology*, 37A(3), pp. 407–425.

English, W. K., Englebart, D. C. and Berman, M. L. (1967). 'Display-Selection Techniques for Text Manipulation.' *IEEE Transactions on Human Factors in Electronics*, HFE-8, pp. 5–15.

Epps, B. W. (1986). 'Comparison of Six Cursor Control Devices Based on Fitts' Law Models', in *Proceedings of the Annual Meeting of the Human Factors Society*, pp. 327–331. Santa Monica, CA: Human Factors Society.

Epps, B. W., Snyder, H. L. and Muto, W. H. (1986). 'Comparison of Six Cursor Devices on a Target Acquisition Task', in *1986 SID Digest of Technical Papers*, pp. 302–305. Los Angeles, CA: Society for Information Display.

Ewing, J., Mehrabanzad, S., Scheck, S., Ostroff, D. and Shneiderman, B. (1986). 'An Experimental Comparison of a Mouse and Arrow Jump Keys for an Interactive Encyclopedia.' *International Journal of Man Machine Studies*, 24(1), pp. 29–45.

Fitts, P. M. (1954). 'The Information Capacity of the Human Motor System in Controlling the Amplitude of Movement.' *Journal of Experimental Psychology*, 47(6), pp. 381–391.

Fitts, P. M. (1964). 'Perceptual-Motor Skill Learning', in A. W. Melton (Ed.), *Categories of human learning*, pp. 243–285. New York: Academic Press.

Fitts, P. M. and Peterson, J. R. (1964). 'Information Capacity of Discrete Motor Responses.' *Journal of Experimental Psychology*, 67(2), pp. 103–112.

Fitts, P. M. and Seeger, C. M. (1953). 'S–R Compatibility: Spatial Characteristics of Stimulus and Response Codes.' *Journal of Experimental Psychology*, 46, pp. 199–210.

Foley, J. D. and van Dam A. (1982). *Fundamentals of Interactive Computer Graphics*. Reading, MA: Addison-Wesley.

Foley, J. D., Gibbs, C., Kim, W. C. and Kovacevic, S. A (1988). 'Knowledge-Based User Interface Management System', in *Human Factors in Computing Systems, CHI '88 Conference Proceedings*, pp. 67–72. New York: ACM Press.

Foley, J. D., Kim, W. C., Kovacevic, S. A. and Murray, K. (1989). 'Defining Interfaces at a High Level of Abstraction.' *IEEE Software*, 6(1), January 1989, pp. 25–32.

Frost, G. (1972). 'Man–Machine Dynamics', in Van Cott and Kinkade (Eds), *Human Engineering Guide to Equipment Design*, pp. 227–309. Washington, D. C.: U.S. Government Printing Office.

Gaertner, K. P. and Holzhausen, K. P. (1980). 'Controlling Air Traffic with a Touch Sensitive Screen.' *Applied Ergonomics*, 11, pp. 17–22.

Gaver, W. (1986). 'Auditory Icons: Using Sound in Computer Interfaces.' *Human–Computer Interaction*, 2(2), pp. 167–177.

Gibson, J. J. (1979). *The Ecological Approach to Visual Perception*. Boston: Houghton Mifflin.

Gillan, D. J., Holden, K., Adam, S., Rudisill, M. and Magee, L. (1990). 'How Does Fitts' Law Fit Pointing and Dragging', in *Human Factors in Computing Systems CHI '90 Conference Proceedings*, pp. 227–234. New York: ACM.

Gillan, D. J., Holden, K., Adam, S., Rudisill, M. and Magee, L. (1992). 'How Should Fitts' Law be Applied to Human–Computer Interaction?' *Interacting with Computers*, 4(3), pp. 289–313.

Glenn, F. A., Iavecchia, H. P., Ross, L. V., Stokes, J. M., Weiland, W. J., Weiss, D. and Zaklad, A. L. (1986). 'Eye–Voice-Controlled Interface', in *Proceedings of the*

Human Factors Society 30th Annual Meeting, pp. 322–326. Santa Monica, CA: Human Factors Society.

Gomez, A. D., Wolfe, S. W., Davenport, E. W. and Calder, B. D. (1982). *LMDS: Lightweight Modular Display System* (NOSC Tech. Report 767). San Diego, CA: Naval Ocean Systems Center.

Gong, R. and Kieras, D. (1994). 'A Validation of the GOMS Model Methodology in the Development of a Specialized, Commercial Software Application', in *Proceedings of the CHI '94 Conference on Human Factors in Computing Systems*, pp. 351–357. New York: ACM.

Goodwin, N. C. (1975). 'Cursor Positioning on an Electronic Display using Lightpen, Lightgun or Keyboard for Three Basic Tasks.' *Human Factors*, 17(3), pp. 289–295.

Graham, E. D. (1996). 'Virtual Pointing on a Computer Display: Non-Linear Control-Display Mappings', in *Proceedings of Graphics Interface '96*, pp. 39–46. San Francisco: Canadian Human–Computer Communications Society and Morgan Kaufmann publishers.

Graham, E. D. and MacKenzie, C. L. (1996). 'Physical versus Virtual Pointing', in *Proceedings of the CHI '96 Conference on Human Factors in Computing Systems*, pp. 292–299. New York: ACM.

Gray, W. D., John, B. E. and Atwood, M. E. (1993). 'Project Ernestine: Validating a GOMS Analysis for Predicting and Explaining Real-World Task Performance.' *Human–Computer Interaction*, 8(3), pp. 237–309.

Greenstein, J. S. and Arnaut, L. Y. (1988). 'Input Devices', in M. Helander (Ed.), *Handbook of Human–Computer Interaction*, pp. 495–519. Amsterdam: Elsevier Science Publishers B. V.

Haller, R., Mutschler, H. and Voss, M. (1984). 'Comparison of Input Devices for Correction of Typing Errors in Office Systems', in *Proceedings of the Interact 84 Conference, First IFIPS Conference on Human–Computer Interaction*, pp. 177–82.

Halliday, A. M. and Redfearn, J. W. T. (1956). 'An Analysis of the Frequency of Finger Tremor in Healthy Subjects.' *Journal of Physiology* (London) 134, pp. 600–611.

Harriman, C. W. (1985). 'Alternatives for Cursor Control: Footmouse, Pad or View System.' *InfoWorld*, 7(38), pp. 48–50.

Haunold, P. and Kuhn, W. (1994). 'A Keystroke Level Analysis of a Graphics Application: Manual Map Digitizing', in *Proceedings of CHI '94 Human Factors in Computing Systems Conference*, pp. 337–343. New York: ACM.

Hay, L. and Beaubaton, D. (1986). 'Visual Correction of a Rapid Goal-Directed Response.' *Perceptual & Motor Skills*, 62(1), pp. 51–57.

Hodes, D. and Akagi, K. (1986). 'Study, Development and Design of a Mouse', in *Proceedings of the Human Factors Society 30th Annual Meeting*, pp. 900–904. Santa Monica, CA: Human Factors Society.

Hoffmann, E. R. (1991). 'A Comparison of Hand and Foot Movement Times.' *Ergonomics*, 34(4), pp. 398–406.

Hoffmann, E. R. (1992). 'Fitts' Law with Transmission Delay.' *Ergonomics*, 35(1), pp. 37–48.

Hottman, S. B. (1981). 'Selection of Remotely Labeled Switch Functions During Dual Task Performance', in *Proceedings of the Human Factors Society 25h Annual Meeting*, pp. 240–242. Santa Monica, CA: Human Factors Society.

Jacob, R. J. K. (1983). 'Using Formal Specifications in the Design of the User–Computer Interface.' *Communications of the ACM*, 26(4), April 1983, pp. 259–264.

Jacob, R. J. K. (1985). 'A State Transition Diagram Language for Visual Programming.' *IEEE Computer*, 18(8), August 1985, pp. 51–59.

Jacob, R. J. K. (1986). 'A Specification Language for Direct-Manipulation User Interfaces.' *ACM Transactions on Graphics*, 5(4), October 1986, pp. 283–317.

Jacob, R. J. K., Sibert, L. E., McFarlane, D. C. and Mullen, M. P. (1994). 'Integrality and Separability of Input Devices.' *ACM Transactions on Computer–Human Interaction*, 1(1), pp. 3–26.

Jagacinski, R. J. (1989). 'Target Acquisition: Performance Measures, Process Models, and Design Implications', in G. R. McMillan, D. Beevis, E. Salas, M. H. Strub, R. Sutton, and L. van Breda (Eds.), *Applications of Human Performance to System Design*, pp. 135–149. New York: Plenum.

Jagacinski, R. J. and Monk, D. L. (1985). 'Fitts' Law in Two Dimensions with Hand and Head Movements.' *Journal of Motor Behavior*, 17(1), pp. 77–95.

Jagacinski, R. J., Plamondon, B. D. and Miller, R. A. (1987). 'Describing Movement Control at Two Levels of Abstraction', in P. A. Hancock (Ed.), *Human Factors Psychology*, pp. 199–247. Amsterdam: North Holland.

Jagacinski, R. J., Hartzell, E. J., Ward, S. and Bishop, K. (1978). 'Fitts' Law as a Function of System Dynamics and Target Uncertainty.' *Journal of Motor Behavior*, 10(2), pp. 123–131.

Jagacinski, R. J., Repperger, D. W., Moran, M. S., Ward, S. L. and Glass, B. (1980a). 'Fitts' Law and the Microstructure of Rapid Discrete Movements.' *Journal of Experimental Psychology: Human Perception and Performance*, 6(2), pp. 309–320.

Jagacinski, R. J., Repperger, D. W., Ward, S. L. and Moran, M. S. (1980b). 'A Test of Fitts' Law with Moving Targets.' *Human Factors*, 22(2), pp. 225–233.

Jellinek, H. D. and Card, S. K. (1990). 'Powermice and User Performance', in J. C. Chew and J. Whiteside (Ed), *Human Factors in Computing Systems CHI '90*, pp. 213–220. New York: ACM.

Jenkins, W. L. and Karr, A. C. (1954). 'The Use of a Joy-Stick in Making Settings on a Simulated Scope Face.' *Journal of Applied Psychology*, 38, pp. 457–461.

John, B. E. (1988). *Contributions to Engineering Models of Human–Computer Interaction*. Unpublished doctoral dissertation, Carnegie Mellon University, Pittsburgh.

John, B. E. and A. H. Vera (1992). 'A GOMS Analysis of a Graphic, Machine-Paced, Highly Interactive Task', in *Human Factors in Computing Systems CHI '92*, pp. 251–258. New York: ACM.

Kabbash, P. and Buxton, W. (1995). 'The "Prince" Technique: Fitts' Law and Selection Using Area Cursors', in *Human Factors in Computing Systems CHI '95*, pp. 273–279. New York: ACM.

Kabbash, P., Buxton, W. and Sellen, A. (1994). 'Two-Handed Input in a Compound Task', in *Human Factors in Computing Systems CHI '94*, pp. 417–423. New York: ACM.

Kabbash, P., MacKenzie, I. S. and Buxton, W. (1993). 'Human Performance Using Computer Input Devices in the Preferred and Non-Preferred Hands.' in *Human Factors in Computing Systems CHI '93*, pp. 474–481. New York: ACM.

Kaiser, J. F. and Reed, W. A. (1977). 'Data Smoothing Using Low-Pass Digital Filters.' *Review of Scientific Instruments*, 48(11), pp. 1447–1456.

Kantowitz, B. H. and Elvers, G. G. (1988). 'Fitts' Law with an Isometric Controller: Effects of Order of Control and Control–Display Gain.' *Journal of Motor Behavior*, 20(1), pp. 53–56.

Kantowitz, B. H. and Knight, J. L. (1976). *Testing Tapping Time-Sharing: Attention Demands of Movement Amplitude and Target Width*. New York: Academic Press.

Karat, J. McDonald, J. E. and Anderson, M. (1986). 'A Comparison of Menu Selection Techniques: Touch Panel, Mouse and Keyboard.' *International Journal of Man Machine Studies*, 25(1), pp. 73–88.

Kawato, M. (1992). 'Optimization and Learning in Neural Networks for Formation and Control of Coordinated Movement', in D. E. Meyer and S. Kornblum (Eds.), *Attention and Performance XIV*, 821–849. Cambridge, MA: MIT Press.

Keele, S. W. (1968). 'Movement Control in Skilled Motor Performance.' *Psychological Bulletin*, 70(6), pp. 387–403.

Keele, S. W. (1986). 'Motor Control', in J. K. Boff, L. Kaufman and J. P. Thomas (Eds.), *Handbook of Human Perception and Performance, Vol. II*, pp. 30:1–60. New York: Wiley.

Keele, S. W. and Posner, M. I. (1968). 'Processing of Visual Feedback in Rapid Movements.' *Journal of Experimental Psychology*, 77, pp. 155–158.

Kerr, R. (1978). 'Diving, Adaptation, and Fitts' Law.' *Journal of Motor Behavior*, 10(3), pp. 255–260.

Kessler, G. D., Hodges, F. F. and Walker, N. (1995). 'Evaluation of the CyberGlove as a Whole-Hand Input Device.' *ACM Transactions on Computer–Human Interaction*, 2(4), pp. 263–283.

Kidd, J. S. and Van Cott, H. P. (1972). 'System and Human Engineering Analyses', in Van Cott and Kinkade (Eds.), *Human Engineering Guide to Equipment Design*. Wash. D. C.: U.S. Government. Printing Office.

Kieras, D. E (1988). 'Towards a Practical GOMS Model Methodology for User Interface Design', in M. Helander (Ed.), *Handbook of Human–Computer Interaction*, pp. 135–157. Amsterdam: Elsevier Science Publishers.

Kieras, D. E. (1995). Personal communication to author Douglas via e-mail, November 8, 1995.

Kieras, D. E and Polson, P. G. (1985). 'An Approach to the Formal Analysis of User Complexity.' *International Journal of Man–Machine Studies*, 22(4), pp. 365–394.

Kieras, D. E., Wood, S. D. and Meyer, D. E. (1995). 'Predictive Engineering Models Using the EPIC Architecture for a High-Performance Task', in *Human Factors in Computing Systems CHI '95*, pp. 11–18. New York: ACM.

Kinkead, R. (1975). 'Typing Speed, Keying Rates and Optimal Keyboard Layouts', in *Proceedings of the 19th Annual Human Factors Society Meeting*. Santa Monica, CA: Human Factors Society.

Kvålseth, T. O. (1981). 'An Experimental Paradigm for Analyzing Human Information Processing during Motor Control Tasks', in *Proceedings of the Human Factors Society*, 25, pp. 581–585. Santa Monica, CA: Human Factors Society.

Langolf, G. D., Chaffin, D. B. and Foulke, J. A. (1976). 'An Investigation of Fitts' Law Using a Wide Range of Movement Amplitudes.' *Journal of Motor Behavior*, 8(2), pp. 113–128.

Lin, M. L., Radwin, R. G. and Vanderheiden, G. C. (1992). 'Gain Effects on Performance Using a Head-Controlled Computer Input Device.' *Ergonomics*, 35(2), pp. 159–175.

Loomis, J. M and Lederman, S. J. (1986). 'Tactual Perception', in K. R. Boff, L. Kaufman, and J. P. Thomas, (Eds.), *Handbook of Perception and Human Performance*, pp. 31:1–41. New York: Wiley.

Lundy-Ekman, L., Ivry, R., Keele, S. and Woollacott, M. (1991). 'Timing and Force Control Deficits in Clumsy Children.' *Journal of Cognitive Neuroscience*, 3(4), pp. 367–376.

MacKenzie, C. L. and Iberall, T. (1994). *The Grasping Hand*. Amsterdam: North-Holland.

MacKenzie, I. S. (1991). Letter to author Mithal.

MacKenzie, I. S. (1992). 'Fitts' Law as a Research and Design Tool in Human–Computer Interaction.' *Human–Computer Interaction*, 7, pp. 91–139.

MacKenzie, I. S. and Buxton, W. (1992). 'Extending Fitts' Law to Two-Dimensional Tasks', in *Human Factors in Computing Systems: CHI '92*, pp. 219–226. New York: ACM.

MacKenzie, I. S., Sellen, A. and Buxton, W. (1991). 'A Comparison of Input Devices in Elemental Pointing and Dragging Tasks', in *Human Factors in Computing Systems: CHI '91 Conference Proceedings*. New York: ACM

MacKenzie, I. S. and Ware, C. (1993). 'Lag as a Determinant of Human Performance in Interactive Systems', in *Proceedings of the CHI '93 Conference on Human Factors in Computing Systems*, pp. 488–493. New York: ACM.

Mackinlay, J., Card, S. K. and Robertson, G. G. (1990). 'A Semantic Analysis of the Design Space of Input Devices.' *Human–Computer Interaction*, 5(2–3), pp. 145–190.

Massie, T. H. (1993). *Design of a Three Degree of Freedom Force Reflecting Haptic Interface*. Unpublished SB Thesis, Massachusetts Institute of Technology, Electrical Engineering and Computer Science Department., May 1993.

Maynard, H. B. (1992). *Maynard's Industrial Engineering Handbook, 4th edition*. New York: McGraw-Hill.

Mehr, M. H. and Mehr, E. (1972). 'Manual Digital Positioning in 2 Axes: A Comparison of Joystick and Trackball Controls', in *Proceedings of the Human Factors Society 16th Annual Meeting*, pp. 110–116. Santa Monica, CA: Human Factors Society.

Meyer, D. E., Abrams, R. A., Kornblum, S., Wright, C. E. and Smith, J. E. K. (1988). 'Optimality in Human Motor Performance: Ideal Control of Rapid Aimed Movements.' *Psychological Review*, 95(3), pp. 340–370.

Meyer, D. E., Smith, J. E. K. and Wright, C. E. (1982). Models for the Speed and Accuracy of Aimed Movements. *Psychological Review*, 89(5), pp. 449–482.

Meyer, D. E., Smith, J. E. K., Kornblum, S., Abrams, R. A. and Wright, C. E. (1990). 'Speed–Accuracy Tradeoffs in Aimed Movements: Toward a Theory of Rapid Voluntary Action', in M. Jeannerod (Ed.), *Attention and Performance XIII*, pp. 173–226. Hillsdale, New Jersey: Erlbaum.

Mithal, A. K. (1995). *Using Psychomotor Models of Movement in the Analysis and Design of Computer Pointing Devices.* Unpublished doctoral dissertation, Computer & Information Science Department., University of Oregon, Eugene, Oregon.

Mithal, A. K. and Douglas, S. A. (1996). 'Differences in Movement Microstructure of the Mouse and the Finger-Controlled Isometric Joystick', in *Proceedings of the ACM Human Factors in Computing Systems CHI '96*, pp. 300–307. New York: ACM.

Monk, A. (1986). 'Mode errors: A User-centred Analysis and Some Preventative Measures Using Keying-Contingent Sound.' *International Journal of Man–Machine Studies*, 24(4), pp. 313–327.

Motoyuki, A. and Soto, S. (1994). 'A Multi-Modal Mouse with Tactile and Force Feedback.' *International Journal of Human–Computer Studies*, 40(3), pp. 443–453.

Newell, A. and Simon, H. A. (1972). *Human Problem Solving.* Englewood Cliffs, N. J.: Prentice-Hall.

Nielsen, J. (1992). *Usability Engineering.* New York: Academic Press.

Oldfield, R. C. (1971). 'The Assessment and Analysis of Handedness: The Edinburgh Inventory.' *Neuropsychologia*, 9, pp. 97–113.

Olson, J. R. and Nilsen, E. (1988). 'Analysis of the Cognition Involved in Spreadsheet Software Interaction.' *Human–Computer Interaction*, 3(4), pp. 309–350.

Olson, J. R. and Olson, G. M. (1990). 'The Growth of Cognitive Modeling in Human–Computer Interaction Since GOMS.' *Human–Computer Interaction*, 5(2 and 3), pp. 221–266.

Oviatt, S. (1996). 'Multimodal Interfaces for Dynamic Interactive Maps', in *Human Factors in Computing Systems: CHI '96 Conference Proceedings*, pp. 95–102. New York: ACM.

Pearson, G. and Weiser, M. (1986). 'Of Moles and Men: The Design of Foot Controls for Workstations', in *Human Factors in Computing Systems: CHI '86 Conference Proceedings*, pp. 333–339. New York: ACM.

Pearson, G. and Weiser, M. (1988). 'Exploratory Evaluation of a Planar Foot-Operated Cursor-Positioning Device', in *Proceedings of the CHI '88 Conference on Human Factors in Computing Systems*, pp. 13–18. New York: Association for Computing Machinery, Inc.

Pew, R. W. (1966). 'Performance of Human Operators in a Three-State Relay Control System with Velocity-Augmented Displays.' *IEEE Transactions on Human Factors, Electronics*, 7, pp. 77–83.

Pfauth, M. and Priest, J. (1981). 'Person–Computer Interface Using Touch Screen Devices', in *Proceedings of the Human Factors Society 25th Annual Meeting*, pp. 500–504. Santa Monica, CA: Human Factors Society.

Polanyi, M. (1958). *Personal Knowledge.* London: Routledge & Kegan Paul.

Polson, P. G. and Kieras, D. E. (1985). 'A Quantitative Model of the Learning and Performance of Text Editing Knowledge', in *Proceedings of the CHI '85 Conference on Human Factors in Computing Systems*, pp. 207–212. New York: ACM.

Porac, C. and Coren, S. (1981). *Lateral Preferences and Human Behavior.* New York: Springer-Verlag.

Posner, M. I. (1978). *Chronometric Explorations of Mind*. Hillsdale, N. J.: Erlbaum.

Reinhart, W. and Marken, R. (1985). 'Control Systems Analysis of Computer Pointing Devices', in *Proceedings of the Human Factors Society 29th Annual Meeting*, pp. 119–121. Santa Monica, CA: Human Factors Society.

Robertson, S. R. (1983). *Goal, Plan and Outcome Tracking in Computer Text-Editing Performance*. Cognitive Science Technical Report 25. New Haven, Conn.: Yale University.

Rosenbaum, D. A. (1991). *Human Motor Control*. San Diego: Academic Press.

Rosenberg, D. J. and Martin, G. (1988). 'Human-Performance Evaluation of Digitizer Pucks for Computer Input of Spatial Information.' *Human Factors*, 30(2), pp. 231–235.

Rumelhart, D. E. and Norman, D. A. (1982). 'Simulating a Skilled Typist: A Study of Skilled Cognitive Motor Performance.' *Cognitive Science*, 6, pp. 1–36.

Rutledge, J. D. and Selker, T. (1990). 'Force-to-Motion Functions for Pointing', in D. Diaper *et al.* (Eds.), *Human–Computer Interaction INTERACT '90*, pp. 701–706. Amsterdam: Elsevier Science Publishers.

Salisbury, J. K. (1995). 'Haptic Rendering: Programming Touch Interaction with Virtual Objects', in *Proceedings of the ACM 1995 Symposium on Interactive 3D Graphics*. New York: ACM.

Schmidt, R. A., Zelaznick, H., Hawkins, B., Frank, J. S. and Quinn, J. T. (1979). 'Motor-Output Variability: A Theory for the Accuracy of Rapid Motor Acts.' *Psychological Review*, 86(5), pp. 415–451.

Schmidt, R. A., Zelaznik, H. N. and Frank, J. S. (1978). 'Sources of Inaccuracy in Rapid Movement', in G. Stelmach (Ed.), *Information Processing in Motor Control and Learning*. New York: Academic Press.

Selker, T. and Rutledge, J. D. (1991). *Finger Force Precision for Computer Pointing*. Technical Report #RC 17342(#76618), 10/30/91. IBM Research Division, T. J. Watson Research Center, Yorktown Heights, NY 10598.

Sellen, A. J., Kurtenbach, G. P. and Buxton, W. A. S. (1992). 'The Prevention of Mode Errors through Sensory Feedback.' *Human–Computer Interaction*, 7(2), pp. 141–164.

Sherr, S. (1988). *Input Devices*. New York: Academic Press, Inc.

Smith, W. (1996). *ISO and ANSI Ergonomic Standards for Computer Products: A Guide to Implementation and Products*. New York: Prentice Hall.

Soukoreff, R. W. and MacKenzie, I. S. (1995). 'Generalized Fitts' Law Model Builder.' *Human Factors in Computing Systems CHI '95 Conference Companion*, pp. 113–114. New York: ACM.

Stammer, R. C. and Bird, J. M. (1980). 'Controller Evaluation of a Touch Input Air Traffic Data System: An "Indelicate" Experiment.' *Human Factors*, 22, pp. 581–589.

Stein, R. B. and Lee, R. G. (1989). 'Tremor and Clonus', in V. B. Brooks (Ed.), *Handbook of Physiology: The Nervous System II. Motor Control, Part 1*, pp. 325–342. Bethesda, MD: American Physiological Society.

Swierenga, S. J. and Struckman-Johnson, D. L. (1984). *Alternative Cursor Control Devices: An Empirical Comparison Using a Tracking Task* (Final Report: Task II.3). Vermillion, SD: University of South Dakota, Human Factors Laboratory.

Thorisson, K. R., Koons, D. B. and Bolt, R. A. (1992). 'Multi-Modal Natural Dialogue', in *Human Factors in Computing Systems CHI '92*, pp. 653–654. New York: ACM.

Tucker, D. (1995). Personal communication to author Douglas via e-mail, April 29, 1995.

Van Cott, H. P. and Kinkade, R. G. (Eds.), (1972). *Human Engineering Guide to Equipment Design* (rev. ed., pp. 345–379). Washington, D. C.: U.S. Government Printing Office.

Venolia, D. (1993). 'Facile 3D Direct Manipulation', in *Human Factors in Computing Systems CHI '93*, pp. 31–36. New York: ACM.

Walker, N., Meyer, D. E. and Smelcer, J. B. (1993). 'Spatial and Temporal Characteristics of Rapid Cursor Positioning Movements with Electromechanical Mice in Human Computer Interaction.' *Human Factors*, 35(3), pp. 431–458.

Ware, C., Arthur, K. and Booth, K. S. (1993). 'Fish Tank Virtual Reality', in *Human Factors in Computing Systems CHI '93*, pp. 37–42. New York: ACM.

Ware, C. and Mikaelian, H. (1987). 'An Evaluation of an Eye Tracker as a Device for Computer Input', in *CHI + GI 1987 Conference Proceedings Human Factors in Computing Systems and Graphics Interface*, pp. 183–188. New York: ACM.

Welford, A. T. (1968). *The Fundamentals of Skill*. London: Methuen.

Whiteside, J., Bennett, J. and Holtzblatt, K. (1988). 'Usability Engineering: Our Experience and Evolution', in M. Helander (Ed.), *Handbook of Human–Computer Interaction*, pp. 791–817. Amsterdam: North-Holland.

Whitfield, D., Ball, R. G. and Bird, J. M. (1983). 'Some Comparisons of On-Display and Off-Display Touch Input Devices for Interaction with Computer Generated Displays.' *Ergonomics*, 26(11), pp. 1033–1053.

Whitmore, D. A. (1987). *Work Measurement*. (Second edition). London: Heinemann.

Wolpaw, J. R., McFarland, D. J., Neat, G. W. and Forneris, C. A. (1991). 'An EEG-Based Brain–Computer Interface for Cursor Control.' *Electroencephalography and Clinical Neurophysiology*, 78(3), pp. 252–259.

Woodworth, R. S. (1899). 'The Accuracy of Voluntary Movement.' *Psychological Review Monograph* (Suppl. 3).

Zhai, S. (1995). *Human Performance in Six Degree of Freedom Input Control*. Ph.D. dissertation, University of Toronto.

Zhai, S., Milgram, P. and Buxton, W. (1996). 'The Influence of Muscle Groups on Performance of Multiple Degree-of-Freedom Input.' *Human Factors in Computing Systems CHI '96*, pp. 308–315. New York: ACM.

Zimmerman, T. G., Lanier, J., Blanchard, C., Bryson, S. and Harvill, Y. (1987). 'A Hand Gesture Interface Device', in *Proceedings of the CHI + GI 1987 Conference on Human Factors in Computing Systems and Graphics Interface*, pp. 189–192. New York: ACM.

Index